The Birds Are Our Friends

Yessengali Raushanov

Whittles Publishing

Published by

Whittles Publishing Ltd.,
Dunbeath,
Caithness, KW6 6EG,
Scotland, UK

www.whittlespublishing.com

ISBN 978-184995-455-6

© 2021 "Ұлттық аударма бюросы" ҚҚ (The National Bureau of Translations)
Project coordinators: Rauan Kenzhekhanuly, Timur Muktarov, Alikhan Tuiebay
Translators: Assiya Issemberdiyeva, Gaukhar Khalyk, Aknur Toleubayeva

Editor: Gale Winskill

A rare theme in Kazakh literature, this book on the life of birds by Yessengali Raushanov should be considered a delightful and valuable treasure that enriches Kazakh culture and literature. The poet creates the impression that he has been writing about birds all his life and this collection can be seen as a legitimate continuation of his poetry collections *Ķara Bauyr Ķasķaldaķ* (*The Cruel Baldicoot*) and *Perišteler men Ķustar* (*Angels and Birds*). The volume includes more than thirty engaging and knowledgeable stories that recount the mysteries of some of our winged friends, including a swan, a gyrfalcon, a swallow and a snowcock. Every reader who cares about beauty and the environment can seek inspiration from this book.

Yessengali Raushanov (1957–2021) was a prominent Kazakh poet and writer. He published numerous poetry collections, securing his place as one of the leading poets in Kazakhstan. His poetry is distinctive because of the way it absorbs ancient motives and oral traditions and reproduces them organically in the contemporary Kazakh language. His allegorical poem 'Ķara Bauyr Ķasķaldaķ' has become an anthem for young Kazakhs, who rose up against Soviet suppression in 1986. Raushanov has also authored a novel, multiple stories and plays, while his 'Ķunanbai  and Abai' was staged at the Nurmukhan Zhantorin Theatre (Aktau) in 2020. His verses have been translated into eight languages, and he translated Uzbek poet Khamza Niyazi's collection and Shakespeare's Hamlet into Kazakh. He was a poet laureate of the State Prize of the Republic of Kazakhstan and the Alash International Prize. He has also been honoured with the orders Ķurmet and Parasat.

The Birds Are Our Friends has previously been translated into Russian, Uzbek and Kyrgyz. Seeing this book translated into English – the language Yessengali Raushanov had a deep appreciation for – is an important endeavour for the National Bureau of Translations. Yessengali aġa's passing was a loss for the entire Kazakh culture and a deeply saddening event for everyone who knew him. We wish this book every success in reaching new audiences.

A Note on Transliteration

The international ISO 9 standard of Romanizing the Cyrillic Characters has been applied while transliterating the Kazakh terms, geographical and personal names. The fact that this norm has been developed by the International Organization for Standardization and adopted by a number of countries in Europe and Asia as a main tool in transliterating the Cyrillic characters into Latin characters has been taken into consideration. Moreover, the Euro-Asian Council for Standardization, Metrology and Certification of 9 CIS countries adopted The System of Standards on Information, Librarianship and Publishing Rules of Transliteration of Cyrillic Script by Latin Alphabet in 2000, authentic to the ISO 9 standard. The Kazakh Government has been developing a Latin alphabet for the Kazakh language which, it is planned, will replace the current Cyrillic script in 2025. Although the new version of the alphabet was published in 2018, the grammar is yet to be developed. The current standard of transliteration of Kazakh terms is used in order to avoid any misspellings and discrepancies in the future.

Russian and other Post-Soviet terms, geographical and personal names have been transliterated according to the BGN/PCGN Romanization System widely used elsewhere.

Contents

Swan

The Caspian Sea has had many sobriquets throughout history – the Caspian, the Giran, the Khvalyn, the Khazar.[1] Kazakhs might also call it the Aķķu Sea (the Swan Sea). The surface area of the earth is about 510 million square kilometres and is home to over one million species of animals. One of these is the swan. To see these elegant birds floating quietly among the huge waves on the shore of the Caspian Sea makes one want to believe in the poet's fantasy that the only sea in the world is the Caspian Sea, and the only bird in the world is the swan. Obviously, they will then want the sea to be called the Swan Sea. Can there be any better place for swans to alight?

There are six species of swan, five of which live in the Northern Hemisphere, whereas the other lives far away on the other side of the Equator. According to scientists, two species that inhabit Kazakh lands are the mute and whooper swans.[2] Lately, this list has also included the tundra swan.

Kazakhs believe there is no bird in the world that can be compared with the mute swan for elegance and beauty and it has been drawn by every animal painter in the East and West. Artists are particularly inspired by its beautifully curved neck. A long time, ago the scientists who invented the Latin alphabet shouted enthusiastically, 'We've found it!' – a meaningful exclamation similar to that of Archimedes – when thinking about the letter 'S' after they saw a pair of swans lazing in a pool. After that, people had called the letter 'the swan's neck'. But this has now been forgotten. In the end, we will also be forgotten.

---

1 The Caspian Sea is the largest inland body of water in the world, and is bordered by Kazakhstan, Russia and Azerbaijan.

2 The mute swan is a species of swan and also a member of the waterfowl family *Anatida*; the whooper swan is a large Northern Hemisphere swan.

The swan is a bird whiter than the snow. Folk poetry says:

In November, several layers of snow fall,

And a black road under the foot turns into a swamp.

Is my sweetheart sitting or lying down?

Like a graceful swan on a lake?

Its beak and legs are red, and its eyelids are black as if painted with kohl. The Eastern poets have used the image of the swan in their lyric poems for many years. According to them, women learned from swans to powder their faces and paint their eyebrows black and their lips red. Who knows? Maybe it is true. It's undeniable that humankind has always worshipped nature.

White, black, red … the swan has a powerful beauty: an indescribable and amazing jewel comprised of three strikingly different colours. Last year I visited Turkmenistan. There was an equine stud in the foothills of Mount Feruza, near Ashgabat. Is it possible to go to Turkmenistan and not visit the Aḵalteke stallions?[3] The world-famous Turkmen stallion neighs as it matures. It is a creature of outstanding beauty, with only one negative attribute – a somewhat discordant soft voice compared to its graceful form. This kind of special creature should possess a wonderful and mighty voice.

The sound of the mute swan recalls to mind the Aḵalteke stallion. What would happen if, alongside its beauty, it were also a singer? For example, the swan could have the voice of a nightingale, a warbler or a starling. This is why the old men say that nothing is perfect in the world.

There are various works such as 'The Swan's Song' or 'The Swan's Farewell Song'. The whooper swan sings in Aeschylus's *Agamemnon*, Plato's *Phaedo* and Shakespeare's *The Merchant of Venice*. There is a singing swan in the poems of Byron too. To keep up with them, some of our Kazakh poets compare the melodiousness of the swan's song to the sound of the *dombyra*,[4] and the melancholy tone of the stringed *ḵobyz* that brings the listener out in goosebumps.[5] A newspaper article about a starlet who stunned audiences with her wonderful voice stated: 'The swan's melody hovers over the wide steppe. What a miracle.' Actually, there is no miracle. The swan is not a songbird. Its song can possibly fill the sky, but it is impossible for its melody to hover over the wide steppe. It is true that sometimes the imaginations of poets or writers are confusing.

The whooper swan is also beautiful. Its voice is more like a goose honk than a bugle call as many often assume. Orazaḵyn Asḵar in 'Ḵazaḵtyṇ Ḵara Ôleṇi' (traditional Kazakh poetry) writes:

---

3 *Aḵalteke* is a thoroughbred Turkmen horse.

4 *Dombyra* is the most popular musical instrument among Kazakhs, made of wood and stringed with animal's intestines. It can be different shapes, with 2–4 strings and 8–24 frets, with the most typical one being oval, two-stringed and with 12 frets.

5 *Ḵobyz* is an ancient Kazakh musical instrument, with a wooden body, two to four strings, and a bow made of horsehair. It is the main component of *baḵsy* rituals for healing people and is considered sacred.

The lone swan on the pure lake hugged by the sun,

Trumpets and beats the water with its wings,

Preens and looks around.

Do not shroud this beauty in a blue silken mist.

What is the difference between this swan and the mute swan?

The difference is in its neck. The mute swan has a curved neck, whereas the other holds its neck straight; it does not bend or bow. Its voice is coarse. It does not swim like the mute swan, but dips its chest in the water and raises its tail.

Once we made our way to the Issyk-Kul Lake in winter, where we saw whooper swans. The surface of the lake was pure white. Every December and January, a thousand birds arrive to winter there, and leave in March. Local children admire the fighting swans and spend all day near the shore. If other birds come too close, the male swan will protect its *šaṇyraḳ* (territory).[6] Sometimes boys make two male swans fight by throwing food between them. Once a Kyrgyz fisherman told the story of how a whooper swan beat a fox that attacked its cygnet, using its wings. This bird can certainly protect itself.

The whooper swan population has decreased over the years. In addition to the Issyk-Kul Lake and the Caspian Sea, this beautiful bird also used to inhabit Lake Bilikôl in the Žambyl region, the Šalḳar and Arḳa lakes in West Kazakhstan, as well as the Aral Sea, Lakes Balḳaš and Zajsan and the River Ile, but today we can hardly find this swan. Of course, both mute and whooper swans are *guests* in the Kazakh land. In general, they live in the Mediterranean, Western Asia and Iran. In the second half of the last century, the city of Aḳtau in Western Kazakhstan has become one of the only places on earth where these swans are common.

Swans live for 30–40 years, although sometimes facts bring this international ornithological opinion into question. For example, a mute swan ringed in 1771 was found in 1887, on a British island – 116 years later! Is it possible for a bird to live that long? There was a similar case in Germany when, in 1492, a German fisherman caught a pike in a pond. The fish bore a ring with the inscription, 'This pike was caught in 1230'. Does that mean that the pike had survived for 267 years? Who would ever believe it? Zoologists still argue about these two facts. According to general belief, crows can live for up to 300 years, although scientists claim they live for 50–75 years. Let's hope it's true that swans can live for 30–40 years, and that this is not too long for them, given that crows can live even longer.

The black swan originates from Australia. A long time ago, the Turkish sultans had ornamental black swans in their palace pools. The late poet Žùsip Ḳydyrov wrote: 'I saw a black decorative swan in Bakhchysarai's garden pool.'[7] His words weren't without basis. Bakhchysarai is the native land of the Crimean Tatars, which few could dispute. Prior to the Russian Conquest, the culture of the Ottoman Turks prevailed there, and it was an old tradition of Istanbul, Bursa and Antalya aristocrats to keep black swans in pools.

---

6 *Šaṇyraḳ* is the circular opening at the top of a yurt.
7 Bakhchysarai is a city in Central Crimea.

In general, there are black swans and white swans. Would you believe it if we said that there is also a grey swan? Near Aķtau, in the Caspian Sea, along with the wintering swans, there are geese, ducks and seagulls. The city's inhabitants don't bother the birds and the swans in particular are so used to people that they eat from their hands. Sometimes you can see grey and brown birds that do not look like geese, ducks or swans. When you see these birds for the first time you may be surprised. Perhaps it is a group of unknown birds. No, it is not. These are cygnets. Kazakhs call them *kôgildir* – the blues. Why blue? No one knows the reason. Clearly their colour is not the light blue of the sky, but grey as if they had been lying in the dust. Swans are not born white. First, they emerge as a bird with grey feathers. The folk song 'Šili ôzen' celebrates a girl, comparing her to a cygnet: 'My dear, my precious, my light, you remind me of the young swan.' Not a gosling or a duckling, a young nightingale, or a stork but a young swan, a cygnet. The beauty of the cygnet is unusual; even if it remained grey throughout its life, it would still be as sweet.

Thus, the swan remains grey until it is three or four years old. According to the proverb, 'A baby in the cradle moults five times', and so the swan also sheds its feathers three or four times before becoming a real white swan.

The enemy of birds is the snake. When it sees eggs, from the tiny eggs of tits and sparrows to larger birds' eggs, it swallows them right away. According to folk legends, however, even snakes don't touch swans' eggs. Scholars argue that swans' eggs are too big (114 × 74 mm) to be swallowed.

According to another legend, we know that predators such as falcons, eagles, kestrels and sparrowhawks feed on all kinds of birds and animals. These predators are particularly fond of chicks. However, none of these 'winged wolves' disturb the cygnets. How can we explain that?

Kazakh falconers never hunt for swans. We have never heard of a falconer whose eagle or falcon caught a swan, and we don't want to.

Swans mate for life.

We are told that cygnets remain by their parents' side until the age of four. Then, when they become the most beautiful of birds with a curved neck, red feet, wide chest,

chiselled beak and long wings, male and female swans mate. When they couple, it seems that they promise to remain together until death, unlike other birds. The female swan is handed to her 'groom' by her father, whereas the mother swan brings the son to his 'bride'. It is a special occasion, similar to the matchmaking and weddings of people. From that day, they remain together. They swim together during the day, and sleep leaning on each other.

An adult swan weighs 15–20 kilograms, and its wingspan can reach up to 2 metres. When they return to the warmer climes from which they came originally, they choose a group leader, then fly up to 8,500–9,000 metres at 95–100 kilometres per hour. The swan is one of the few birds that can fly over the famous Himalayas.

Female swans lay between three and nine eggs. The baby swans hatch out of their eggs after an incubation period of 38–40, sometimes 45, days. The width of the nest can be up to 2 metres. During this period, the male swan does not sleep at night and brings his mate food. It is interesting that the mute swan cannot dive. It is difficult for a large bird to dive deep because of its thick feathers and giant wings. Therefore, it just bows its neck and finds its food between the bulrushes.

It is quite difficult to distinguish male and female swans. The only difference is in springtime, when a dark spot on the beak of the male swan enlarges and is visible from a distance as if inflicting fear into their rivals. The female swan has a similar beak but with a smaller black spot. In addition, female swans tend to be smaller than their male counterparts. They are very amicable and do not argue, fight, cackle or gang up on each other like other birds. They are silent. They understand each other tacitly, in peace and tranquillity. Their beauty thrills not only people, but also other birds. When a couple of swans pass by, ducks sail to the side and give way. You may call it 'beauty worship', or fear of a giant bird – as you wish! Make a point of trying to see the swan when it lifts its neck from the water and raises its wings slightly. It is the swan at its most beautiful. When two swans float together gracefully, it seems to me to be a great shame to think that birds can be polygamous.

There are many legends about how the swan throws itself on to the rocks and dies after the death of its mate, as if saying, 'What do I have to live for after this?' There are plenty of songs, *kùjs* and poems with the same plot.[8] *Swan Lake* by Pyotr Tchaikovsky, a long poem *Aķķular u̇jyķtaġanda* (*When the Swans Sleep*) by Mu̇ķaġali Maķataev and the *kùj* 'Aķķu' ('The Swan') by Nu̇rġisa Tilendiev all prove this.

I do not understand why Russians usually refer to the goose first and then the swan in the popular fairy tale '*Gusi-lebedi*' ('Geese and Swans'). In the nineteenth century, the feathers and the skin of swans were very expensive in Russia. According to historical records, 450 swan skins were sold in 1893 at the Constantine Fair in the Aķmola region, and 1,600 in 1894. How can we talk about kindness and mercy when we learn this?

Another adversary of the swan is the shaman, the healer. There were times when they encouraged many crazy hunters to commit a crime, saying that swan bile was a cure for thousands of diseases.

Chinese people made various dishes from swan meat, as well as using their skins and feathers as raw materials to make valuable ornaments. In traditional Chinese medicine, the bile of the swan is dried, then ground and burned, with the ashes used to heal burns. A long time ago, the Chinese considered the swan a sunbird and named it 'Yang'.

Many Greco-Roman legends about Zeus, Aphrodite and Orpheus mention the swan. An Ancient Indian myth recounts a beautiful story of two swans, Ham and Sam.

The Turkic people from the Altaj-Sayan region believe they originate from the swan. That is why Buryat and Yakut women attach a swan's feather to their headwear. When they see the first swan in the spring, they splash milk to the sky and sing:

Our mother, the swan bird,
have you reached your native land?

---

8 A *kùj* is a Kazakh instrumental musical composition performed on Kazakh instruments such as the *dombyra*, *ķobyz* and *syrnaj*.

Siberian Tatars say:

> At first, Tengri, the Heavenly God, sent Ak Kosh [White Bird] to bring the
> soil from the bottom of the sea. Ak Kosh stretched its long neck, pulling out
> a piece of ground, and brought it to Tengri. Tengri breathed into the soil
> and created the devils. The demons spread all over the world and began to
> wail. Having seen this, Tengri became angry, and sent the devils over the six
> mountains into the woods and created the Tengri people from the second
> piece of ground brought by Ak Kosh. The Tengri people were the ancestors of
> today's Turkic people. That is why Turkic people consider the swan a sacred
> bird.

If you go to Maṇġystau, go there in winter. Firstly, the beautiful city of Aḳtau on the
Caspian shore is warm in winter. There are no raging storms, snow or slippery ice. The saying 'the warm winter when butter doesn't harden' probably refers to this phenomenon. No
wonder that elderly men sigh, 'Maṇġystau has a black ravine, with no snow in winter.' It is
a pleasure to walk near the sea at new moon. One can also see the amazing scene of swans
staying on the Caspian Sea at that time.

Swans first arrived in Maṇġystau in 1974–75.

If we look back at history, it seems that there were waters with swans in the land of Ûš
Ḳiân hundreds of years ago,[9] at the time when Aʼz-Žaʼnibek demonstrated the beauty of the
then prosperous city of Sarajšyḳ to the world.[10] The khan's beautiful daughter decided that
the magnificent city lacked a pool with swans, and she diverted the Žajyḳ (Volga) River
from its course to flow through the city. Thus, slaves, overseen by engineers, worked hard
to make a lake, not a pool. It seems as if going too far and overstepping the mark has always
existed. Did the saying 'I fear the khan's daughter's manners, not the khan's command' originate in those times, or recently?

The khan's daughter didn't stop there. Having said that the swan was fond of sweet
things, she ordered caravans of sugar to the lake, to pour their cargo into the water. That's
why its name became 'Seker Lake' (Sugar Lake). As a result, swans started to land on Seker
Lake. Nobody disturbed them. Anyone who scared the birds was punished by the khan's
daughter. In a short time, the surface of Sugar Lake was covered with swans. Girls floated to
the middle of the water on golden boats and and gently pushed away the numerous swans
to allow the boats to move.

There were such wonderful places in the Kazakh land. Where are those towns? Who
destroyed them? Not *who*, but *what* destroyed them? Greed, arrogance or stupidity? Perhaps laziness, wastefulness or boasting? We do not know. It is a mistake to say that we know
our history. We create history to suit our needs.

---

9 Ûš Ḳiân is the arm of three rivers, the Ojyl, Ḳiyl and Žem, in the Atyrau Valley.

10 Žaʼnibek Khan was a Kazakh khan, who ruled 1478–80. Sarajšyḳ was a medieval city located in what is now
the Atyrau region.

The Birds Are Our Friends

Think about the past; look at the future. Those swans reside on the other side of the Caspian Sea today. At the end of the 1970s and the beginning of the 1980s, about 10,000 swans wintered there. According to publications during the Soviet Era, 'the ecology of the sea on the Kazakh side was healthier, and the birds that moved from Iran enjoyed particular care'.

In fact, there is another matter. One of the functions of the Maṇġystau Energy Complex was the desalination of seawater. Fortunately, the atomic device did a good job. A certain amount of warm water from the energy station was discharged into the sea. The swans came in search of warmth. They acquired the habit of living in this warm water for a couple of months, sometimes laying eggs, and eventually returning to warmer places.

'Only groups of swans visit the Kazakhstan shore of the Caspian Sea every year. Other birds don't come to us,' newspapers reported.

'No, various birds visit our shores annually,' argued some scholars.

We are inclined to believe the first version. Any white bird that plays in the waves, that approaches the shore or fades away into the distance, seems to belong to Maṇġystau. How can a bird that has never seen or known Maṇġystau appreciate it?

Every year, sometimes every few years, I visit my homeland. I stay in Aḵtau on the way there and on the way back. The airport is always crowded when I fly to Almaty.

'Sir, are you from the City Administration?'

When I looked back, I saw a young girl who spoke Russian. She was like a swan. In her left hand, she held a 1–1.5-metre-long box. A travel bag was in her other hand. Apparently, she thought I was someone else.

'Do you work at the City Administration?' she laughed again. Her smile was pure.

'No, no,' I said, as if guilty. 'No, not in the City Administration.'

'I'm sorry you left the City Administration. I thought you were still there.'

'Sorry?'

'I have to pay extra for my luggage. Could you please take this box with you to the plane? Just take it with you. Nobody will check.'

'Okay,' I replied. How could a student pay extra? Moreover, I had no baggage.

The box was heavy. I did not pay much attention to it. There were many girls who were buying and selling different things at that time.

We landed safely in Almaty.

'Goodbye, *aġa*,' said the girl gratefully.[11] She got into the Jeep of a swarthy guy with rough skin.

'*Arzymajdy*. You're welcome,' I said in the southern dialect.

So, the story came to an end. There are insignificant encounters, and this was one of them. If I had seen her on the street again, I wouldn't have recognized her, and may God protect her. I would have forgotten that story, but once one of my friends and from now on the spoken words are not mine, but those of my friend *lived in the most beautiful house, in the most beautiful part of Almaty, had the most beautiful car and the greatest position*, and invited me to a party. I went there. We had some drinks. We ate. I praised and was praised. Then I left. Oh God, hold on, I almost forgot:

'Hold on' said my friend, as others were leaving. 'I have something to show you. They won't appreciate it, they're stupid.'

My friend, of course, didn't include himself in that category.

He had created a small zoo on the riverbank behind the house. There were partridges and quails in one cage, pheasants in another, parrots in the third, and a white goose hiding in the corner of another cosy room.

'Ajman, stand up. Your *aġa* has come. Won't you greet me?' said my friend in a loud voice.

The white goose first craned its neck, then lifted its chest. This wasn't a goose, but a swan. What a swan it was! I looked around. My friend had blocked the mountain river with stones, made a narrow canal that passed through his yard and built a large covered pool. That poor swan swam in the pool during the day and went to the warm room to sleep in the evening.

'Do you recognize it?' asked my friend.

'Of course! This is a mute swan.'

'I was sure that you would recognize the Maṇġystau swan.'

'What?'

'Yes, the swan was brought from Mangystau. I called it Ajman: Made in Maṇġystau. How did I bring him? It wasn't difficult. You can buy swans. It's an expensive pleasure. They put it in a box and transferred by plane.'

When I saw the box, I must have been wide-eyed. It was the same box that I had carried myself on the plane from Aḳtau airport. I did not ask the name of the beautiful girl I had encountered. But what could I have done if I had known her? According to my friend, there were many 'new Kazakhs', who were creating private zoos at their villas and haciendas. He was determined to talk about the 'tough guys' who owned the animals, but

11 *Aġa* – respectful form of address to an older man, which can be translated as 'brother', 'uncle'.

I did not question him. I did not want to hurt my heart. If there are things that a man can't handle, his heart would be one of them.

'Don't shoot a swan'; 'Swans are the jewels of waters'; 'Do not compare a swan and an owl'; 'If you become friends with swans you will have a good luck'; 'Geese might be white, but they are not swans' – these are the proverbs that our ancestors used to say. Do modern Kazakh children still learn these proverbs as we did?

'If trade enters your country, then the enemy and discord will enter the country,' said Maťžan Bi.[12] With the advent of trade, Kazakhs began to trample their sacred, reverent things; things that our seven generations and seventy-seven ancestors did not look away from, not to mention lift their hands against. Who is the enemy that went to trade? Not who, but what? First and foremost, it was our greed.

I was tired when I returned from my friend's home. There was the image of the poor swan in front of my eyes. Its eyes were red. I saw not a queen of birds, but a poor bird used to calamity, violence, harshness and darkness, that no longer feared disaster and was thirsty, greedy … that would eat everything it was given.

---

12 Maťžan Bi Tileumaġanbetuĺy (1841–1929) was a Kazakh *bi* (judge, politician, diplomat, orator). A *bi* would consult rulers on matters pertaining to the common people, passing judgments on crimes, given the absence of written law in nomadic societies, and negotiating with enemies – like a modern-day diplomat.

Gyrfalcon

Gyrfalcon, why don't you bring yourself to my net?

Folk song

An image that eludes me.

Ġabit Mùsirepov

When did it leave us?

Where is it now?

Perhaps it has forgotten where we are. Otherwise, why would it abandon us? 'To the slave who is alive, the summer has arrived at last!' as they say. All other birds return from Maġaryp to Mašyraḵ in groups, and on the allotted day, they fly from Mašyraḵ to Maġaryp in flocks – but not the gyrfalcon. It did not come here either last year or this year, and we waited in vain the year before that. It is hard to believe that it won't return.

Why do we miss the gyrfalcon? Because of the hunting? Maybe. Falconry is one of the first types of hunting that humanity ever invented. In history, it is likely that Ancient Indian peoples used to hawk and hunt for animals about 2,500 years ago. Moreover, falconry was one of the favourite entertainments of the Egyptian pharaohs, who hunted birds, hares and foxes using trained birds of prey such as gyrfalcons and hawks.

Ziyauddin Nakhshabi (a thirteenth-century Persian poet) compared the gyrfalcon to the new moon in his *Tuti Namah* (*Tales of the Parrot*). The book *The Secret History of the Mongols* tells us that Genghis Khan's future courage and prestige were foretold when his father dreamed of a gyrfalcon. That is why our Mongolian brothers do not hawk today. There is an interesting legend about it, perhaps a discussion for another time. There is an unusual picture on one of the tombs in the Ancient Egyptian city of Thebes, built approximately in the late fourteenth century BCE. Historians refer to it as 'Nabamun's Fowl Hunting'. A copy of this illustration with a duck, a goose, an avocet and some other birds is stored in the British Museum in London.

In the Middle Ages, this art came to Europe. As Irish playwright Oliver Goldsmith writes in his *A History of the Earth, and Animated Nature* about hawks:

> (…A)nd such was their value in general, that it was made felony in the reign of Edward III, to steal a hawk. To take its eggs, even in a person's own ground, was punishable with imprisonment for a year and a day, together with a fine at the king's pleasure. In the reign of Elizabeth, the imprisonment was reduced to three months; but the offender was to lie in prison till he got security for his good behaviour for seven years farther.'[13]

Alfred Brehm, a German zoologist, wrote in the nineteenth century: 'Hawking with sparrowhawks still prevails in England and Holland'.

The Kazakhs also revere the sparrowhawk. See how a six-year-old protagonist was described in the eponymous poem, 'Ḳobylandy Batyr' as riding a bay and having a hawk in his hands, with a hound following him.

In my childhood, there was a popular book called *Batyrlar Žyry* (*Heroic Epics*), in which it seems that the late artist K. Baranov illustrated Ḳobylandy on a horse with a hawk in his hand after reading these verses. (Later, this picture was reprinted in the edition of *Batyrlar Žyry* published by Žazuśy).

Perhaps he imagined Ḳambar Batyr, who had been 'ringing the bell and hawking', because Ḳambar was a poor man, who fed 'sixty Arġyn families and ninety different crowds'.[14]

The heroism of the goshawk to fight ducks and geese, baldicoots, black grouse, pheasants, the chukar partridge and even bustards, which are the largest birds of the steppe, amazed *sal-seri* – singers, composers and poets of the past. The famous singer Muḥit praised his friend, saying: 'Our Muḥtar is sleepless. He sleeps as the sparrow-hawk.' Ḳanapiâ the *sal*, said, 'I have been hawking since my childhood, and the beads of sweat have fallen from my forehead ever since.'

Muḥtar A'uezov in his novel *Abaj Žoly* (*The Path of Abai*) described Tákežan, an aristocrat, as follows: 'Tákežan approaches the shore. The handsome young man, beautifully dressed, is riding a horse and has a goshawk in his hands … he has caught a yellow goose, two ducks …'[15]

As much as Kazakhs enjoy falconry, they have never killed a human being for a bird. Moreover, if falconry is harmful to anyone, it is considered a crime, *haram* (forbidden in Islam).

---

13 Goldsmith O., *A History of the Earth and Animated Nature*, Philadelphia: John Grigg, 1870, Vol 3, p. 71.

14 Arġyn is a Kazakh tribe.

15 Muḥtar A'uezov (1897–1961) was a Kazakh writer, a social activist, a Doctor of Philology, a professor and an honoured academic of the Soviet Union. He is most famous for authoring the novel about the poet Abaj Ḳunanbajuĺy (Abai Kunanbayev, 1845–1904), called *Abaj Žoly* (*Path of Abaj*), from which the quote is taken.

It is clear that the hunter never becomes rich.

In general, one never hunts because of poverty or wealth; it is the business of neither the rich nor the hero. What if it is the business of an unsettled mood that flies as a bird and cannot find a place to land (or does not want to land)?

Does the unsettled mood belong only to the hunter?

Is a bird more swift-winged or the imagination?

The dreamy spirit of humans always lacks something. It is prone to mood swings and looks for something that does not exist. It feels sick from a fantasy that clings to it and runs like the wind in the air. Let us look at the example in the following verse:

In my twenties I am like a gyrfalcon that's eager to hunt,

A kestrel is a minor bird owned by the poor.

Even if a goshawk catches ten ducks and thirty geese,

A white hawk is way more precious.

What can we say about this? We have just praised the goshawk, so why do we disparage it now? There are more examples of deprecating the bird, such as: 'Fascinated by the saker falcon, you'll whip the goshawk.' There is a reason for it: 'The goshawk is a thief among birds.' There is one more saying among people: 'The goshawk fills your pots; the saker falcon makes your hems dirty.' As if denying this proverb, they praise the saker falcon further:

With a golden whip in my hand,

With an unspoken word in my mind,

I'd sacrifice myself for your treasured eyes

Shining like a saker falcon, unblinded.

If you think this is not enough, then here is another: 'Like the saker falcon of Ķaroj that can catch a wolf, the able young men are favoured by ladies.' Obviously, it is unlikely that the saker falcon would hunt a wolf. Sometimes, we can overpraise something, but it is clear that the saker falcon is a brave, stubborn and irritable bird.

However, it cannot be compared to the gyrfalcon. The gyrfalcon is superior anyway.

It's clear that we long for the gyrfalcon not because we desire wealth and heroism, but because of the yearning originated in the worship of beauty.

There are about sixty species of gyrfalcon. All of them are beautiful and excel at hunting. As the folk poem says:

A grey Peregrine looks like a grey arrow.
A white hawk flies like a bullet.
A hapless man breeds a barbary falcon,
And the one who counts a Hobby among raptors
Will breed as less valued a bird as a Merlin.

Again, there is a contradiction! If a man lacks luck, he raises a barbary falcon, the poem insists. A famous Kazakh poet, Aķan Seri, in contrast, held a barbary falcon in high esteem: 'My beauty, worthy of a barbary falcon, are you going to be tied to a red-footed falcon?', he used to sing.[16]

By the way, about the barbary falcon …

There is the house of A'bilhaķ the falconer on a beautiful slope in east Almaty. In troubled times, he fled from China's iron grasp and, with difficulty, moved to Kazakhstan. Although well educated, he tended sheep and did physical labour after his arrival in Kazakhstan. But he was content to suffer because, most importantly, he had returned to his ancestors' land. He is a strong, resilient, wise and noble man, well versed in his business, knows the value of the word, and isn't frail. It's been a long time since he was hawking. Today, there are few Kazakhs who know the secrets of birds as well as A'bilhaķ. He is like an encyclopedia.

According to A'bilhaķ, the bird that we call 'šahin' is not in fact a barbary falcon.[17] The term 'bidajyķ' in Kazakh, sometimes translated as 'barbary falcon' used to be an adjective for tenacity and dexterity. For example, we say, 'Oh, his bird looks like a real *bidajyķ*'. Hence, a peregrine, a saker falcon, a hawk, even a goshawk, can be a *bidajyķ*. The language changes over time. Certainly, a bird called a *bidajyķ* existed at some point in history, but after its disappearance, falconers used this word as an honorific term, but we erroneously translate it as 'barbary falcon'. When it comes to the gyrfalcon, A'bilhaķ sighs like the poet Abaj: 'You made me angry escaping me perpetually.'[18] The gyrfalcon is a dream.

In folklore people praise or blacken something easily, but there is not a single bad word about the gyrfalcon. It is a rare occurrence; a phenomenon! Even the best human being who 'can catch flying birds with his teeth', as they say, is subject to criticism, let alone birds. Even Nausharuan, the most just Padishah in world history, was subjected to numerous criticisms. It's the same with the prophets. However, you won't find anything bad about the gyrfalcon. It's unbelievable, but the only bird that people have not questioned or slandered is the gyrfalcon. The Kazakh folk poet Šerniâz said: 'The crow won't dare to land on the feathers of a dying falcon.' Gyrfalcons stay clean even when they die. In addition, as Šalkiiz, a Kazakh *žyrau* (poet and storyteller) remarked boastfully, 'When the gyrfalcon sheds feathers, the crow dares not to come near it.' True, how would it dare to? According to a folk poem,

---

16 Aķan Seri (1843–1913) was a Kazakh poet, singer and composer; the quote is from his song 'Syrymbet'.

17 Šahin is a synonym for the barbary falcon (*Falco pelegrinoides*).

18 Abaj Ķuňanbaju̇ly (Abai Kunanbaiuly, 1845–1904), the most influential of all Kazakh poets, also a composer and philosopher, considered to be a reformer of Kazakh literature on the basis of enlightened Islam. His works also reflect traditions of European and Russian culture. The quote is from his poem 'Šoķpardaj kekili bar, ķamys ķulaķ' ('The horse to which I refer').

I have long been in love with you,
A beauty with shiny black braids.
If you had fallen on my palm,
I would court you like a gyrfalcon.

It is clear that the gyrfalcon is a highly revered bird.

Much can be said about the beauty of the falcon species. Seven or eight species of falcon live in the bountiful Kazakh land, and were studied in detail by Soviet ornithologists. Unfortunately, there is no gyrfalcon among them. Where is it? Why do Kazakhs no longer breed and train the gyrfalcon? At times like this, I remember the line from the famous folk song performed by the late Ġarifolla Ķurmanġaliev: 'Gyrfalcon, why don't you alight?' in which he figuratively addresses his sweetheart, comparing her to a gyrfalcon.[19]

Gyrfalcons are easily recognizable. They have a grey back (blue-grey or dark grey), a bent beak, grey eyes and a striped chest. People confuse the gyrfalcon with other birds because of its striped chest. In fact, each bird has a different stripe. For example, it is not for nothing that Russians call the Eurasian sparrowhawk a 'sailor's shirt': if its chest is covered with horizontal stripes, then the stripes of the Eurasian hobby and the common kestrel begin in the groin. However, the most distinctive feature of these two birds is a stripe along the two sides of the mouth, which are directed downwards like a 'moustache'. The moustache of a Eurasian hobby is dark black in colour, whereas the kestrel has a light-yellow moustache, which is difficult to see from afar.

These last three birds are the size of a pigeon, but they easily attack birds bigger than themselves. Therefore, people say 'to attack like a hawk'.

In general, eagles are regarded as the foremost birds of prey, followed by the families of hawks (Accipitridae) and falcons (Falconidae). The latter is described 'as beautiful as the falcon'. Nevertheless, hunters and falconers are not drawn to gyrfalcons because of their beauty. What are they after?

The gyrfalcon is the largest among its kind. It is 2 kilograms in weight and has large wings. It is beautiful and strong. It has a yellow band around the eyes and feathered limbs. Males and females fly together, as the folk song notices: 'I wore a *bešpet* of the finest silk, two gyrfalcons fly out of a single nest.'[20]

They hover, gathering up their legs when they fly. In that moment, they resemble a white stone, which has been thrown upwards. They pounce directly on their victim when they hunt. They unbend their legs so quickly that the poor goose does not understand how its head was cut off. They do not watch their victim from a shelter, but pounce when hovering in the air.

When I listen to the famous song of Žaâu Muŝa called 'Kôgaršyn',[21] performed by Žùsipbek Elebekov,[22] I always remember the gyrfalcon, especially when he says, 'When they

---

19 Ġarifolla Ķurmanġaliev (1909–93) was a popular opera singer (tenor), composer, actor, musical performer and teacher. The quote is from the folk song 'Aķsuņķar nege ķonbajsyŋ?'.

20 *Bešpet* is a light, embroidered, knee-length garment worn over a dress or t-shirt.

21 Žaâu Muŝa (1835–1929) was a Kazakh poet, folk composer and singer.

22 Žùsipbek Elebekov (1904–77) was a Kazakh singer (tenor) and People's Artist of the Kazakh SSR (1942).

sing about their favourite pigeons calmly', I imagine how the gyrfalcon flies up. Of course, the poet Maġžan's song 'Aḳsuṅḳar Ḳu̇s' ('The Gyrfalcon') is another matter; his lyrics are as beautiful as the gyrfalcon itself.[23]

The poet Iliâs Žansùgirov wrote, in his article of 1927: 'Zatayevich went to Ḳarḳaraly through Semej last summer and brought not only songs, but also *kùjs*', and then he listed 113 *kùjs*.[24] One of them – 'Kenesarynyṇ Kôkbalaġy' ('Kôkbalaḳ of Kenesary') – must refer to Kenesary Khan, and 'Kôkbalaḳ' may refer to his gyrfalcon. It suited the khan to hunt with a gyrfalcon rather than with a golden eagle. Of course, this is just a guess. It is not the only possibility. Another problem is why people do not play this *kùj* today. Maybe it is lying on dusty archive shelves. In his article Žansùgirov also cites the example of about forty *kùjs* among the Mataj tribe of Aḳsu and writes about *kùjŝi* – composers and performers of *kùjs* – such as Nu̇rsapa, Egeubaj and Molyḳbaj. One of these *kùjs* is 'Ḳu̇direttiṇ ḳu̇sy' ('The Bird of Power'). What kind of bird is it? Does this *kùj* exist now or has it been forgotten? Perhaps there are stories, legends associated with this *kùj*. In the end, we want to believe that it has not been lost.

The gyrfalcon loves open spaces. It must see everything: animals that run on the earth and birds that fly in the sky. When the gyrfalcon is about to breed, it chooses the high nests of the crow, like a wolf that takes the den it likes. Of course, it drives off the crow. The gyrfalcon incubates eggs in exactly 28 days, and from the first days of hatching imposes a strict upbringing. Usually the number of chicks does not exceed four or five, sometimes even fewer. Gyrfalcons hatch few chicks. Whereas other birds feed their chicks every hour (for example, a tit feeds its chicks 500–550 times a day), a gyrfalcon only feeds its chicks twice a day. Therefore, a tit feeds every 2–3 minutes, and a gyrfalcon every 10–12 hours.

Its favourite dish is goose meat. Russians call it the owner of the goose. By the way, Yaroslav the Wise, according to the collection of laws known as the 'Russian Truth', imposed a large fine on those who stole gyrfalcons.[25] The Russians remember not only this, but also the way the Golden Horde khans forced them to bring not only jewels as a tribute when they were in power, but also gyrfalcons.[26] In the sixteenth century, matchmakers gave each other gyrfalcons. In the Russian Chronicles, a lot was said about gyrfalcons. For example, Russian falconers traded one falcon for three stallions with Bashkir lords.

Historical accounts of the conflicts between the Kazakhs and the Turkmen, which began a long time ago and ended in the 1920s, are controversial. According to some, the Kazakhs asked the Ambassador of the Turkmen for 'twelve gyrfalcons in exchange for twelve parts of the body' of Lord Annadurdi, who the Kazakhs had captured. The Turkmen searched for gyrfal-

23 Maġžan Žu̇mabaev (1893–1938): one of the most influential Kazakh poets and a member of the Alaš Orda Party. He was persecuted and ultimately shot in March 1938.

24 Aleksandr Zatayevich (1869–1936) was a Russian music ethnographer and exponent of Central Asian folk music.

25 Yaroslav the Wise (*c*.978–1054) was Grand Prince of Veliky Novgorod and Kiev three times.

26 The Golden Horde was originally a Mongol and later Turkicized khanate established in the thirteenth century, and originating in the north-western sector of the Mongol Empire.

cons all winter and finally found ten of them. Then the Kazakh *batyr* said, 'I asked for twelve gyrfalcons.[27] They brought only ten. I will gouge out two parts of this scum (two eyes). Then we will be even.' However, at that moment *aksakals* intervened in the dispute, so they acted prudently and released Annadurdi to his homeland.[28]

'I'll be back,' he said. Two months later, he returned to the Kazakhs with two gyrfalcons on his shoulder. The Kazakh *batyr* shook his head in awe when he saw a stately, courageous and handsome man in a white *šapan* coat, riding a horse alone through the Maṇġystau steppe. The legend says that the *batyr* thought to himself, *Oh, what a real man he is! A real gyrfalcon! How fortunate that I did not kill him.* He met the man with full honours and presented him with nine camels. According to Eastern tradition, Annadurdi was nicknamed *Aḵsuṇḵar* (Gyrfalcon).

Russians refer to the gyrfalcon affectionately as the 'red falcon'. The word 'red' in the Old Slavic language means 'good, chosen'.

The Russians had an interesting method for taming the gyrfalcon. They let the gyrfalcon into a closed room half full of water. In the middle was a falconer. The bird flew from side to side until tired and finally landed on the hand of the hawker.

'Looking for the gyrfalcon' means looking for something that does not exist. For example, Kazakhs talk about the giant mythical Samu̇ryḵ bird. We honour it, compose songs about it and depict it on state symbols but it does not exist.

The same can be said about the Humayun bird, which is found in oriental literature and art. No one has ever seen it. It is like happiness: we all talk, dream, think about happiness, but none of us has seen it. Perhaps you have. If so, tell me, because I have been looking for it for too long.

Is it possible that gyrfalcon is a fiction? No way! The gyrfalcon exists. Unfortunately, it has been a long time since it abandoned the Kazakh steppe and flew away. No one has seen it in the last ten years. To be honest, it did not often fly to our lands even in the past. Probably, there were many of them when the Kazakhs were strong and powerful, but it is true that in recent centuries it has been difficult to encounter it. This is the bitter truth.

When the elders of the past were disappointed, according to the poet Mahambet, they said: [29]

> *I am a noble gyrfalcon bird*
> *I will leave you again if I grow vexed.*
> *What other choice do I have?!*

We are so accustomed to *haram* that we do not even feel disgust. The great Mahambet was a true poet, and following his footsteps, we are bound to consider ourselves inferior.

---

27 *Batyr* – originally term for 'hero' or 'valiant warrior', roughly equivalent to the European knight; nowadays the term signifies military or masculine prowess.

28 *Aḵsaḵal* – traditionally, a well-respected and powerful elder in charge of the community. Nowadays, a reverential form of address to elderly men in general.

29 Mahambet Ôtemisu̇ly (1804–46), Kazakh poet, also known for leadership in rebellions against Russian colonialism. This activity is believed to have resulted in his murder in 1846. The exerpt is from his poem 'Bajmaġambet su̇ltanġa aitḵany'.

What birds are found in Kazakhstan now? There are so many crows that we are even afraid to tell the crows that they are crows. There are also imperial eagles, which have giant wings; water eagles that swallow algae like fish and fish like frogs; vultures that fatten on their own shadows; harriers; brown vultures; kites; snake eagles … It is clear that these birds are the owners of today's fauna and flora. All eat carrion. However, the gyrfalcon would not eat them. A century ago Eset Bi declared:[30] 'Snatching the birds flying in the distance, I was the real gyrfalcon.'

The gyrfalcon would feed itself with dignity. As the saying goes: 'The vulture eats greedily and covertly; the gyrfalcon eats sparsely and openly.' The vulture eats greedily, covering its prey, burying it underground, until it begins to rot and stink, fouling the air and spreading disease, whereas gyrfalcons soar gracefully into the sky: they stand and remain tall.

We have been told that the gyrfalcon lives in the forests of the Far North, beyond Siberia. The mass media and scholars say so. We are upset not because they live so far away, but because they don't live in our land.

Why don't they live in our land?

Gyrfalcon

---

30 Eset Bi Ḳarauly (1779–1869) was a Kazakh *bi* – a judge and politician excelling in oratory and steppe law.

Swallow

It is someone's child too.

Saği Žienbaev, 'Ķarlyğaš' ('The Swallow')[31]

*E*renķabyrġa! (Tien Shan)

The caravan of bare walls, plains, turbulent rivers, clean ponds, dark forests, strong winds, cold hollows, pastures, bare steppes and dunes stretches from east to west for 1,000 kilometres. The poet Ôtežan Nuŕġaliev admired Kazakh lands for good reason, exclaiming, 'These places have no end and no boundaries. What secrets do they reveal?' This is all Kazakh land; a heritage that we will leave to future generations.

One of the special mountain ranges of Erenķabyrġa is the Šaķpaķ Pass, a beautiful mountain that lies between Taraz and Šymkent. Here, the Talas Alatau mountain range continues into the Ķaratau range, like an elder, who gives way with the words 'I am tired. It's your turn to rise'.

Šaķpaķ has a special wind. Scientists have calculated that it reaches speeds of up to 30–40 metres per second. Sometimes it is the wind that brings down pillars, tears off the roofs of houses or misleads a lone traveller, but it is very important for science, as there is a station, built in 1966, where birds are ringed. This wind, which can knock down a rider, prevents birds from flying. The Kazakhs, whose ancestors lived here for a long time, learned about this feature of Šaķpaķ long before the biologists of the Soviet Union. If they didn't know about it, they wouldn't sing in the following way (from the folk song Šaķpaķ-Mašat'):

My native parts are behind Šaķpaķ and Mašat.

The wind in Šaķpaķ is as strong as a beater.

To reach the place where my darling lives,

I will fly through a pass that birds can't fly over.

---

31 Saği Žienbaev (1934–94) was a Soviet and Kazakh poet and translator; 'Ķarlyğaš' was the lead poem of his 1959 collection of the same name.

Ornithologists and hydro-meteorologists searched diligently for a place 'so high that birds cannot fly over with the wind like a beater' for a very long time. Our ancestors sang about this place many centuries ago. Kazakhs do not pay attention to the biblical phrase, 'In the beginning was the Word', otherwise, we would know that folklore is the source of all science.

From the proudest bird, the eagle, which can cover the whole sky with its wings, to the smallest sparrow, no bird can fly high over Šaḳpaḳ; they fly closer to the ground and become like the obedient son-in-law who's been introduced to his in-laws for the first time. Scientists realized that this is the best place for ringing birds when they saw that the rooks and crows did not fly over Šaḳpaḳ, but simply crossed over on foot. On the pass, there is the mouth of a net 8–12 metres high and 35–40 metres wide. We call it a 'net-mouth' because tired birds, which have flown several kilometres, fall into this net on their own. The length of this net-mouth is 100 metres. The large mouth narrows and turns into a narrow oesophagus. Birds can no longer get out. There are many stories about Šaḳpaḳ; for example, according to a song, 'Abylaj [himself] would not have been able to pass through the Arḳa's Pass'.[32]

Thus, Šaḳpaḳ, one of the famous stations for ringing birds, was founded by a Danish scientist, J. Mortenson, in 1899. Of course, its current state is another matter. About 200 species of birds are being studied anew. Sometimes no birds fall into the net-mouth, and sometimes hundreds of thousands of birds do. On 6 May 1974, 12,832 birds were ringed, and 14,428 birds on 3 May 1977; thus Kazakhstan was mentioned twice among the world's ornithological organizations.

The first time, Kazakhstan was glorified to the whole world by the Šaḳpaḳ Pass, and the second time by a tiny swallow. Yes, the common swallow.

In the autumn of 1978, scientists from the Institute of Zoology at the Kazakhstan Academy of Sciences were engaged in daily activities at Šaḳpaḳ. They ringed and released a swallow that had fallen into the net. This swallow was discovered by Russian ornithologists in distant Khakassia four days later and they were surprised to find that the bird had flown over 800 kilometres a day. Until then, no one had paid attention to swallows, considering them 'an already studied object'. It means that this particular swallow had flown at more than 30 kilometres per hour. The magazine *Yunyi Naturalist* expressed surprise about the acclaimed 'Kazakh swallow' in its August issue, and the *Sel'skaya Zhizn'* newspaper reprinted the article.

The Kazakhs have always considered the swallow to be a nice bird. In the oral tradition, where the same characters can be described as greedy, rich, evil and kind, a benevolent attitude towards the swallow remains unchanged.

A tale called 'Ḳarlyġaš' ('The Swallow') begins as follows:

> 'The damned Ùš Ḳiân is the land of our ancestors. If you ask who our ancestors were, they were the bold Noġajly. These lands are vast, in the Maṇġystau hollow, near the Ash'yagar ponds. Only few people lived by the Ash'yagar ponds, but they were very strong, and the equal of many. Once upon a time, a local boy was grazing the lambs. Gangsters from the tribe of Ajladyr, who were returning

Swallow

---

32 Abylaj Khan was a Kazakh khan who headed the national liberation struggle against the Dzhungar conquerors during the seventeenth and eighteenth centuries; the liberator of Kazakh lands and unifier of the three žùz (tribal unions headed by their own khan).

sad, tired and empty-handed from a *barymta*, noticed that boy, knocked him down with an iron whip and took him away with them.'[33]

As the saying goes, 'a slave won't be looked for, a metal won't be twisted', and the boy was forced to graze cattle, chop wood, make fires – he did absolutely everything. One day, a flock of crows landed near the boy, who was weeping sorrowfully. The boy expressed his sadness to a crow and implored it to deliver his amulet to his father. The callous crow did not respond. Then a magpie arrived. The boy made the magpie the same request. The magpie also did not respond. Cranes arrived, but they did not even look at the boy and flew away noisily. Two swans landed on a lake nearby. Hearing the voice of the sobbing boy, they responded:

> When the sun rises, look to the east:
> It is an orphan just like you.
> When the swallow comes
> make your plea, and you'll be blessed.

The next day, the swallow arrived:

> My dear swallow, I am sad and desperate,
> I fell victim to merciless soldiers.
> I am left alone though I have six siblings.
> You are as kind as anyone's sister.
> Take my amulet, fly to Maṇġystau,
> And pass on the message to my poor parents, please.

Then the boy hung his amulet on the wings of the swallow.

The swallow flew, as the boy had told it to, over the wide lakes, over the uninhabited steppes; it hid from hawks in the mountains; it flew over the endless mountains, over the steppes of Ùstirt, over the chalk cliffs of Oġlandy and the Šopan Ata pastures. The kind swallow was like the dearest sister. It flew day and night, its voice heard in the dark. This tiny bird's courage turned out to be greater than that of the entire clan.

The swallow brought the amulet safe and sound to the boy's parents. The old man and the old woman recognized the amulet and gathered all the people, urging them to go and rescue their blood unless they had no heart. Hearing their plea, eighty horsemen from the Adaj tribe followed the swallow, and found and rescued the boy. They shot six men of Ajla-

---

33 *Barymta* is the seizure of cattle as a means to obtain revenge for an offence or reward for damage caused, among Turkic nomadic peoples.

dyr for the boy's six months of imprisonment, returned with six camels loaded with sixty carpets and achieved their goal.

Now, there are no mighty men like these.

Everything is gone; everything sounds like a lie. Only the tale of the swallow remains. Not only in this, but also in other tales, people considered the swallow a friend. No wonder they say: 'Like a swallow that put out the fire with its wings.' Speaking of comparison, the Kazakhs compare their dear ones, daughters and sisters, to swallows.

A brother, saying goodbye to a marrying sister, says:

> The water dripping into a hollow accumulates,
>
> But the wealth acquired dishonestly doesn't.
>
> We have one hand, but different fingers.
>
> We were born together, but do not live so.
>
> My dear swallow, wherever you are,
>
> Be safe and sound, my beloved sister.

The swallow is a symbol of beauty: 'Your eyebrows are like the wings of the swallow; may all sisters be like you.'

Kazakhs never destroy a swallow's nest. Our prominent writer Tynymbaj Nu̇rmag̣anbe-tov called one of his books *Ķarlyg̣aštyŋ uâsy* (*The Swallow's Nest*).

The prominent poet Muķag̣ali Maķataev wrote:

> My swallow, have you come? Didn't a hawk hurt you?
>
> Did you return safe, my bird with a forked tail, to your own nest?
>
> Have you returned, my dear, with your mate?
>
> How come you're alone? Where is your mate?
>
> My harmless one, who offended you?[34]

You feel sorry for the hapless bird that has lost its companion, like a young widow.

The song 'Ķarlyg̣aš' ('Swallow') by the academic Ahmet Žu̇banov is still popular today. In addition, the eponymous dance was first performed in his opera *Abaj* (1944), and is considered a national treasure.

> White neck, thin eyebrows, broad forehead,
>
> your beautiful face looks snow-white.
>
> Your gentle and light character,
>
> shines as a light, my swallow.

---

34 The quote is from Maķataev's poem 'Ķarlyg̣ašym keldiŋ be?' ('My swallow, have you come?')

Here the great composer compares a beautiful girl to a swallow, conjuring the image of his beloved, imagining the swallow.

Aḳan Seri says, 'Swallow is the name of the song.' In fact, Ḳarlyġaš (Swallow) is one of the most common Kazakh girls' names.[35] Kazakhs rarely call girls Aḳḳu (Swan); one hardly encounters Lašyn (Falcon), Üki (Owl) or Torġaj (Sparrow). Nevertheless, there are many girls called Ḳarlyġaš.

The swallow has long been considered one of the few birds believed to be our inseparable companion.

All four holy books include the same story about the Prophet Noah, who escaped a world-engulfing flood in his Ark. When the vessel arrived at Ḳazyġurt (Jeddah, Mount Suleiman, Ararat, Mangystau, etc.), he sent a dove, instructing it to 'find out if the Flood has stopped and the land is dry'. In some sources, the dove is replaced by a swallow.

'The Story of the Prophet Noah' in *Kisas-ul Anbiya* by Rabghuzi tells the story of being on board the Ark during the Flood![36] When the water seeped through a hole and the boat began to sink, the snake said, 'I will stop the water. Just give me the most delicious meat.' The Prophet Noah, in a bind, ordered the bee to sting everyone and try their meat to identify the most delicious one. The bee flew away and, on the way back, intended to say that the most delicious meat was that of humans, but then it met a swallow and told it everything. The swallow said, 'Show your tongue.' When the bee opened its mouth, the swallow ripped out its tongue. No one has understood the buzz of a dumb bee since then. The swallow said, 'The most delicious meat is that of a frog.' Since then, the bee has buzzed, the snake has fed on frogs, and the swallow that saved people from death has been considered as dear as a sister.

It is known that the great Tôle Bi, was buried in Shaykhantauyr, Tashkent.[37] His grave is located next to that of Žùnis Khan.[38] If you delve into history, you will discover that Žùnis Khan was a relative of Zahir ud-din Muhammad Babur.[39] In the 1970s, a Tashkent Uzbek named Muhammed Saly guarded the grave. His children grew peanuts and were engaged in farming in the Myrzašôl district of the Zhizak region.

I used to visit Tashkent often for work in those days. Each time I'd visit the grave of Tôle Bi. One day, Muhammed Saly asked why I visited this grave so often. I explained to

35 Aḳan Seri Ḳoramsauly (1843–1913) was a Kazakh *seri*, poet and composer; the quote is from his song 'Ḳarlyġaš' ('Swallow').
36 Rabguzi, Turkic writer and poet from Khorezm at the end of the thirteenth and beginning of the fourteenth centuries.
37 Tôle Bi Alibekuly (1663–1756) was a Kazakh *bi* (judge) of the Great *žùz*, and a statesman, orator and advisor to Táuke Khan.
38 Žùnis Khan (1416/7–87) was a khan of Moghulistan (1469–87).
39 Zahir ud-din Muhammad Babur (1483–1530) was the founder and first Emperor of the Mughal Dynasty in India.

The Birds Are Our Friends

him who Tôle Bi was, that Kazakhs revered the spirits of their ancestors and visited their graves. The old man said that his ancestors were also Kazakhs. I said, 'In that case, you're not an Uzbek at all, but a Kazakh.' He asked slyly, 'What is the difference?' I had met Kazakhs who had become Uzbeks not only in Tashkent, but also in Samarkand, Zhizak, Syr Dariâ and Bukhara. They had forgotten their origins and language, and married their children to their brothers' offspring. Moreover, they considered this the right way, in keeping with the Prophet Muhammad (peace be upon him).

In general, Uzbeks have no custom of knowing one's ancestors up to seven generations as Kazakhs do. Uzbeks know only three or four of their ancestors. Nobody blames them for this. The conversation dragged on and the guard told us the story of Koldirgoch Bi ('Swallow Bi'; that is, 'Tôle Bi'). 'The Kazakhs lived in yurts and roamed the pastures. Once Kalmyks attacked the Kazakhs and the latter moved to the mountains. However, Koldir-goch Bi did not move. When Kalmyk Zajsan asked him why he did not move with the other people, he pointed his whip at the šaṇyraḳ – the upper dome of the yurt. It turned out that a swallow's nest with chicks was there. Without uttering a single word, Tôle Bi made it clear that he was not going to move anywhere until the chicks got stronger. Then Zajsan, realizing that in front of him stood a holy man, dismounted from his horse and greeted the elderly man. After that, he was nicknamed "Ḳarlyġaš Bi" [Swallow Bi] and was honoured by being buried in the Pantheon of Khazret Yunus Khan, or Žùnis Khan.'

In the Hermitage in St Petersburg, there is a room of ancient jugs. On one of these jugs, a baby girl and a boy are depicted happily greeting a swallow that presumably has returned to its native land. The return of the swallows means the return of spring, goodness, warmth, grace and joy. According to Ancient Egyptian mythology, beautiful Isis turned into a swallow when searching for her dead husband to the ends of the earth.

The Christian world associates the swallow with the Prophet Jesus. It is known that Jesus was crucified on the order of Pontius Pilate. It is said that a swallow postponed his death by removing a nail and a hammer from a Roman soldier.

Latvians have an even more beautiful legend about the swallow. From the beginning of time, when the earth and the water appeared, and humans became humans, God became angry and began to punish everyone. The ground was covered with thick snow and slippery ice; there was a terrible frost and blizzard. According to Latvian oral tradition, the swallow pitied the people, and stole fire from God's hearth and made a fire for humans for the first time.

Swallows arrive late from their migration, but depart early in the autumn. They arrive late because they eat flying insects, attacking them, even drinking on the wing, flying low to sip water. It is known that flying insects do not appear immediately after the snow melts but wait until late spring when everything is green. Swallows leave our lands early in the autumn for the same reason: they stay as long as the flying insects remain. Swallows usually nest on the front of a house or on the roofs of sheds. They are not afraid of people and are quite amicable. Their song is special and pleasant; there's nothing else like it.

It is true that in the last five to six years, swallows have started to fly less frequently to the southern regions, especially to Almaty, and some years they haven't been seen there at all. A prime reason is that people have had a negative and noticeable effect on the environment, destroying everything – woods, ponds and mountains.

It is said that swallows do not make nests where ill-intentioned and deceitful people live. In Almaty, around the 'huge houses that were built at the foot of the mountain and prevent breezes blowing' (Žumeken Näžimedenov), everything is green, but there are very few birds.[40] If you climb a little higher and walk around the yards of houses in Gornyi Gigant, you may notice swallow and sparrow nests. Why? One reason is that in the last twenty to thirty years there are more mynah birds in the city. All the swallows flew out of our city because of the mynahs. What can we do?

It was Alfred Brehm, a German zoologist, who spoke about the value of the swallow from an academic point of view. He was the first to disprove the improbable legends spread by religious groups. Brehm highlighted the vigilance of the swallow. He wrote that the swallow clearly sees its prey, even when it soars high in the sky. A person might be surprised by its sharp-sightedness when attacking a moving object, and amused by its clumsiness when catching an insect that is sitting still on the grass. Therefore, on rainy days, the swallow flies back and forth to scare insects away from grass in order to catch them in flight.

The swallows arrive in May along with cuckoos and nightingales. Early May offers pleasant nights. During such calm and quiet evenings, according to folk legend, cuckoos scream to announce that the swallows have arrived. Immediately on arrival, the swallow begins to build its nest. Soon, it lays four to six white eggs with brown speckles. In early August, it lays eggs for a second time. Its chicks grow strong within fourteen to sixteen days.

Speaking of nests, it is fascinating how city barn swallows make their nests on the flat and slippery concrete surfaces of multi-storey buildings in the cities. The common house martin also makes great nests. The male and female protect their nest together, as well as their eggs, which hatch one by one. Therefore, swallow families are strong.

According to a medieval legend, 'swallows avoid plague'. People knew that plague, cholera, smallpox and malaria were receding and the population was beginning to recover when they saw the swallows return.

In Dagestan, there is a village called Pudahar. According to legend, it originated when, once upon a time, young men who were keen to fight went in search of the enemy and stopped at the foot of a mountain to take a nap. They stuck their waving flags into the ground and fell asleep, only to wake up late for morning prayer. When they awoke, they saw a swallow's nest at the top of the flag. These mighty men, unafraid of armies, were stopped by this holy bird and settled there, engaging in farming and animal husbandry and eventually founding a village.

Estonians are fond of swallows as well. The swallow has been the national bird of this country since 1962. Let us see what Estonian folklore says about how the swallow's tail came to be forked.

A long time ago, a young man who was famous for his intelligence, courage and dexterity lived in the city of Tallinn. He had a sweetheart of indescribable beauty. When they walked along the shore hand in hand, people stared in awe of them. The devil, jealous of the happiness of the couple, turned the beautiful girl into a swallow, and using witchcraft, matched his own cunning, talkative and awkward daughter to the young man.

The days passed.

One day the young man decided to marry the devil's daughter.

They had a magnificent wedding. During the wedding, a swallow flew swiftly towards the young man, destroying everything on the table. People chased it away. Soon the swallow landed on the groom's shoulder and pulled out the bride's earrings with its beak. The

The Birds Are Our Friends

40 Žumeken Näžimedenov (1935–83) was a Kazakh composer.

bride cried bitterly. The bird that had spoiled the wedding was chased with knives, axes and pitchforks. The swallow's tail was cut with a sharp axe, and since then it has been forked.

Now let us consider various superstitions about the swallow:

- If the swallow lands on a barn, then a ewe will give birth to twin lambs and there will be an abundance of food; if it lands on a house, expect a new arrival to the family.
- Bullets miss the swallow.
- A mantis will gouge out the eyes of a child who destroys a swallow's nest, because swallows and the mantis are relatives.
- Swallows are made of clay just like humans, and, therefore, should not be disturbed.
- If you dream of a swallow, you will be happy.
- If you see a swallow, then shake your pocket, because you will get a lot of money.
- If a young man dreams of a swallow, he will marry his beloved.
- When you see a swallow for the first time in spring, look at your feet. If you have a white hair stuck to you, then you will marry a blonde; if a dark hair, then a brunette.
- A swallow makes its nest for forty days. The person who destroys it will be doomed to forty evils.
- When you first see a swallow in the spring, put coal in your pocket. That year you will find happiness.
- If you dream of a dead swallow, then someone close to you will die. Do not forget to give alms.
- If the swallow does not return to its nest, be careful; there may be a fire in that house.
- If the swallow flies around a house for a long time, then the daughter of that house will marry.
- If the girl you love does not let you close, then buy a gold ring and put it in a swallow's nest for nine days. On the tenth day, give it to the girl. By God's will, your wish will be fulfilled.
- 'Man learned to build a house from a swallow, and to knit from a spider' (Democritus, Greek philosopher).
- A swallow drinks poppy juice to save children from being born blind.

As the saying goes, 'The favourite of the people has many names', and there are many tales and legends about the swallow, starting with such improbable Christian myths as 'The swallow sleeps under the swamp in winter' and ending with such *scientific discoveries* as 'The swallow sits on the wings of a crane, or clings to the stork to fly to warm lands'. In Western Ukraine, to this day, there is a legend that the swallow sleeps at the bottom of a lake in winter. According to another superstition, if you miss the swallow during the wintertime, then press your ears to the ice and you will hear its voice.

Is there any literature in the world where there are no legends about the swallow?

Is there a country in the world where people do not like swallows?

According to another legend, every person has their own swallow. It hovers over our head day and night and wishes us health and protects us from evil. People are so stupid that they are unable to find this bird throughout their life. If they did, they would live happily ever after.

Have you found your swallow?

Snowcock

Did you climb U´lytau?
Did you try the snowcock meat?

Folk song

When I hear about snowcock, it reminds me of La´zzat Asanova, who perished young during the Želtoķsan Uprising of Kazakh youth in December 1986. She chose death over imprisonment. May Allah open the gates of the eight heavens to her. She perished, but proved that Kazakh girls' free spirit would never die.

The snowcock also dies immediately if it is caged. Therefore, there are no snowcocks in any zoo in the world. You can tame the chicks of a partridge, which plays in the mountains, of a quail, which lives in the wilderness of the forest, even of a pheasant, whose eggs can be hatched by a domestic chicken. Nestlings forget about their origins and run after a chicken. However, the snowcock cannot be tamed. A hen will not be able to hatch its eggs, and if a person touches its chicks, then they die immediately.

Maybe the snowcock is the spirit of the ancient free Kazakhs who flew away to the sky, leaving us behind.

An innocent bird that lives in the high mountains, it is a symbol of snow-white fidelity, true beauty and pride, and cannot remain in a sinful world where there is no freedom. Yes, the earth is a place where we – that is, sinners – live, and only angels and birds can live in the sky.

Honour and glory to the birds!
In the whole wide world,
I see only sky, and
I obey your justness, O Allah,
since birds and angels fly over my head.

Here, the morning came again, a joyful day.
You did not give wings to me,

but granted them to the birds,
how wise you are.

If only I became Edil, or Žajyķ,
one day, unexpectedly,
even if I acquired wings,
I would still give them away to the birds,
saying, 'My beautiful ones, only you deserve the sky'.[41]

Everyone should know their place. It is true that snowcocks fly low, but they live at an altitude of 3,000 metres above sea level. There are even those who report seeing them at a height of 5,000 metres above sea level. Slightly exaggerated, it's above the clouds. It is clear that at such an altitude there is very little grass. Everywhere there is white snow, high mountains covered with ice, strong wind. There are no trees, flowers or leaves at all. What does this bird eat? Even in the harshest winter, the snow on the sunny side melts quickly. When the snow melts, the snowcock immediately finds food. Imperceptible mountain garlic, juniper buds, even moss are food for the snowcock. (By the way, it is worth noting that the Ancient Kazakhs called mountain garlic 'snowcock onion' – *u'lar piâz*. To my mind, this is the correct name. We use the scientific name – 'mountain garlic' – a direct translation from Russian.) This graceful bird is not voracious; it is content with what it has and always keeps its body clean. As for purity, crows and magpies do not come near where there are snowcocks, which feeds alongside the proud argali: horned mountain goats. It is said that the argali pierce the snow in search of food not only for themselves, but also for the snowcock. How nice when noble animals co-exist peacefully.

As for its rare appearance, firstly, it is a very careful bird, and trying to catch it in a cage or a net is useless. The red-footed falcon, the Eurasian hobby, even the sparrowhawk itself cannot catch it, only the mountain eagle. In addition, no normal falconer will hunt the snowcock and shoot it. If they see a dead snowcock, they take its claws and feathers to hang on the cradle of a baby or on a lintel. Secondly, like all precious things, snowcocks are very rare. They do not multiply. Perhaps that is why we cherish them.

Many ornithologists who have wanted to see the snowcock with their own eyes and touch it with their own hands have returned from the mountains empty-handed and exhausted. For those who appreciate the value of birds, hearing its voice is joy enough. Ten years ago, the media said that hospitals had appeared in India where doctors treated patients with the snowcock's song.

There is an assumption that the first tune appeared in the Kazakh steppe. It might be true. We are sure that the person who recreated the first music loved birds very much. Probably, music was originally called 'bird language'. Every musical instrument has signs of bird songs. It is known that Kazakhs do not shoot swans, owls or snowcocks, but honour them. For example:

In Kazakh songs there are sound combinations, such as 'Ugaj-aj, ugaj-aj, u-g-a-j'. I think this imitates the sound of an owl. 'U-u-u-ug-aj' is a separate melody that does not resemble the voice of a single bird. The snowcock's song is a separate topic. Usually, five to ten, sometimes twenty, snowcocks fly together, and early in the morning they start to sing in unison.

41 From the poem '*Perišteler men ķustar*' ('Angels and Birds') by the author of this volume.

Probably it is better to say they are *talking*, not singing. At such moments, we unwittingly recall such a phrase like 'to make noise, like the snowcock'. Of course, this does not mean that the best a snowcock can offer is to make noise. They have a special song. Naturalist and writer Boris Shcherbakov, from East Kazakhstan, states that their song resembles the voice of a muezzin when they stretch 'Ah-ah-a'. As far as I am concerned, it is more like the sound of the *sybyzǵy*, a Kazakh instrument, than the sound of the *azan* (call to prayer). It seems that the Kazakh who invented the *sybyzǵy* was familiar with the voice of snowcock.

In Kyrgyz folk songs there are lines such as: 'Voice like that of a snowcock …', 'language like that of a snowcock'. One of the most popular songs of the Kyrgyz people is 'My youth, you are like a singing snowcock'. It's a beautiful song. And when they praise Alatau, the songs declare: 'My Alatau, whose high ranges shelter singing snowcocks.'

In Europe, a lot of work is being done to protect and to breed birds. However, in those countries there is no snowcock. The snow-covered mountains, long rivers and green forests of Italy, Switzerland and France seem somewhat incomplete to us, because snowcocks don't live there, and never have. Since this bird only lives at altitude, I had hoped that it might live in the Alps. Alfred Brehm wrote about mountain (*Chukar*) partridge (*Alectoris*) and mountain grouse who live there, but they are not snowcocks. European scientists have been confused, proclaiming that snowcocks have been found in the Alps or the Pyrenees, but they have been proven wrong. In fact, snowcocks do not inhabit those areas.

How did Allah create the land and mountains? How did he create the earth and water? Everything is masterfully described in detail in a book called *Noor Namah* (*The Book of Light*). In addition, we certainly know the story of 'Kisass-ul-anbiyan'. It seems that God was particularly merciful to Central Asia when it came to the mountains. Just look – there are a lot of animals and plants in Central Asian and in the Himalayan mountains. If we go westward, and look at the mountains in Europe, the number and diversity of animals diminish like morning stars. Moreover, the mountains get lower towards the west. Therefore, in Europe there is no snowcock. Of course, we are not trying to boast: this is a scientifically proven phenomenon.

Speaking of science, zoogeographers concluded that there are five species of snowcock in the world. The Caucasian snowcock lives in the mountains of Kaf, the Caspian snowcock lives in the mountains of the South Caucasus and the Kopet Dag mountains in Turkmenistan. These snowcocks are rather small in comparison with the snowcocks that live in Alatau and Altaj. Our Maṇǵystau saker falcon is great at hunting them. The Tibetan snowcock lives in the south-east of the Pamir mountains. Snowcocks, which live in Tien Shan and the Himalayas, are found in the mountains near Almaty too; that is, on the Ile Alatau ridges, Right Talǵar, Left Talǵar, Middle Talǵar, Buʼlaṇbel (Dzungarian Alatau), Belžajlau, Sarybel, in Tekežaṇǵaḳ and the Piskent cliffs of Talas Alatau. It would be more correct to say that they do not *live* there, but they can be *seen* there. They disappear when they feel the slightest danger. They fly very fast, but walk on the ground like turkeys. Therefore, in some scientific literature they are called 'mountain turkeys'. In fact, they are not at all like turkeys. The white snowcock is found in the Altaj and Saân mountains. When Kazakhs speak of them, they ask, 'Did you climb a high mountain? Did you try the snowcock meat?'

Let us clarify something. We are not talking about Uʼlytau, which is located in the south-west of Saryarḳa, more precisely in the **Žezḳazġan** region. The snowcock does not live in these mountains at all. The highest point of Uʼlytau is at 1,134 metres, and the average altitude is only 400–600 metres. For comparison, the highest point of Tien Shan is Victory

Peak (also known as Peak Pobedy) at 7,439 metres and the height of Khan-Tengri (Han Táṇiri) is 6,995 metres. The peaks of Muʺztau, Aḳbastau, Aḳtau and Bolukha in Altaj are no higher than 4,506 metres. It is clear that the Ancient Kazakhs were not talking about lower ridges of 400–600 metres as 'mountaintops' when they sang: 'Is it a snowcock that screams on the mountaintop? Will it cry if I catch its chicks?'

We honour the Kazakh poet Ḳasym Amanžolov deeply, but his lines about snowcocks flying over Ulytau must be just the fruit of his imagination: 'A snowcock of Ulytau will fly like a cloud,/ A huge fish will frolic in the Aral.'

In addition, in one of the songs that is now broadcast on the radio or on TV, the poet describes a beautiful woman with whom he fell in love, as, 'She looks like a snowcock from Ulytau'.

Tastes differ. How can you compare a girl to a snowcock? The snowcock has a dark grey back, short toes, a chiselled beak, a round head, a short neck, a sharp tail and a plump chest that does not match its body. However, our subject is not the appearance of the snowcock, but the fact that it does not live in Ulytau.

Nevertheless, this does not diminish sacred Ulytau, or its authority. For a true Kazakh, the very name 'Uly-Tau' – that is, 'the Great Mountain' – is something precious and holy. What about the age-old stories of its Ḳarakeṇgir, Sarykeṇgir and Edige ranges? Saying that there is no snowcock in Ulytau does not mean that there are no animals at all. This can be inferred from the geographical names in this area: Bùrkit (Eagle), Buʹldyryḳ (Sand Grouse), Aḳsuṇḳar (Gyrfalcon), and Ḳarlyġaštau (Mountain of the Swallow). In the end, who knows for sure that snowcocks did not live in Ulytau centuries ago, along with the falcons?

The name *Ulytau* is found in all Turkic peoples. The bluish mountain near the city of Bursa, which was the first capital of Turkey, is called Ulytau. Ottoman Turks believe that this name comes from the word for 'sacred, holy'. '*Uly*' is a Turkic word. Kazakhs pronounce it '*uly*', but in other Turkic nations the word is '*ulug*'. The name Ulyḳbek (Ulugbek) comes precisely from this word.[42] Today in the Kazakh language, the word '*ulyḳ*' is found very rarely, only in some proverbs, and indicates a high-ranking position, like 'ruler' ('Be humble whatever high position you hold', '*Ulyḳ* and *tôre* tormented the people …' etc.).

The Turkic people use the word *Buyuk* (high) along with *Uluk*. Kazakhs only use the word *uly* (great). It seems that Kazakhs overdid it when fighting against Pan-Turkism during the Soviet times and lost a lot of their heritage, including some precious words from their language. So, when our ancestors said, 'Did you climb Ulytau?' they probably meant the sacred mountain, the holy place, its height and purity in

---

42 Ulugbek: Mirza Muhammed Taraghay
    bin Shahrukh (1394–1449) was a Timurid
    ruler, astronomer and mathematician.
    '*Ulugbek*' is a moniker, loosely translated
    as 'Great Ruler'.

general, not the actual geographical name, Ulytau. Then why did they say, 'Did you try the snowcock meat?'

Here we want to dwell on a superstition. They say that sailors and anglers had a custom that if among drowning people there was a man who had tried the meat of the snowcock, then he would be thrown into the water as a sacrifice and the rest would reach the shore unharmed.

According to another legend, long ago, local residents asked merchants who visited China, 'Did you climb Ulytau? Did you try the snowcock meat?' If someone answered positively, then he was killed immediately, and his flesh was cooked to be used as a cure for a thousand diseases.

So, what is it? Is it a way of honouring the snowcock or a method that was used to excuse unreasonable hunters? You may think whatever you like, but it is true that such conversations exist to this day.

Let us forget about legend and return to the truth. There is a lot of information that Eastern healers, shamans and chiropractors used the snowcock's meat to treat many diseases. It is said that the secret medicine called '*mumiye*', which can be found only in high mountains, was found thanks to *kal-murik* ('snowcock' in Tajiki Persian language). We assume that the black oil mentioned in the tale is a *mumiye*. Dear readers, I urge you to read another fairy tale.

> Long ago, when the pheasant was red with a long tail, the fox was a guard, the tortoise weighed goods in the market, the partridge played *kernej* and the woodchuck was a harmonist, the following happened at the very top of Ulytau, in the snowcock's nest.[43]

> At that time, an old man named Ulanaḳ lived in Ulytau. He was destitute and childless: he dressed in leaves, slept on bare ground, had festered eyes and shaky hands. He had an old wife named Uldanaj. When the snowcock began to sing in the morning, they cried: 'When the snowcock sings, it reminds us of the son we don't have, and of the daughter we don't have. Is there anyone more miserable than we are?'

> God pitied Ulanaḳ and Uldanaj and granted them a son. They called him Ularbek. Ularbek grew up fast and became a huntsman. He had a string trap, and neither a high-flying golden eagle, nor a fast-running kulan could escape it. Therefore, he was nicknamed 'Hunter Ularbek with the string trap'. He wandered in all the mountains and caught all the animals. 'His shelter was a hut. At the sight of him, animals would run, a saiga would kick its baby and run too, its milk spilled on the ground,' as they say.

> When Ulanaḳ became even older, he warned his only son:
> The snowcock bird of Ulytau lived on the top of the mount.
> The baby of a mother deer was next to her.
> Why did you hunt them?

43 *Kernej* is a wind instrument, resembling a small pipe, which is made from copper.

Was the nestling in the nest your enemy?

Would you eat it, a newborn chick?

The young saiga fell off a cliff and died.

Animals and birds all ran away.

When your mother was pregnant, she craved for snowcock.

It is a sacred bird. If you don't stop scaring away the animals,

if you don't understand how sacred the snowcock is,

you are courting danger, my son.

No one can reach the top of Ulytau, no one can find the snowcock's nest. But Ularbek was stubborn.

It has long been said that, 'It's impossible to stop the girl who wants to get married and the hunter who wants to hunt'. When Ulanak died, it was a favourable day for hunting. Instead of paying his last respects to his father, Ularbek went to Ulytau for the snowcock's nest, taking with him his string trap and a gun, saying, 'If a camel dies, it will be slaughtered, if the father dies, he will be buried, but it would be foolish to miss such a hunting season …'

Then the huntsman started to sing:

> If I do not climb Ulytau, why do I need a road?
> If I do not catch the snowcock, why do I need my hands?

He had just uttered these words, when he slipped, fell and broke his arm.

> You were masterful and tireless,
> what is wrong with you, my hand?
> My flat sole, my strong toes,
> My quick heels, my long feet,
> what is wrong with you?

No sooner had he said this when he broke his leg.

He lay there for two days, overwhelmed by pain. No one came to him. He lay for four days and could not descend the mountain. No one rescued him. He shouted in pain. No one heard except the unforgiving mountain and the deserted steppe. He made crutches out of his gun and traps and made his way back home with difficulty. When he returned, he saw that his father had already been buried, the camel had been slaughtered, and the people who had gathered for the funeral prayers had already gone. There was no one who sympathized with him. Who but a mother would feel sorry for a spoiled son? She cried, hugging her son: 'I cried my eyes out, my dear. You were a sharp-shooter; nothing escaped your bullet. Why did you become so insatiable, my son?'

Months and years passed, but Ularbek could not get up. His broken arm ached every night, his broken leg did not move. One day his mother said, 'This won't do, son. I will go to Ulytau. I will look for the snowcock. It helped me overcome my craving when I was pregnant with you. Maybe it will help me again to overcome my grief.'

> You hide at the sight of us, snowcock, don't be afraid, come here.
> Look at poor me. Look at my crying son.
> Pluck my forty ribs, take my thirty vertebrae, but help my only child.

She walked day and night. On the fifth day, her back ached. On the sixth day, her leg ached, but she didn't stop. On the seventh day she saw a mountain and, on its slopes, there was a nest, and in the nest, there was a single nestling. She wanted to touch it, but dropped it and the chick broke its leg. The poor old woman ran back and hid in the shadow of the stone. She fell asleep with fatigue and awoke to the voice of a bird in alarm. Then she saw how the snowcock was giving black substance to the chick, whose leg was broken. She peered closely, but could not see the black substance, then returned the next day. She saw that the chick had become quite strong, as the mother bird had smeared black oil-like substance on its leg and wrapped it with leaves, and there were soiled leaves all around.

> During my sunset years
> I had to walk through the mountains.
> My only son almost died, breaking his arm and leg.
> I am asking neither for your meat nor for your bone.
> Give me some of your waste.
> I am ready to die for the sake of my child.

Uldanaj collected all the waste without dropping a single drop and returned home. She immediately wrapped Ularbek's arms and legs in it. Her son slept well that night. The next morning, she added snowcock's waste to tea and gave it to her son, while saying: 'Drink for three days, to the bottom; drink for seven days, and be patient; drink for eight days, then stand up; drink for nine days and go and celebrate.'

Soon Ularbek recovered fully and made friends with the snowcock, pulled out the string from his trap, attached it to the *ķobyz* and therefore the *ķobyz* melody was called an *Ular*; that is, 'snowcock' in Kazakh.

The Birds Are Our Friends

Clanging Cranes

*N*ow does the old song begin, that people sang?

> *Our people move early, come back late,*
> *the bird returns alongside them.*
> *There is a grief in the voice of the departing bird,*
> *that reminds us of our sorrow.*[44]

What kind of bird is it? What is the song that recalls old wounds buried deep in the heart? I think that this song, which makes one cry involuntarily, was inspired by the sad melody of cranes, which they sing on their departure.

This autumn is very favourable. There is no rain, no snow, no piercing winds. How long will these carefree starry nights and warm days last? At this time, the birds leave us every year for warm lands.

Scientists call the period from 21 September to 21 October the first month of autumn, and sometimes 'the time when the birds migrate'. At this time of year there may be an Indian summer; Kazakhs call it a 'yellowish summer'. In southern Kazakhstan, this time of the year is called 'the season of watermelons and melons'. The second month of autumn lasts from 21 October to 21 November. Kazakhs call this time 'brown autumn' (quiet autumn). The third month lasts from 21 November to 21 December. As Abai wrote, 'November and December are the beginning of winter, sometimes it comes sooner, sometimes later'. It is late autumn, unpleasant and cold.

This year the birds stayed until late autumn. Speaking of birds, our winged friends migrate at different times. Not all birds fly away at once. The very first birds to fly away are the singers, 'interesting red-and-green-feathered birds'. By late September, they are nowhere to be found. They are also the last to arrive in spring.

---

44 The first line refers to the Kazakhs' nomadic lifestyle. They used to move four times a year: from winter pastures (*kystau*) to spring pastures (*kôkteu*), then to summer and autumn pastures (*žajlau* and *kùzeu* respectively).

The second to leave are those birds that are afraid to fly during the day because of falcons and hawks; small birds such as ducks, quails and Eurasian woodcocks.

As the saying goes, 'The last camel in the caravan has the heaviest load': large birds like cranes, swans, herons and storks fly last. The stork is a silent bird; herons and pelicans have an ordinary voice. Is it because they fly to warm lands together, or because we do not always pay attention to them, but often confuse them?

It is true that long-legged birds look alike. Therefore, some foolish hunters get into trouble by shooting a flying heron, thinking it is a goose. The heron throws back its head and bends its neck during flight, whereas the goose pulls its head forward, like a swan. Perhaps that is why Kazakhs called a good horse a 'gooseneck', a 'pure-bred gooseneck'.

The crane is very easy to identify. If the swan flies with its knees bent, the crane flies with its head stretched forward and its legs stretched back. Now add to this image its aforementioned woeful voice. It seems that God instructed cranes to sing a farewell song to their

The Birds Are Our Friends

native lands on behalf of all the birds flying off to warmer climes. As they say, 'If six brothers are born to one mother, only one of them can be the leader.' It seems that among all the birds, only the crane flies with such grief.

This year they returned in the second half of November: Clang, clang, clang …

This song has a secret power that can wake sweetly sleeping nature, like the sound of the *azan* in the early morning. Therefore, people say: 'There is grief in the voice of the departing bird.'

Our ancestors sang 'I couldn't say farewell to my distinguished people'. Nature does not have ugly moments, it's always singing and celebrating life. Nomadic people knew this very well. There is true majesty in finding the meaning of existence in the cranes' short song, which disappears in a split second!

The *dombyra* can reproduce the voice of a swan; the accordion can reproduce the voice of a nightingale; the *ķobyz* can reproduce the voice of a goose; the pipe can perfectly reproduce the sad voice of a crane. Bashkirs have a *kùj* called 'Synrau Torna' – 'Lonely Crane'. This is the heart-breaking melody of the returning crane. A long time ago, when the Bashkirs roamed near Edil's (the Volga's) ponds, they came across the Russian cannon. They were trapped, with Edil to the rear and a gun in front. At this moment, dark clouds covered the sky and the enemies could see nothing. They were bewildered. The Bashkir *batyrs* passed by the Russian soldiers while they were confused. It turned out that the clouds were *cranes*. Legend has it that the aforementioned *kùj* is dedicated to white angels that came from nowhere.

A similar legend can be found in the 'Ar-Risala' ('Accounts') by the Arab historian ibn Fadlan, who visited our lands in the first half of the tenth century. Legends and fairy tales collected by ethnographers Sergei Rybakov (1897) and Karim Diyarov (1987) recount the same thing. The first Bashkir ballet was called *The Crane Song*. The famous Bashkir poet Rami Garipov has a poem with the same title. The song 'Zhuravli' ('Cranes') was almost as popular as the state anthem during the Soviet Era. Its lyrics are written by the prominent Avar poet Rasul Gamzatov. Gamzatov was a friend of Kazakh literature and regarded Muḣtar Aʻuezov as his mentor. The lyrics in combination with the beautiful melody of Soviet composer and performer Yan Frenkel are touching indeed. It was translated into Kazakh by the late poet Saġi Žienbaev, and one of the most successful English translations was produced by American poet Leo Schwartzberg in 2018:

> Sometimes I feel that all those fallen soldiers,
> Who never left the bloody battle zones,
> Have not been buried to decay and molder,
> But turned into white cranes that softly groan.
>
> And thus, until these days since those bygone times,
> They still fly in the skies and gently cry.
> Isn't it why we often hear those sad chimes
> And calmly freeze, while looking in the sky?
>
> A tired flock of cranes still flies – their wings flap.
> Birds glide into the twilight, roaming free.

In their formation I can see a small gap –
It might be so, that space is meant for me.

The day shall come, when in a mist of ashen
I'll soar with cranes, and final rest I'll find,
From the skies calling – in a bird-like fashion –
All those of you, who I'll have left behind.[45]

Rasul Gamzatov died and was buried on Mount Tarki in Dagestan on 4 October 2003. The monument 'White Cranes' was erected just above his grave. The people of Dagestan call 22 November 'the Day of the White Cranes'.

Recently, an 8-metre bronze monument was erected in honour of the people killed during a hostage crisis at a theatre located on Dubrovskaya Street in Moscow, and carried out by Chechens, who Russians have regarded as terrorists. The monument depicts three cranes leaning towards each other and about to fly up into the sky. Russian people have long honoured cranes.

During the reign of the tsar, the St Petersburg cadets and soldiers, even officers, lovingly sang the song 'The Crane' ('*Zhuravl*'). The chorus of this song is sung in a sad voice. People say that the lyrics of this song were composed by the distinguished nineteenth-century Russian poet Mikhail Lermontov; others say that they were authored by another prominent poet, Alexander Polezhayev. In recent years, they have said that this work belongs to an eighteenth-century poet, Gavrila Derzhavin.

As the saying goes, 'Children of the same mother can be as different as chalk and cheese', and such a sad song does not distinguish all cranes; there are cranes that fly making a very unpleasant sound. There are fifteen crane species belonging to five groups: the blue crane, the black-necked crane, the white-naped crane, the black-crowned crane and the demoiselle crane, as well as the Eurasian, hooded, Siberian, wattled and whooping cranes, etc.

The black-tailed, slate-grey-coloured Eurasian crane has the saddest voice of all fifteen cranes. It is 1.5 metres in height, weighs 4–4.5 kilograms and can be seen from afar. Because of its bitter voice and long legs, the grey crane often falls prey to hunters and predators.

The poet Baḳytkerej Ysḳaḳov collected the following folk song:

Cranes, long-necked lords,

considerate sisters-in-law

who buttoned an old fur coat for me,

stretch the lasso and carpet,

send my regards to the lame girl.

---

45 Translated by Leo Schwartzberg © 2018, available at: https://lyricstranslate.com/en/zhuravli-журавли-cranes.html-5.

The return of cranes in the spring is described in the folk mythology as follows:

> There is a long, long road.
> A large troop is coming
> on the long road.
> Who is the commander?
> It's a long-legged giant named 'The Lanky'

'A large troop is coming' because Eurasian cranes usually fly in flocks. When the leader (a giant named 'The Lanky') gets tired, the second-in-command, another 'long-legged giant with short feathers', assumes the position. Until recently, scientific literature claimed that the number of Eurasian cranes in a flock could reach 70–80. More recently, the Russian media wrote about the *scientific sensation* that about 500 Eurasian cranes landed simultaneously on crops on the border of the Menzil and Aktanysh regions of Tatarstan.

They stop in Aķmola, Ķostanaj and the Pavlodar regions of northern Kazakhstan in August and September, to refresh themselves before flying to warmer lands. Cranes spoiled 1,500 hectares of cropland belonging to the Krasnoyarskaya Company in the Aķmola region recently. It would be wrong to conclude that these birds should be exterminated though. The Ahmet Bajtu̇rsynov Ķostanaj State University studies Eurasian and white-naped cranes, and serves as an example for protecting and resettling them.[46] Teachers and students at Ķostanaj are introducing an initiative to celebrate 'Crane Day' annually each autumn. I believe God protects those who protect the birds.

George Archibald has been co-founder and President of the International Crane Foundation in the United States since 1973. In the beginning Mr Archibald was just an ordinary

person who had grown up with no interest in birds, biology or ornithology, but then he joined the US Army. In those years America did not know how to get out of the Vietnam War. Mr Archibald's company suffered many losses in battle. The two sides shot at each other mercilessly. It was very noisy. As soon as the battle subsided slightly, two Eurasian cranes landed between the opposing sides and began to dance. Cranes usually dance during the breeding season. However, there are people who have seen cranes dance on

46 Ahmet Bajtu̇rsynov (1873–1937) was a prominent Kazakh poet, linguist, educator and member of the national Alash movement. He was shot by the USSR authorities in 1937.

other days. These noble birds, that looked as if they were trying to mediate between the troops who were fighting to the death, inspired the soldier. He swore, 'I will dedicate my life to the protection of the cranes if I survive this war.' His wish came true and he returned home safe and sound from the bloody battle. He spent all his money to launch a foundation dedicated to the protection of cranes and eventually succeeded in opening the International Crane Foundation.

By the way, these Eurasian cranes have been immortalized on screen, in Soviet director Mikhail Kalatozov's film, *The Cranes Are Flying*, which is still popular after fifty years.

This famous crane dance, which has acted for good so many times, occasionally turns into a fight. Although storks are famous for fighting among themselves, cranes have a special method of fighting. One unarmed combat method, invented for self-defence by the students of the Shaolin Temple in China, is called the 'White Crane Style'. Where did this method come from? Legend has it that a monk who was tired on a long journey rested by the roadside. After some time, he saw cranes fighting with each other in the fields. The monk, watching every movement, forgot his fatigue for a moment and began to dance. The goal was to memorize the cranes' fighting movements. Thus, a new style appeared among the Shaolin fighters.

Kazakhs do not eat cranes, therefore, they do not shoot them. The late Táken Álimḳulov, in his story 'Alǵyrdyn tamyry' ('The Root of Alǵyr'), made his hero Bóribek eat a crane:[47]

> When he was eating crane's meat at noon, Bóribek pulled a juniper out of his purse and snorted: 'This worthless crane did not drink enough milk when it was a chick. Its meat is stuck between my teeth.' *Did not drink enough milk.* How could Bóribek know that birds do not produce milk? The cranes speak beautiful language. When they bid farewell, goosebumps run through one's body. That is why, perhaps, the Kazakhs do not eat the crane.

Táken Álimḳulov was describing the years of the Great Famine (1930–33) in this story. Have you heard about those who stole a crane from the zoo to eat a little while back, when there was no famine or other extreme conditions?

In the Novosibirsk Zoo, the Japanese crane (red-crowned crane), which cost US$7,000, disappeared. The Head of the zoo, Mr Shilo, reported the situation to the public on local television and asked for the return of the crane. Soon, they had a message about crane's feathers scattered in the yard of a man named Sergei, who lived in the suburbs. When guards attended the scene, they found unemployed Sergei and his beloved Masha frying the crane.

'Where did you get that?' they asked.

'I had a headache and went to the zoo, and then I noticed a bird with long legs. When the guards were not at their stations, I twisted its neck and put it in my bag. I've exchanged half of its meat for vodka, and that's the other half,' he said as if it were nothing.

Some people just don't care.

There were suggestions about making the white-naped crane the emblem of the fauna of the Republic of Kazakhstan, and like many good initiatives, this story has also been forgotten. In truth, the most precious bird for Kazakhs is the bustard. Unfortunately, there are very few bustards left today on the vast lands stretching between Altaj and Atyrau. The

---

47 Táken Álimḳulov (1918–87) was a Kazakh writer and literary critic.

most common bird after the bustard was the white-naped crane, but today it is included on Kazakhstan's Red List.[48]

I personally do not understand why Kazakhs call the white-naped crane 'white-headed'. In fact, it is 'black-headed'. Its forehead, crown, neck and chest are black. This is what distinguishes it from other cranes. Yes, it has white eyebrows that grow just above the eyes, like the bustard. Perhaps that is why it was nicknamed the white-headed, or white-naped, crane. Of course, this bird deserves a more beautiful and meaningful name. The *Kazakh Soviet Encyclopedia*, published in the Soviet Era, names it the 'graceful crane', which is more suitable than 'white-headed crane'.[49] Well, it isn't the first and won't be the last gorgeous creature to bear an unsuitable name.

Kazakhs have honoured the white-naped crane. People predicted the weather by observing them in flight. If they flew low, it meant that the cold was approaching. If they flew high in the sky, then autumn was forecast to be warm and favourable. If they migrated late, the winter would be warm. If they left quickly in groups and in a neat formation, then it meant in one week's time there would be blizzards and thick snow, so people began to enclose their weak and sick cattle in barns and prepare fodder and hay for them.

One nomadic people, the Mongols, never bothered cranes. White-naped cranes lived unmolested and were not afraid of anyone in the Mongolian land, much as cows roam freely in India. Unlike in Kazakhstan, their numbers haven't declined in Mongolia. They almost died out during the Virgin Lands Campaign in Kazakhstan, but now their number has reached 50,000–60,000.[50]

The number of white-naped cranes is growing every year, but the number of Siberian or snow cranes, which number about 3,000 throughout the world, is decreasing. This is a snow-white bird and can be easily confused with the white stork. However, if you look at the red feathers near its beak and the black feathers on its tail, you can determine that it is a crane. Those who could not define it initially called it a *Storch* in German (simply meaning 'stork'). Russians call it *Sterkh*.

Long ago, these cranes lived along the Tobyl and Esil (Ishim) rivers, but now we hardly see them at all in Kazakhstan. However, sometimes in the autumn they stop on our land to spend a night or two while flying to India and Iran.

---

48 The International Union for Conservation of Nature (IUCN) Red List of Threatened Species.

49 *Kazakh Soviet Encyclopedia*, Volume II, p. 253.

50 The Virgin Lands Campaign was Nikita Khrushchev's State Development and Resettlement Campaign (1953–63) to turn the lands located mostly in the steppes of the Volga region, northern Kazakhstan and southern Siberia into a major agricultural region.

They fly over nine countries to get to warmer lands. It is especially dangerous to fly over Afghanistan and Pakistan, because in these countries they are allowed to shoot Siberian cranes. But we also have some rich people who like to put a 1.5-metre-tall snow-white crane on display, as a decoration. The Siberian crane is considered the bird of happiness, a holy bird, in many countries. Its distinctive feature is that it lives longer than other cranes. In Japan, for instance, one well-looked-after Siberian crane lived for seventy years.

A'biš Kekilbaev, a great Kazakh writer of our time, talks in his travel log *Tyrau-tyrau tyrnalar* (*Clanging Cranes*) about the Japanese love for Siberian cranes:[51]

> 250,000 of the 400,000 inhabitants of Hiroshima were killed in one day … The then-four-year-old girl Sasaki Teyko, finally died in 1955, after fighting cancer for ten years. Since Siberian cranes are one of the longest-living birds, the Japanese believe that if a person who has been diagnosed with an incurable disease makes thousands of cranes on their own, they will get well. Sasaki also made 600 paper cranes believing this … People say that she would have survived if she had been allowed enough time to make one thousand cranes. A monument in her honour was erected in the park in 1958, with money raised by children. A little girl sits on a bumpy beak that resembles the atomic bomb. Several flying cranes hang on the monument. Thousands of children throughout the world send millions of paper cranes every year to put on Sasaki's monument …

The Siberian crane does not make a nest. It hatches its eggs on ice and snow. Only one of the two eggs survives. The law of natural selection is relentless. This is a very careful bird, a noble creature. It is cherished in any country.

Ķuandyķ Šaṅġytbaev, a poet as handsome as the Siberian crane itself, describes in his poem 'Kytalyk' ('Siberian crane') that this bird is respected by the Yakuts too:

> We paid a visit to Bului,
> we were guests for a few days.
> In a hospitable home,
> we met a Kazakh girl.
>
> *Kytalyk*, come here, *kytalyk*,
> an angel bird of happiness,
> let us drink from the *choron*
> for the health of the Yakuts![52]

We would like to finish the story about the white crane with a Japanese fairy tale entitled *The Crane Wife*:

Once upon a time, there lived a farmer. He was very poor. He had a tiny plot of land, where he worked tirelessly from morning to evening, but remained poor. His life was dark and dull. Once he stood leaning on his hoe and thought, *Why was I born to suffer? I wish I*

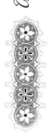

---

51 A'biš Kekilbaev (1939–2015) was a prominent writer, literary translator, poet and literary critic, as well as a notable public and political figure, People's Writer of Kazakhstan (1987) and a Labour Hero (2009).

52 *Kytalyk* is a Yakut name for the Siberian crane, sacred bird for Yakuts. *Choron* is a national Yakut vessel for the storage and consumption of *ķymyz* (fermented mare's milk).

had died. Suddenly something fell from the sky in front of him. It turned out to be a crane, with a broken wing. He thought, *You are a hapless bird, just like me*, and took it home. He washed its wound with rice water and bandaged the wound. Days and months passed. The wounded bird started to recover. When the bird grew stronger, the man led her out into the street and allowed her to fly away wishing her, *Good luck! May troubles pass you by! Take care!* The crane circled over the farmer's house three times and then disappeared. The farmer went to the fields with his hoe. In the evening, as usual, he returned home tired and sweaty. He was so tired that he fell asleep on the way. He hit his head on a wall and saw in front of him a girl of indescribable beauty.

'My dear, who are you? Where did you come from?' the farmer asked in disbelief.

'Don't worry, don't rush,' the girl replied. 'I am your wife, bestowed on you by God.'

'Stop it, darling. Do not mock me. Go away. I am a poor fellow unable to feed himself, let alone a wife. There is no grain in my house,' said the man and turned away.

'Don't worry,' uttered the girl. 'If you untie this bundle, we will have enough rice. Come on, open the door.'

The farmer agreed with God's will. They began to live together, two halves forming one whole. The poor man started to find some luck. He began to wear new things, renewed his house, ate enough, slept comfortably and woke content. He was no longer thin and poor. One day his wife said: 'Now, build me a room next to our house. I will put a spinning wheel there to add to a spindle. But you must not go there until I let you. Do not even dare peek through the door. Agreed?'

'Agreed,' he said.

For seven days and seven nights, he heard his wife turning the spindle in the next room. For seven days and seven nights, his wife did not leave that room. On the eighth day, she signalled. The farmer got up and walked to the door. He saw his wife holding a carpet of extraordinary beauty.

'Take it and sell in the bazaar,' said the wife. 'God will help. You will get a lot of money.'

All her words came true: one immensely wealthy merchant bought the carpet for a large sum. The farmer ran home, and saw that a second carpet was ready. That rich man bought this carpet too. The farmer walked out of the bazaar and thought, *Where does my wife get the thread for the carpet from? Where does my wife get these beautiful dyes from?*

He could not help it and looked through a hole in the door: there was no wife, but the wounded crane in front of the spindle. It was pulling out its feathers to make the thread. Its feathers turned into white threads, and the crane's blood turned into red dye on the carpet.

'Hey, what are you doing?' the farmer screamed. The crane took fright and sat down tiredly.

'No, it can't be so, dear,' she said in the voice of his wife. 'Now we are finished. What did I tell you? Not to enter without permission. Yes, I am the crane that you saved. I am the daughter of the King of Birds. I fell in love with you and came to you to be your wife. I kept my promise. You broke our vow. I cannot stay here. Goodbye. Take care of this last carpet from me, let it remind you of me.'

Then the crane flew three times round the farmer's head and disappeared. Forever.

Why can't a man keep his promise?

What are the faults of birds?

Pelican

A distinguished Kazakh writer, Ġabit Mùsirepov, in his story 'Ataķty áňši Majra' ('The famous singer Majra'), quotes Majra:

There was a lousy poet named Ķydyraly, and he used his poor verses as a bargaining tool for favours from others.[53] He walked from one *auyl* to another, earning a living.[54] If you saw Ķydyraly perform, you might think that poets are the nastiest people in the world: tedious, annoying and rude. Neither his song nor his poems were pleasant. He always praised the rich and belittled the poor and the weak.

The high-speed Almaty–Moscow train in which I happened to be a traveller had its own Ķydyraly. The main difference was that the guy who was singing while hurtling through the compartment, unlike Ġabit Mùsirepov's character Ķydyraly, was a beggar. As for the similarity – he was intrusive and approached passengers by hunching over and sitting down on the edge of the seat.

'Uncle, let me sing you a song with the *dombyra*,' (he mispronounced it).

He began to sing, without waiting for an answer. His voice was miserable and sad. His songs combined Kyrgyz tunes and elements of *ashula*, an original Uzbek song style. His *dombyra* suited him; it was as lazy and sluggish as a worn-out horse suffering from back pain. Listening to him, you might think that there was no instrument more wretched and pathetic than the *dombyra*. You would have felt like giving alms to the owner of the *dombyra*, so that he no longer played. It seemed that its melody would make you depressed and nauseous and that this horror would never end.

---

53 Ķydyraly, a man's name, can be loosely translated from Kazakh as 'someone who is fun-loving, enjoys paying visits to others' or 'an idle person'.

54 *Auyl* is traditionally a cultural union of nomads, now a rural settlement; synonymous with sacred concepts such as 'native land' and 'homeland'.

The train went fast. There were two of us in the compartment: an old woman, who had visited her nephews in Almaty, and me. We did not get on well from the beginning of our journey. The old woman seemed too fashionable and fun-loving for her age. Sometimes she spoke Russian. *Ķydyraly* greeted us when he passed by each time.

'I am trying to feed my family,' he said, smiling inappropriately.

'That's right,' said the old woman, supporting him.

Why it was the right thing to do? Now, when a guest arrives in any district, *auyl*, even school or institution, more often than not a hired poet appears to greet them by singing a song. How difficult it was to be poor and decent at the same time.

Ķydyraly came again:

'Uncle, one song on *dombyra* …'

I handed him the money in advance, and then pointed to the door:

'Let's pretend that you have already performed the song on the *dombyra*, and I have already listened to it. Happy travels. Go.'

The old woman lifted her head as if she had been waiting for this moment.

'Don't bother him, son, let him sing,' she said, coughing. Then she called the *singer-poet* close to her.

'Sing us the song that you sang yesterday. If you sing well, then I will give you money. Yesterday you didn't sing it very well.'

'I don't take money from retirees and policemen,' grinned the *singer-poet*. Shameless poets, cheap artists, annoying artisans have such nasty, clichéd words. They annoy you, be it at weddings or when watching TV.

I hurried out. When I returned after having dinner in the dining car, I saw that many people had gathered in front of our compartment. They crowded round and stood together. A song was coming from inside; a pleasant and beautiful song, not an annoying one. That wretched *dombyra* had a delicate sound now and combined gently with a beautiful song. I thought, *God! Is this guy, sitting on my seat with his legs crossed, the same Ķydyraly I left half an hour ago? That same Ķydyraly who sang plaintively? How did he suddenly change?* I could not believe my eyes.

> I am singing to amuse you along the way,
> if you want to, then put dollars in my hand.
> If you do not want to give dollars and give *tenge*,
> I will still be pleased with you.[55]
> *Alaj, alaj, alaj-aj-au-rahym-aj,*

Oh, life … I thought, this annoying song, which he had sung the day before when wandering around the carriages, was all he is capable of.

The old woman looked thoughtfully through the window. She seemed like a calm and respected matron, not a frivolous old woman, which was my first impression of her. The song grew louder and louder. This was a completely different song. The deep wrinkles under the singer's eyes had already smoothed out, his thin neck had become even longer. It seemed that his hissing words, due to a missing tooth, had already been corrected. He seemed somewhat familiar when he sang the refrain, as if I had already seen him some-

55 *Tenge* is Kazakh currency.

where else. Where had I seen him? How long had I known the singer or song? Was this the same guy who'd annoyed us yesterday with his vile songs? How did he know such wonderful poetry?

It was a ballad about a young man madly in love with a beauty: he lost peace of mind because of his love. He suffered because of the request of the girl: 'The day you bring your mother's heart to me, I will be your wife,' she said. He struggled with the request, but in the end, he got up at night and tore his mother's heart out. The young man walked and stumbled, and dropped the heart that was in his hands. The heart that lay on the ground uttered, 'My son, watch your step, be careful.' 'Mothers' love is infinite' concluded the song. People applauded.

'Well done!'

'What a pity!'

'Sing another song!'

But he did not sing. The poet grabbed his *dombyra* and left, despite his old hat overflowing with money. He did not even acknowledge the applause of the people; he walked quickly, gasping for breath. I grabbed the old hat and ran after him. When I caught up, I saw him smoking in the vestibule. He was very pale. He massaged his heart with his right hand.

'I know you,' he said, shading his eyes. 'You did not recognize me. I was different. Who would have thought that things could turn out this way? I've been unemployed for thirteen years,' he said breathlessly. He put out the cigarette, crushing it with his heel.

'Excuse me,' he said with a guilty voice, 'My quick work feeds me. I will leave at the next station. Farewell. My heart hurts, damn it!'

He clutched his heart again. I lit a cigarette and looked outside.

'It was the famous ballad "Ana *žùregi*" ["Mother's heart"] by Aķuštap Baķtygereeva.'[56]

'I know,' I said, 'it is one of her great verses.'

'I entered the Conservatoire thanks to that song. I always get ill when I sing that song now,' he said sadly. 'You can't sing such a song carelessly, and so I try my best. Then I definitely feel unwell, like this.'

I handed him the old hat.

'Go to the doctor,' I said.

'The doctors will not attend you unless you give them money,' said the poet with a grin. Why was this poor man grinning?

Ivan Bunin's character says: 'Only a Chinese man will say that his wife died yesterday and laugh ruefully.'[57] Have we all become like that? The train stopped. It was a small station. The playful conductor girl, who had been angry all day, smiled. She patted him on the shoulder

56 Aķu štap Baķtygereeva (*b.* 1944) is a poet, and winner of the State Prize of the Republic of Kazakhstan (2018).

57 Ivan Bunin (1870–1953) was the first Russian writer to win the Nobel Prize for Literature.

with her huge hands and said, '*Ciao*'. The guy walked, occasionally panting, in the direction of the first-aid post, clutching his heart.

The train went fast. It was hotter and stuffier inside than outside. Looking at the bent, submissive trees alongside the road, one could understand that there was not the slightest breeze.

'Did we pass Birḵazan?' asked the old woman.[58]

'I don't know,' I replied.

The old woman muttered something and wiped her face with her palms. All old women were alike: she had just recited the Qur'an for the benefit of departed souls, or had remembered something and recited *kalima* to herself.[59] She wished health to her grandchildren in the *auyl* and her nephews in Almaty. The whole world seems to be well and unharmed thanks to the prayers of people like her.

The conductor came with a kettle and said: 'Drink tea, Grandma. We've just passed Birḵazan station.'

'Long life to you, daughter.'

The girl made her way out. I moved the teapot towards me to pour the tea. The old woman straightened her headscarf and sat up.

'My dear, are you from Žaṇaḵorġan or Türkistan?' she asked. 'You are not a stranger to me. You have turned out to be a *ḵuda*.[60] I know that the men pour tea in your area. Thank you, but I can pour the tea myself. Give me the kettle.'

I gave it to her. The old woman first poured tea for me, then poured herself a full cup and looked out of the window with astonishment.

'Birḵazan. These are all our lands,' she said, glancing at the elevated hills. 'When I first got married, I lived next to that lake.

'The Second World War was over. My husband came back safe and sound. The people feasted, but not with abundance. Everyone hoped that the wounds of war would soon heal. That was the spirit. The head of the collective farm was my distant brother-in-law. He summoned my husband and said:

'"My good man, we want to send you to Ḵambaš, so that you can be in charge of the fishermen. The old female cook's fingers were infected by whitlow and she can no longer work. Take your wife. She will prepare food for the fishermen."

'In those days, unlike today, the word of an older person was law for the young people. We collected our belongings, loaded them onto a black camel and set off in the evening. When we arrived, we found there no anglers, but old men and women, women with children. They were tired, exhausted and nervous. At the slightest dispute, they immediately began to swear. Let her rest in peace, my mother-in-law was from the Žaḵajym clan and had given me quite a lot of pure-bred dromedary meat in the autumn. I cooked it the day we arrived. After the people cheered up, having eaten meat, they handed me a book, saying, "Dear sister-in-law, read us a story," and I read. People were happy. We went to bed late.

---

58 Birḵazan: lit. 'Pelican' – a small town in West Kazakhstan.

59 It is common practice among Kazakhs to recite Qur'anic verses assumingly for the benefit of departed souls; *kalima* is the formal content of the declaration of faith: 'There is no God but Allah, and Muhammad is his messenger.'

60 Usually parents and relatives of a married couple refer to each other as *ḵuda*, and have a particular warm and respectful relationship; in Kazakh society one would be honoured to be called *ḵuda*, and pleased to treat their *ḵuda* with all due respect in response; in addition, people from the same area as their *ḵuda* could be treated with the same reverence.

The Birds Are Our Friends

'The moon was shining brightly. There were no mosquitoes.

'"It seems that the pelicans have arrived," my husband said, listening in to the sounds coming from the lakeside.

'I did not pay attention. I knew that the pelican was a bird, but I could not distinguish its voice from the voice of other birds. To me, all the birds seemed the same.

'The next day I headed to the lake, but it was swampy on the shore, and I went further in search of drinking water. I passed by the field of purple loosestrife with my full bucket and suddenly it seemed to me that something massive had flown over my head. I screamed. It seemed that something huge, like the flying roof of a house, landed on the water with a crash. I looked and saw a spotted bird with a long white beak, a grey tail, a yellow craw and a white breast, which sailed next to the reeds. I had never seen it before, but I realized that it was the pelican that my husband had been talking about.

'The pelican was an impressive bird indeed. It was smaller than a bustard, but twice as big as a swan. God knew, it swallowed two or three buckets of water at once and kept the fish and a frog, and spat out the rest of the water. When it had drunk the water, its gular pouch expanded and fell down. Perhaps that was why I immediately guessed the answer to the riddle, when later, guys and girls were entertaining themselves by asking riddles:

> Our people spend their summers in the highlands,
> this is their native place, where they are accustomed to.
> A respected matron gracefully fattens on the lake,
> hanging on her neck a large *saba*.[61]
> Who is she?

'From that day on, I hated my new *neighbour*, who scared me to death. It was an ugly bird with thick, short claws and short legs, which looked ridiculous against the backdrop of its huge torso. Other birds sang beautifully, frolicked, played on the shore of the lake, but the pelican buzzed like an old muttering woman. It ate frogs, crayfish, small fish and insects. It was very gluttonous. It clearly saw the small fish in the water, even when flying very high, and immediately swooped down. It picked up its prey at the speed of light and swallowed it whole, immediately. I told my husband everything.

'He said sadly: "This damned war affected the birds too. At the end of March and the beginning of April,

61 *Saba* is a large vessel to ferment mare's milk, usually made of smoked horse skin.

there used to be so many pelicans that the surface of the lake would not be visible at all. I saw 500–600 birds fly to the lake together. Now there are very few of them left." He sighed.

'He was such an agitated man that he felt sorry even when a raven died. That was probably why he died so early, let him rest in peace. Other people's husbands, his contemporaries, are still restless.'

The old woman cried a little. The train was rushing fast. The tea had long since cooled. The conductor had disappeared without a trace at the right time. I wanted to make hot tea, but I was afraid that the old woman would scold me again and sat silently. The image of the singer who'd sung 'Mother's heart' by Aқuštap Baķtygereeva was still before my eyes. Where was he?

The old woman continued her story.

'Once I noticed a circle resembling chain mail in the centre of a lake, woven from trees, reeds and the remains of cat's tail. Pelicans lived in those areas, so this was its nest. As soon as I thought about it, the bird immediately headed towards me, making a terrible sound. I ran away. The next day I returned to that place. The two birds had united and made their nest even bigger. However, I did not linger and left. There was an unbearable smell. It was impossible to get close. Soon, three eggs appeared in the nest. I was so sorry that such beautiful eggs lay in such a terrible nest. After some time, my mother-in-law fell ill and I left for the *auyl*. On my return a month later, I saw that those eggs were still resting in the nest. The pelican sat on its nest all day long. Another week passed. Early in the morning, I came to fetch some water and saw three newborn chicks leaning towards their mother.

'"The pelican is indeed an impressive bird. It is probably the only bird that incubates its eggs for thirty to forty days," my husband laughed.

'It seemed to me that the chicks were very weak, tender, thin and sickly. In addition, in May, it became very hot. The lake began to dry up. The pelican was not only unable to catch fish near the shore but also began to carry water from quite a distance. The hottest days had started. Not only man, but also beast could not stand still when the chicks began to chirp desperately. I brought them some water. The gluttonous creatures immediately drank a bucket of water and began to chirp again. Two pelicans rushed around the lake. They fetched water one by one, brought fish, spat out a frog, which the chicks swallowed, but the chicks still did not eat enough.

'One day, the pelican opened its mouth wide and began to swallow its greedy chicks. I grabbed a stone and threw it at it. It bounced off. The poor chick rushed back to its parent. The pelican tried to swallow it again, and opened its mouth. I drove the malicious bird away again. Suddenly a male pelican flew in and opened its mouth. An agile chick stuck its head into its open mouth and pulled a small fish from the pelican's throat. Only then did I understand the pelican's trick: it had filled its throat pouch with water and was trying to give it to the chick, and I was driving it away by mistake, thinking that it was going to devour its own chick.

'July came. It was said that in July the sun would start to move slower. It was true. The sun rose high overhead before lunch and remained there until five o'clock in the evening. Everything turned yellow because of the heat. Even sparrows did not chirp. The bottom of the well dried out during the day, but with the onset of the evening a small amount of water accumulated, but dried up again in the morning. It was terribly hot, terribly hot. Even though the chicks had been born two months earlier, they had just started to grow stronger. They still could not fly. They grew very slowly. My husband said knowingly that the pelican

The Birds Are Our Friends

was "the camel of the birds". A collective farm water machine filled the well with water every two days, but warm water did not quench thirst. The elders said that such an incredibly hot summer had happened once before, in 1916, when the Reds and Whites started fighting amongst themselves.

'I forgot that I had hated and been disgusted by the pelicans and carried water to their chicks. The male pelican died, with the tail of a rotten fish sticking out of its mouth. The poor bird had died before it reached the nest. The female pelican was very weak. She flapped her wings and walked around the nest in confusion when the chicks chirped. As luck would have it, I tripped over a tree and spilled water from a bucket. I burst into tears. The female pelican looked at me, and then at the overturned empty bucket, and returned to the nest. "Please, endure a little more; I will bring water now." The pelican returned to the nest and clung to the chicks. She began to scratch at her chest with her long beak. The chicks started chirping even louder and pushing out their necks. I felt sorry for the poor bird and said to myself, "Oh, please, endure a little more".

'When I got up, to take the bucket, I heard a sudden sound. I immediately looked around and saw the pelican split its chest open with its sharp beak and give his young birds its blood to drink. It was not blood, but something thick that looked like a mixture of blood and milk. "What did you do, poor thing? I will bring water. Here, I'm leaving. I'll be right back," I said sobbing. I ran as hard as I could. The well that was near seemed so far away. I finally got there. I filled two buckets and rushed back to the nest. "Don't die, don't die. Here I am," I said, talking to the poor bird. I prayed to God. As I approached, I saw the three chicks flee, stumble, and then they flew away. They landed again and then flew off again. I got to the nest. The huge pelican sat with its head bowed, as if floating on water. The blood that flowed from its chest had been absorbed by the yellow sand. I put the buckets in front of the bird. It did not move. I saw that it was already dead. Its lifeless eyes were directed to the west, from where its chicks flew away …'

The old woman was silent.

I began to imagine the pelican before my eyes: a massive white-grey bird that swam with its mouth open. What else did I know? It ate a lot of fish. What else?

'Now go,' said the old woman. 'My husband considered the pelican a holy bird.'

At that moment, I remembered that Alfred Brehm had written that Muslims did not eat pelican meat, as there is a legend that the pelican helped the Companions of the Prophet on their way to Mecca, by carrying water to them. Probably, such a legend actually exists, but I have never read it either in the Hadith or in Eastern sayings. However, there are many books that I haven't read yet. Therefore, I could neither agree with the words of the old woman nor object. I conjured up the images of the mother bird who died saving her chicks, and the singer who suffered by singing the song 'Mother's heart'. I felt uneasy and began to look for the similarity between them.

The train was travelling fast.

The road was long and the Kazakh steppe wide.

Pelican

Bustard

'As soon as I left the village and got to the area with sparse vegetation nearby, the rain began to come down in buckets,' said Ḳajreḳeṇ. 'God Almighty. I sat down under the bushes of the common salt tree. Some time had passed. The rain was still pouring; quite a lot of time had passed. It was still pouring; a lot of time passed. The rain had not stopped yet. Everything was wet. I was standing in a narrow ditch, which immediately turned into a canal. The old men said that during the Flood of the Prophet Noah, first, burned leather that was hanging on the wall split and water flowed from it to the stove, from the stove to the threshold, from the threshold to the hollow, from the hollow to the mountain.

'I hoped that the rain would not turn into a flood. The hollow under my feet turned into a canal in an instant. I glanced at the water and saw a dead hare floating in it. After that, pheasant chicks swam by, emerging and sinking. I didn't pay attention. Then a fox swam, holding its black nose out of the water. I thought that I wouldn't need the fox's skin in the summer and didn't extend my hand to it. Then pigs swam near me grunting. I drove them away saying, "Go away, dogs." At last, I was tired of sitting and waiting, and my loins started to hurt. When I was about to get up, something flew over me, hitting the reeds. It scared the hell out of me. As they say, "Even a hero will hold on to the rope for dear life." I looked carefully and saw a huge grey bird moving in the stream of water. The bird walked clumsily, like a drunken man. I sat down and took a deep breath. When it swam beside me, I grabbed it and pulled it to me saying, "Oh, viper, I have caught you!"

'It turned out to be a bustard. A second bustard came immediately. And then a third one. I grabbed them one by one and put them beside me. I am not kidding you. At that time, I caught five bustards bare-handed, without any net, then drove them to the village.'

'Well, well, son-in-law, can you stop exaggerating?!'

'No, I can't.'

'Five bustards, you say?'

'Five bustards. If you don't believe me, ask my mother. She is off to the bazaar in Tùrkistan, but she will be back tomorrow. Then you can ask her.'

'So poor bustards can't swim? Or did they all have broken wings?'

'I don't know. I'm not the Prophet Solomon.'

'Maybe it's because of the bug juice, brother-in-law?'

'I last drank vodka on 9 May 1945. Since then, I haven't touched the stuff.'

'No, I'm not talking about you, but about bustards.'

'You ought to ask the bustards. But at that time you were not born yet.'

'I think they were drunk.'

'Who would give them vodka? You amaze me.'

'No, it's you who amaze me. You must be the only person in history who drove birds like sheep.'

'Why am I the only one? My matchmaker, Serik, in Šieli, also caught two bustards last autumn after heavy rain and exchanged them for petrol with Russian forwarding agents.'

'Are you talking about that liar Serik? They say, "The liar has a witness nearby …"'

'What?'

Every *auyl* has its Sudyrahmet – a compulsive liar. This unique image created by the writer Aʹbdiżamil Nuʹrpejisov is fascinating. The only person in the *auyl* who could lie convincingly was our brother-in-law, Ķajreķeņ. After this story, he was called the 'bustard brother-in-law'. People laughed at him. We stopped believing his words, but he still stood his ground. He said stubbornly: 'I can tell you before God that I drove the bustards to the *auyl*.'

Our sister, the late Ķibat, was a very calm and laconic person: 'The horse's secret is clear to its master', as they say. She didn't even listen to her husband's words. Let her rest in peace. She smiled at the corner of her mouth and continued to do her chores.

Today Ķajrekeṇ is no more; even the people who knew him are no longer in the *auyl*.

During my childhood, there were a lot of bustards on the shore of Syr Dariâ, especially during the autumn rice harvest. We saw bustards in the paddy fields all the time, grazing like sheep. In 1885, V. Plotnikov, a Russian zoologist who passed through Sauyr and Tarbaġataj, wrote: 'Even an ordinary hunter can shoot 10–15 bustards every day without any problem, and you see how many bustards there are.'

At present, the number of bustards in Central and South-East Kazakhstan has declined by a factor of ten. It is likely that there was a special place for bustard meat production fifty to sixty years ago, on the Šaķpaķ Pass (the border between the Žambyl and Tùrkistan regions).

In the epic poem about the legendary eponymous warrior 'Ķobylandy Batyr', it states:

> At the crooked end of the hamlet,
> on the forest side,
> the *batyr* born to be a lion,
> having shot a bustard,
> was chewing it, cutting it to the waist.
> Ķùrtķa noticed him.[62]

Ķùrtķa said to the *batyr* chewing the raw bustard: 'Couldn't you snatch the bustard's feathers and pluck it, and eat it fried?'

This means that Kazakh hunters have known for a long time how delicious the bustard's meat is. Arabs say that its meat is not only tasty, but also has tremendous power to heal diseases. Sheikhs worship it like ginseng, because they consider it a medicine that soothes the human body and gives strength.

Rock carvings were discovered in 1972 along the Arpa River, 25 kilometres south of Šolaķķorġan, in the South Kazakhstan region. The main part of the petroglyphs, found by such scientists as M. Ķadyrbaev and A. Mar'yashev, consists of images of camels, horses and onagers (a type of Asian wild ass), and most importantly, a hunter hunting a wild bird. You can easily see that the wild bird is a bustard. It was supposed that these pieces were created in the late Bronze Age, which means that the ancient story of Ķobylandy Batyr could be way more recent.

62 Ķùrtķa was Ķobylandy Batyr's wife.

The bustard is the largest of the steppe birds. The heaviest ones weigh 18 to 21 kilograms. According to *Guinness World Records*, the heaviest bird is, of course, the African ostrich, which weighs up to 100 kilograms. Another name for the bustard is a '*tokṭybalak̦*'; that is, 'as big as a hogget'. Ancient Kazakhs sang: 'Toḳtybalak̦ will run after the grass …'

These words make a point. 'Run after the grass' proves that they basically feed on plants, and of course there are times when they snack on insects. They avoid human beings and are very cautious. Owing to their exceptionally tasty meat, they were hunted excessively. As a result, they were put on the Red List of Threatened Species several years ago. They used to come in April and May, but recently they have not returned to their usual pastures.

There is a well-known zoo in Frankfurt, Germany, where once I saw the inscription 'Bustard' (Latin name *otis tarda*) and it reminded me of Ḳajreken̦ from the remote *auyl*. We had mocked him unfairly. According to modern biology, bustards do not have sebaceous glands on their tail, so they have dry feathers due to a lack of oil. As a result, during heavy rain, or when it is cold, their feathers stick to their body and it becomes difficult for them to move around. Therefore, we read in the Russian, Ukrainian and Bashkir literature, or hear epic stories, about how some heroes, like Ḳajreken̦, drove bustards with sticks.

I am convinced now that it is absolutely plausible that Ḳajreken̦ drove the bustards to the village like sheep, and had really grabbed the MacQueen's bustard by the feet while he was hiding in the bushes. The MacQueen's bustard is also a steppe bird. We can call it the bustard's 'younger brother'. According to scientists, there were many MacQueen's bustards on the shore of Lake Balk̦aš, in the south-west of the country, alongside the Ojyl, Ḳiyl, Žem and Ḳajnar rivers, in the Maṇġystau and Torġaj regions, as well as in the Betpak̦-Dala Desert. In 1971, only one or two MacQueen's bustards were found in about 3,300 km of the Betpak̦-Dala Desert. In Maṇġystau, a survey was carried out in 1986–89, which involved searching for, recognizing, counting and documenting birds using a plane or helicopter. There were only 216 MacQueen's bustards in a few thousand kilometres, and no bustards. In the south-west Ustirt and south Maṇġystau areas, only a few MacQueen's bustards were found every 2,000–3,000 kilometres.

Male MacQueen's bustards dance to attract females during the breeding season, sometimes running around the rare bushes that grow in the steppe, calling and inviting its *beloved* to dance. At this time, it forgets about everything else. It dances and runs until it falls to its knees. It raises the white feathers of the head and throat, and steps on the ground as if dancing. There is a national Turkmen dance, in which men dressed in white clothes tap the ground and sing 'Let's do the steps'. Kazakhs are not inclined to dance very much, so they call the Turkmen dance 'the MacQueen's bustard mating dance'. Let them laugh. The Turkmen dance is very beautiful and it suits them well. When the MacQueen's bustard dances, in its madness and ecstasy it sees nothing. This is probably when they can be caught by people – like Ḳajreken̦ hiding in the bushes.

The second way to catch a MacQueen's bustard is to set a trap where they dance. During the dance, of course, they do not see the trap. But the MacQueen's bustard is not like its 'older brother'; it can take flight very quickly. When it escapes at speed, no one can catch it. It both takes off and lands swiftly. When it comes to the bustard, it is not true that it cannot fly. It can fly, but takes off with very heavy beating wings and, after a while, it lands again. There is a line describing the pace of Tajburyl, a winged horse of Ḳobylandy, in 'Ḳobylandy Batyr': 'While the grey heron and the glossy ibis try to take off, Ḳobylandy catches them easily'; this description could be equally true of bustards.

Speaking of bustards …

It's the nineteenth century, in the Turkmen bazaar. Unlike Uzbeks, Tajiks and Persians, Turkmen do not know how to bargain and are laconic. They do not have traditions such as telling funny stories, playing the clown or dancing. They do not speak a lot, but they can keep a promise. Usually they come to the bazaar to make purchases. If you see a Turkmen seller, you can immediately guess what he is selling, one of only three or four things. The first is a horse, the second is a carpet, the third is a camel and the fourth is a pedigree dog, which the Kazakhs call the Turkmen hound.

Turkmen especially appreciate horses, which are cherished like the apple of their eye. But Uzbeks do not need them; they use an ass or a bullock for farming, not a horse. Only Kazakhs buy horses. Turkmen usually ask for two camels or a rifle with a hundred bullets. They are not convincing. They do not argue, bargain or swear. Kazakhs also do not like to beat about the bush and immediately give an answer. What do they say?

'I will give you five sheep; not simple sheep, but fat ones, which are the same height as you.'

'Hey, Kazakh, aren't you ashamed? You are telling me a load of codswallop,' replies the Turkmen.

'I will not give you more than five sheep, otherwise it will be too much,' the stubborn Kazakh insists. 'And will your fucking horse crap golden dung?'

'You can scold me, my grandfather, but not my horse,' says the ragged Turkmen. 'This is a sacred horse.'

'What's so sacred about it?' asks the Kazakh. 'This year there are many bustards in Ùstirt. If I buy this horse, then my children can happily chase after bustards. Otherwise I would not buy this horse. Tell me, why else I might need it?'

'Ah, you make me sick,' says the angry Turkmen. 'If you're going to chase bustards, then you need a dray horse. Why do you want to torture your Adaj horse?'[63]

'The thoroughbred Adaj horse is a sacred creature. You cannot ride it just for fun and games. Only real men ride them on special occasions,' the Kazakh says. Then he turns away and pretends not to understand anything while he knows perfectly well a good horse's worth. He bargains to suppress the spirit and pride of his rival. Then another Kazakh arrives.

'Hey,' he says immediately, 'I will give you four rams and one goat. It is not a simple goat; it is as unique as your horse. Let's do a trade.'

'No, you can't,' says the Turkmen.

'Why not?'

'You want to buy it too cheaply.'

'Hey, son, what do you want with a horse that will be chasing bustards for a couple of months? Otherwise, I have no use for it. I will return it to you in the autumn. Don't worry that I will ride it! Your horse is not adapted to our winters. It will freeze during the first storm.'

The Turkmen left the bazaar in a bad mood, with his Aḵalteke stallion and a large pedigree dog. Of course, the Kazakh was also sad. The Turkmen was sad because he could not sell his goods, whereas the Kazakh was sad because he would have to tease his Adaj horse to make it chase bustards.

If he had managed to buy the Aḵalteke stallion, then he would have been lucky. At dawn, a huge number of bustards in Ùstirt scatter at the sight of a rider emerging unexpect-

The Birds Are Our Friends

63 Adaj horse, bred by the Adaj tribe of West Kazakhstan, is a highly regarded, thoroughbred horse.

edly from behind the saxaul trees. They cannot take off immediately. When they are just starting to take off, they feel as if they are being beaten ruthlessly on a back with a whip. The swift horse rushes forward. A second bird does not have time to take off and collapses onto the ground. In a while, you will see a satisfied Kazakh, returning happily to the *auyl* on a Turkmen horse, laden with four or five bustards.

'Enough,' says the Kazakh. 'I don't want to exterminate all the bustards. Besides, Aķalte-ke can't be ridden continuously.'

I remember this story every time I come to Maṇġystau. Today, there are almost no pedigree Adaj horses and no Aķalteke stallions at all. Kazakh children, who do not know how to bargain, now sell oil on the world markets, and whether oil is good or bad for the fatherland remains uncertain and obscure.

An obscure history, a misty life, a steppe enveloped in a misty mirage … Now there are very few bustards left. Each time we produce oil from the ground, animals on earth die. One of them is the bustard. Oh, if only God had created something inexhaustible …

As for the 'benefits of oil' … in the summer of 2003, the terrible news appeared that local camels had been infected with plague. Not only Kazakh newspapers and magazines, but the foreign media also wrote about this. The Maṇġystau region was again disgraced in front of the whole world because of the stupid authorities. I thought about the bustards. It was worth remembering that they are called the 'nurses of the steppe'. When bustards disappeared, many different worms, insects, frogs and gnawing pests appeared en masse. As a result, the cattle began to die out from plague during peacetime. What would happen to people who ate meat and drank their milk?

One day in 2003, an Arab sheikh visited Maṇġystau. Many guests came to the oil region. But this guest did not bring prosperity, only expenses. Jeeps and armed Arab hunters arrived in planes that landed at Aķtau airport. Then they went to Ùstirt. Their goal was to hunt great bustards and MacQueen's bustards. One sheikh had ten to fifteen saker falcons. They hunted bustards that were hiding in the bushes, chasing them out by firing blanks from Kalashnikovs, then pursued them in cars. When they got close enough, they released the saker falcons. The whole steppe smelled of blood. There was no pity, no humanity. Precious Kazakh poultry was food for the Arab falcon, then for the Arab him-self, and the remains were delivered to the Arab minions. The sheikh's companions and servants attacked the table, and in a matter of seconds the table was devastated 'as if licked clean' by the viper'. The Tajik writer Sadriddin Aini, in his novel *Bukhara*, described the Bukharians, who came to Amir Alimkul to feast. A hundred years have passed since then, but nothing has changed.

What about Muslims who commit un-Islamic actions? What can we say about the authorities of the region, who allowed them to 'shoot, eat and exterminate birds?' Where is the shame, compassion and humanity? Is this all we have achieved since the declaration of our country's Independence? Does this mean we have fostered a generation that only knows how to take the American dollar and discharges other values? What is sacred for such a generation? Bustards and houbaras are not the only creatures exterminated by foreigners.

Previously, the autumn shooting season in 2000 was approved by Government decree to be from 20 September to 31 October. You might ask why a highly respected sheikh from the United Arab Emirates wanted to hunt bustards in South Kazakhstan. Our distinguished officials, who were ready to sell their mothers for money, gladly agreed to this. Seeing that Kazakh officials had bowed their heads before him, the Arab sheikh also asked to hunt in

Bustard

the special Šardara region for a period of ten years. What was wrong with that? Our humble people only asked for US$1,107 for each bustard.

Earlier, in 1996, the same sheikh had gone to the Republic of Uzbekistan to ask their authorities for permission to hunt bustards. The Uzbeks took the rich Arab sheikh by surprise, saying that each bustard would cost US$5,000, that this money would go towards the Republic's economy, and that he could only hunt 20–25 bustards. At one time, sheikhs who hunted in Afghanistan paid US$7,000–10,000 for each bustard.

After the Kazakhs allowed him to hunt 100 or more bustards, for roughly US $1,000 for each bird, the Arab sheikh treated them with disdain. Why was the price difference so great between Kazakh, Uzbek and Afghan bustards? This shame was published in the Russian newspaper *Delo*. Corruption in Kazakhstan has become the stuff of legend. Who should we blame after this?

During a scientific–practical conference of the International Society for the Protection of the Bustard, which was held in Kherson in 2001, one of the South Kazakhstan officials was mocked by a crowd of people because of the following statement: 'Firstly, the bustard is not Kazakh, but a migratory bird. Secondly, what's wrong if we get US$1,107 for each bird?' It seems that we have confused sovereignty with bad manners, outrage and ignorance.

For such sheikhs who do not understand such terms as 'conscience', 'modesty', 'goodness' and 'pity', as stated in the Holy Qur'an, in the Hadith of the Prophet Muhammad al-Mustafa, Kazakhstan has become the easiest country. In no other country is there a Government that is so careless with the environment. For example, the last bustard in the British Isles was shot 175 years ago, yet a previous United Kingdom Minister of Culture, Media and Sport sent ornithologists to the Russian Federation, allocating special funds for the recovery of these birds. Thus, bustard chicks were brought from Russia for a huge amount of money and are now being raised on a special farm in Wiltshire.

When they discovered this, the French began to search their archaeological and biological archives to define which species of bustard had lived in their land (there are twenty-three species in the world). Taking into account the soil, water and climate conditions, they also consider the establishment of bustard-breeding farms an important public event.

The activity of the Germans, who cannot tolerate negligence, has become an example for all with regard to breeding bustards. The wet summer of 1977 could be considered a *žut*.[64] Endless rain damaged the earth. All birds were almost brought to the verge of extinction. It was especially hard for bustards, as 65–70 per cent of their nestlings tend to die even during a favourable summer. The ornithologists of the German Stackby bio-station collected all the eggs from abandoned nests and placed them in incubators. Soon sixty chicks were born. They had to feed each chick twelve times a day.

It's not for nothing that the Kazakhs say that 'Orphans have seven stomachs', meaning they are greedy. This experience has become known to the whole world and now

64 *Žut* is the massive loss of livestock owing to starvation caused by adverse weather conditions.

ornithologists in the UK, France, Italy and Russia are engaged in raising bustards. Yet Kazakhstan is doing nothing in this area.

Bustard reserves in the Saratov, Astrakhan and Penza regions of Russia are protected by the Government. Russians not only raise and breed them, but also make them a source of income in line with the requirements of society. Russian ecologists have raised the issue of bustards' extinction in Baikal, Bashkortostan and Tatarstan as a matter of national importance and have been organizing specific events. The *Piterskiy Okhotnik* was pleased to announce that bustards hatched a clutch of eggs at St Petersburg Zoo. Sergei Voronin, the Chief Observer for Environmental Protection for the Republic of Uzbekistan, said in an interview with the Russian newspaper *Delo* that it was strictly forbidden to shoot critically endangered great bustards and MacQueen's bustards in the regions of Horezm and Karakalpakstan. Arabs cannot shoot Uzbek bustards any more, even if they pay rather more than US$5,000 per bird.

The bustards inhabiting the Ukrainian steppes, are under the protection of the Government. Martovoe village, in the Kherson region, is also called 'The Village of Bustards'. Here, alongside the education of young ecologists, practical measures are being taken in relation to raising bustards.

What can be said about the ecological culture of Kazakhstan? How can we embarrass the police and the foresters that detain old people as poachers, who are only guilty of fishing from ponds on the outskirts of their towns, rather than protect endangered bustards from foreign hunters?

Birds have the same right to live in the steppe as the Kazakhs do.

Bustard

Stork

(A story by my friend)

If storks come, then summer comes too.

Folk song

Şynaz is the city in which water is scarce as honeysweet.
Life rushes as if it is a stork, let's enjoy it while we can.

Folk song

Those were wonderful days.

Spring in Tashkent arrives in the second half of February: like white-flowering apricot trees and box-thorn it blooms, like the weeping willow it rises in a day, like the Lombardy poplar it shoots up. Roads, streets, gardens are filled with music. Spring sounds like a starling, soars like grey pigeons, and like a great tit, does not calm down all day.

Oh, spring nights.

Remember the beginning of Fyodor Dostoevsky's short story, 'White Nights'. If I'm boring you, I beg your pardon, but if you are tempted to listen to a few moments, then please do:

> It was a wonderful night, such a night as is only possible when we are young, dear reader. The sky was so starry, so bright that, looking at it, one could not help asking oneself whether ill-humoured and capricious people could live under such a sky. That is a youthful question too, dear reader, very youthful, but may the Lord put it more frequently into your heart![65]

---

65 Dostoevsky F., 'White Nights', translated by Constance Garnett. Available at: http://www.online-literature.com/dostoevsky/4394/

That was the night as described above, my friend.

The nightingale sings in the garden. Have you ever heard the nightingale sing? There are sixty-two versions of the '*Aķželeņ' kùj*, aren't there? The 'twelve *muqams*' of the Uyghurs are different from each other.[66] And how much the singing of the nightingale changes in one outing – I wish I knew. A warm wind blows. Brisk spring, songful spring. Oh, my God, will those days really not come back? I don't want to believe it.

I do not remember where I came from, I went home late, across the street, and headed to the post office.

66 *Aķželeņ* is a traditional musical genre of Kazakhs, short form of *kùj*, distinguished by cheerful mood; *Muqam*: melody type and set of melodic formulas of the Uyghurs, used to guide improvization and composition – there are twelve of them.

Post office. Beautiful pool full of water,
pilaf is being cooked a little further on.
A restless boy walked here,
waiting for the Almaty newspaper.
The Kazakh verse is like a group of saigas rushing to the lake reeds.
Whenever possible, everyone tried to catch them.
Or it's like a camel wandering once near the stream,
whose calf was at grass further away …

It was a magnificent garden with chinar and elm, blooming willow and white poplar. The Garden of Youth, the Garden of Love. There was a girl sitting demurely on a long bench at the entrance. I stared at her beautiful eyebrows and eyes as I passed by. Her oblong face, overbearing stature and black curly hair indicated that she was a mountain girl, apparently a Tajik, or she may also have been Uzbek. It is usually difficult for a person when they first arrive in this country to distinguish two nationalities by appearance. You notice the difference a while later. However, their *dastarhan*, clothing, the relationship between people, traditions and customs, and hospitality are very similar to each other.[67] Among Uzbek intelligencia there are many people of Tajik origin. Mixed marriages are even more common. As the saying goes, 'A stranger nearby is dearer than kin in the distance', and the feeling of kinship between the two nations living in close proximity is natural. For me, coming from a Kazakh *auyl*, it was outlandish. It's interesting when it's outlandish.

The girl was looking down. She furrowed her brow. The kohl make-up on her eyebrows seemed too thick. Either she was hurt and had been crying, or she was unwell. Moreover, Uzbek and Tajik girls don't go out in the twilight. I turned around:

'Miss, can I help you?' I said in Russian.

The girl didn't let me finish speaking and turned away.

'Can you speak Tajik or Uzbek? I don't know Russian,' she replied in Tajiki Persian.

'Just look what this girl says,' I said, and looked her straight in the face. 'Well, what about Kazakh?' I said in Tajiki Persian.

She understood my joke, smiled and laughed loudly. Her smile was bright.

'Oh, she is only seventeen, you can read it in her eyes,' I murmured, repeating the words of the poet Ôtežan Nurġaliev.

'Well, well.' She looked at me and a yet another reply in Tajiki Persian followed: 'I would wholeheartedly like to learn Kazakh.'

'Right,' I smiled. 'Thank you.'

'Thank you very much.'

Her name was Mahlaraiym. '*Mah*', from Persian, means moon, and '*aiym*' is also 'my moon' in Turkish. 'My father is Tajik, my mother is Uzbek. They had been thinking about my name for a long time when I was born. Eventually they settled on Mahlaraiym. It sounds like both an Uzbek and a Tajik name.'

The girl came from Chirchik and was studying in the Faculty of Language and Literature, at Tashkent State University. We became friends.

Once she invited me to her native *kishlak*. Following along the clay fence, we arrived at

67 *Dastarhan* is a traditional concept concerning all dining- and hosting-related practices and etiquette. Inviting someone to a *dastarhan* means hosting according to the norms of hospitality. More specifically, *dastarhan* is a synonym for a dining table or tablecloth.

62

The Birds Are Our Friends

a house with white roofs, right next to the River Chirchik. The first thing to catch my eye was a dried mulberry tree in the yard with a stork's nest at its top. From a distance, it seemed like a Mexican sombrero, worn on a slender young man's head.

She was a beautiful girl.

I was young too. I wrote poetry. Mahlaraiym loved poetry. I wanted to be a poet just because of her, to win her favour. 'Of course,' – I spoke in her native Tajiki Persian to encouraged her to talk – 'Mirza Alisher Navoi is a great poet.'

'*Sız buzurg akynsız,*' she said, somehow trying to speak Kazakh. You are a great poet.

I was offended initially when I misheard the word *buzurg* as *bużyk* (hooligan). Later, she began to speak Kazakh fluently. Unfortunately, I was not able to improve my Persian. There are too many regets, my friend, to reveal them all.

The girl's parents were educated, open-minded, cultured people. They were glad to have us. I stayed there for two or three days. After the unbearable heat of Tashkent, this house on the mountain slopes looked just like paradise. And below, the River Chirchik was flowing.

> When girls appeared dressed
> heading to the Chirchik to swim,
> under the scorching sun
> the body and soul were looking for refuge.
>
> The Chirchik was flowing, flowing and splashing,
> it was a babbling stream.
> The Chirchik was flowing, flowing and biting
> the coast's white and naked thigh.

Subsequently, I visited different countries of the world. I do not even remember the names of some of them, but I'm still delighted with that trip to Chirchik. I got on well with the girl's father. In his youth, he had worked as a driver in Tselinograd. He had pleasant memories of the Kazakhs. We both slept in the *iwan* in front of the door.[68] Every day I woke with the flapping of two storks' wings.

When the stork arrives, the children of the *kishlak* clap their hands and scream enthusiastically: '*Laılek keldı – ıaz býldı, qonatlorı qoǵoz býldı.*' The stork has come, summer has come, their wings have turned into paper. I heard this couplet from folk singers. Considering that Uzbek verses don't always rhyme and don't have a fixed number of syllables, unlike Kazakh verses, these two lines are not that bad.

The stork is a beautiful bird indeed. Uzbeks call it '*lailak*'. Southern Kazakhs use both the word '*laĵlek*' and '*degelek*'; that is, stork. When the sun rises in the east, it remains on its nest, opens its wings and bends its neck towards its back. It's a wonderful picture. In the first few days, Mahlaraiym and I fed them, going to the nest in turn. They eat small fish, gobies, grasshoppers, meat, beetles, frogs and crustaceans.

'I love storks very much. These are my storks,' said the girl playfully.

'Your storks are really beautiful,' I said, smiling back, 'just like you.'

'Thank you, I am grateful,' said the girl. 'Do you know that I gave the male the name Tahir, and the female the name Zuhra? They are loyal to each other, loving birds. Tahir

Stork

comes first. He flies over the *kishlak*, locates our house and flies to last year's nest. Then he sets to work. He patches all the flaws and holes. In the evening he makes a noise and stretches, which means he is missing Zuhra. Zuhra comes soon after. Together they clean, expand and enlarge the nest. Tahir is incredibly hardworking, but very jealous. If other birds enter this area, he is always ready to fight. Jealousy is not good, is it?'

'He loves her. He would not be jealous otherwise,' I said, as if I was listening to a fairy tale.

'Zuhra is faithful. Many times I have seen her expel other birds from the nest with her wings when Tahir was not around. Another disadvantage of Tahir is that he is a fighter. I saw him fighting with birds from a nearby *kishlak*. Despite the fact that he was injured, he fell, got up and again rushed back into battle. Several times my father separated the birds, otherwise Tahir would have died long ago.'

'Surely, many flirt with her because Zuhra is beautiful,' I said jokingly. 'Otherwise, why would Tahir fight them?'

'Zuhra is not guilty just because she is beautiful,' said the girl, 'but Tahir is very kind-hearted. He caresses Zuhra very gently, especially during the season of love. He rattles his beak and strokes Zuhra from head to toe. You should see Zuhra. There is no happier bird at this moment. She hides her head in Tahir's embrace, starts to preen. Beautiful spring nights will begin for them. Both of them go to the bottom of the nest and are not visible for some time. Tahir comes out for a moment, then Zuhra appears. They pamper each other and start cleaning again. Later, two or three eggs will appear in the nest; sometimes five or six eggs. You yourself have seen eggs the size of ostrich eggs – 100 grams. Incubating the eggs is the duty of both the husband and wife. Like Zuhra, Tahir also spends a lot of time on the eggs. Last year, the chicks were born in twenty-seven days, this year in thirty-four days.

'Looking at the chicks is pure entertainment. Blinking, tiny, puffy white chicks go to their mother immediately after hatching on their little red legs, and begin to oppress her with their little black beaks. However, unlike other birds, storks do not usually bring their chicks food in their beaks, but regurgitate unprocessed food, which the chicks then eat. I have not seen more good-natured birds than storks. If the weather is cold, then they press the chicks to their chests, and on hot days they fill their beaks with water or pour water on their children like a cool shower. When Zuhra leaves for the *bazaar*, Tahir stays at home. And when Tahir goes hunting, Zuhra does not leave the nest for a second.

'Another interesting fact about storks is that they are taciturn. If there is danger or if they are joyful when their chicks start to fledge, they don't make any sound. Even when they fight, these birds remain silent and die in silence. The only sounds they make are those of flapping wings and clacking beaks. That is all. The stork's songs, music, sorrows and laughter are all silence.'

Mahlaraiym could have talked about storks all night long. I wouldn't get tired of listening to her.

'It is time for you to go back to the city,' said her father, the day after the first chick hatched. Concern could be seen on his face. The girl's mother entered the kitchen. Tajik and Uzbek women are not supposed to argue with men. Young girls don't communicate openly with their fathers, but deliver everything via their mothers.

'Every year the same thing happens. Once the chicks start to hatch, you send me back to the city,' the girl complained to her mother. 'I want to stroke the little stork chicks. When I come back, the birds will have grown up already. It's boring. Some of them may find other nests and leave.'

'The chicks won't grow up so quickly. It takes one and a half to two months, you know that. When they start to fledge, I will bring you home myself,' said her father, comforting the girl.

'Okay, Father'.

We went to the bus station together. The mother and daughter went to get tickets. Her father and I headed to the beer house.

'Don't be sad, young man,' said her father, sipping a cold beer. 'But our daughter has had heart disease from birth. There are times when she doesn't sleep a wink. We don't sleep either, but sit beside her from dusk to dawn. Don't offend her, may God fulfil your wishes ...'

I recalled the night I had first met Mahlaraiym. I intended to say something, but he raised his hand as if to say, 'You don't have to.'

'You may think it is not correct for a Muslim to say "leave us" to guests,' he said. 'Don't be offended; you are totally welcome here. You have already seen that our female stork brought us nestlings. Mahlaraiym loves her so much because she has been used to her from childhood. But you don't know, young man ...'

He stopped short.

'What do you mean?'

'Eh, young man,' he said and looked out of the window. 'It is hard. After a while, our female stork will start killing her chicks. If you put the ones that survive into the nest, she will bite their stomachs and crush their body in two. Fucking nasty bird! Mahlaraiym is not aware of this. She thinks the stork is the most beautiful, kindest bird in the world. I am afraid if she sees how the female bird kills its own chicks, that she will have a heart attack. Who knows, it is believed that the disease will disappear if she gets married.'

Later ...

Later I went through lots of things.

> Haze covered the yellow meadow,
> my sorrowful autumn has returned.
> We have shared secrets, my weeping willow,
> but now it is time to go, let's say goodbye.
> I am that kind of person, don't be offended,
> please, neither call me, nor say to leave you.
> My precious, even if you look long at the road,
> a bird of yours won't return in spring…

I returned to Tashkent ten years later. The next day I looked for Mahlaraiym. I could not find her. I went to Chirchik, but her father had moved elsewhere. There was no mulberry tree where storks nested, but there was a donkey carriage without a wheel. A large man with a hawk nose appeared from a hut and said: 'I swear to you, Uncle, I do not know where they are.'

So, I lost Mahlaraiym.

Since then, much water has passed under the bridge. Wherever I go, I look for a stork. If I happen to see a nest, I look at it for a long time. Different thoughts come to my mind. I have encountered storks in the Šymken, Žambyl and Almaty regions of Kazakhstan, but nowhere else. The bird is rarely found in our parts.

Ten or fifteen years ago I saw some nests in the *auyls* of Ķarnaķ, Sauran, Šornaķ, Uranķaj, Satymsaj, and districts of Sajram, Keles, as well as Bôgen, Maķtaral and Žetisaj in South Kazakhstan. The *auyl* of Žuantôbe in the south is a gateway to the Sozaķ district. Unfortunately, the last stork flew away from this *auyl* in 1978. There was a song saying, 'Didn't you see a white or black stork? Didn't you come here as we agreed?' A prominent Kazakh writer, Táken A'limķulov, used to love this song, but it is long forgotten.

There are some precious moments in the far corners of our mind in everyday life that we do not care about. Have you seen the old canals in the deserted steppes, in the mountains? Don't they lie unnoticed, inconspicuous? Suddenly, they are washed by a stream of heavy rain. After the flood, agates come to the surface. The stork is like a flood in my heart. I see it very rarely. But when I see it, it torments my forgotten, distant feeling of sorrow and anxiety, my pleasant memories. I can't hide them:

> There is a song, I am scared to listen to it,
> the wave of my grief may break the dam …

As written in this song, I had times when I tried not to see and think about the stork. Man cannot escape from himself.

That year I went to Bukhara on a guided tour. A local historian said that the height of the Kalyan Tower was 46.5 metres, equal to a twelve-storey house. But this was not a surprise. I was surprised, however, by the fact that storks nested on the roof of that tower. My heart sank, because all the time I was thinking about Mahlaraiym.

Since 1644, the city of Nabburg, in Germany, has been world famous for its white storks. I have been to this city as well. A Turkish boy named Mehmed, who was a guide, said: 'In our language, this bird is called "*leilek*", sometimes it is called "*haji baba*". Then I recalled that Ukrainians call them '*lelek*' or '*leleka*'. Tatars call it '*leklek*'.

In our youth, there was a Russian song that began like this: 'The white stork flies, flies over the whitish Poles'e' … Once when I was listening to this song, a journalist from Maņġystau, Vladimir Sh'itov, said that the black stork wanders in the Šetpe and Oġlandy districts of West Kazakhstan, and the local Kazakhs call them *ķarabaj*, confusing it with glossy ibis.

The Birds Are Our Friends

I have read about the black stork in the Marķakôl, Kùršim and Zajsan districts of East Kazakhstan. I haven't met a person who has seen the black stork in other regions. According to some people, this must be an *introverted* bird, just like me. That is probably why I did not look for it. What can its desolate existence do except break my heart? I have enough loneliness in my life.

Sometimes I am amazed at myself. As Mahlaraiym's father told me, this is a cruel bird that kills its own chicks, throws them out of the nest … Yet my senseless habit is looking for the tender bird that Mahlaraiym adored so much.

As a rule, poets devote poems to their loved ones: 'Wherever I am, whenever, I think of only you.' This is probably true. I am not a poet. When I was young, I used to write poems. Later, when I was more than thirty years old, writing poetry was not fun and not difficult. Today we have reached an age where we read poems written by young people, especially young girls, and smile at them thinly. I don't believe in anything. I don't even want to be-lieve. If anyone was loyal, it was me. If anyone was honest, wasn't I that person? I remember the times when I believed in nonsense and lies, and my eyes filled with tears. I am generally a person who cries often. But I don't show tears to anyone, and I've never talked to any-one about my youth, so I'm probably not going to talk for the rest of my life. What is the meaning of superfluous words? If I had been born in ancient times, would I have been a warden, because I love loneliness? Loneliness and silence. Whenever, wherever I go, I think of Mahlaraiym. Whatever trip I take, I keep the image of Mahlaraiym in my mind. That is probably why I don't like sitting at home.

Where are you, Mahlaraiym?

I am very old. If you saw me today, you might not recognize me. But I would recognize you in the crowd even after forty years.

You used to say, 'Write a *dastan* called "*Lajlek*", "The stork".'

I couldn't do it.

Why write about it and make it known? You are in my heart, white *lajlek*.

I miss you. And I am so sorry.

Quail

*T*here is an old saying: 'There's a high mountain, no other would be higher. A baby sparrow won't be able to reach its peak.'

Here another tale begins. Let's have a look at it.

Once upon a time, there was a high peak located by the Ķarasu River, near the city of Ķaratau. Its peak couldn't be reached even by the Lord of Birds, eagles, let alone baby sparrows. The birds' attempts to fly over it all failed, since that superior peak continuously aspired to greater heights.

All the greatest songs had been sung long ago, before us; the only thing we can do is listen to them. The narrative above might have been born in those times.

'I can reach its peak,' the swan said, but halfway up it started weeping, as its wings became powerless. The swan soon disappeared into the reeds.

Then the snowcock made an attempt as well. However, it came back when halfway there and remained in its nest, ashamed.

The saying 'The liveliest of birds – the hawk – will go down if its wing is twisted' comes from this.

After the question 'Who's next?' the modest quail appeared.

'Let me! I am going to fly.'

Other birds kept saying: 'Stop it. You will hurt yourself, poor you. You will injure your breast, your bones will remain scattered in the black rocks.'

'Even if I fall, that will happen in my homeland, and I would like it to happen here. Sink or swim!'

It discharged itself like a bullet from a sling. It soared high, turned around and touched the black rocks with its breast. The quail found itself on the other side of the mountain. Mountains and rocks started crumbling and breaking up, finally turning into sand and meadow-land. Since then, quails, unlike other birds, when landing, embrace the ground with their breast and not with their tail. The quail with its injured breast that conquered the peak paved the road for many other birds. Are you searching for justice, when it was unattainable even then?

Unquestionably, not every traditional saying is a reasonable one. As you can see, the proverb stating that 'a bird flies with wings and lands with a tail' has nothing to do with quails.

That was the quail ready to sacrifice itself for its native land …

What mercy did we show towards that quail?

Every year, there is open season on wildlife at the end of August and the beginning of September. At this time of year, when the mountain slopes serve as slaughterhouses, the first to find itself at the end of a gun is a quail. So, shooting them is allowed. Quails are like scapegoats. Their only fault is that they grow up and migrate to the south earlier than other birds. They have no other fault.

In his work *Brehms Tierleben* (*Brehm's Life of Animals*) Alfred Brehm wrote:

> Instead of saying that they migrate to the south, it is better to say that they go on a dangerous journey. The danger here is humans. During that season the people of the Mediterranean islands swarming all over the place go fowl-ing. They set nets, bait traps, and smear glue. If worse comes to worst, hunters beat birds with sticks and kill them. The ones that return miraculously safely, fly over boundless rivers nearly falling into the waves, their wings becoming numb. With this in mind, I am wondering how they still exist.[69]

Brehm was the first to write about the existence of twenty types of quail throughout the world.

When it gets colder, quails migrate to neighbouring Siberia, and then on to Crimea. They form groups and wait for the rain to stop. When the weather clears up, the birds leave Crimea, pass by Qaf Mountain, and reach Turkey. After staying there, they then head to Africa, all the time flying at night. This is the dangerous journey mentioned by Brehm.

Another proverb states 'Quails have no home'. There is no reason for this at all. Quails have places to live, fly to and land on. The female lays 20 to 30 eggs at a time, and watches the eggs night and day.

As a result of this unrest and struggle, in 15–16 days the eggs hatch. One domesticated quail hen can lay about 300–320 eggs annually. Do you know of any other bird more fertile than this ?

The saying 'Quails have no home' may have something to do with the fact that its nest is usually located in places not easily visible to the eye, and the fields where they look for food are vast.

Households in the lower reaches of Syr Dariâ grow alfalfa as part of their rice-crop rotation, and for fodder. People living near Tùrkistan call it clover (*bede*). There has been an assumption that the word for quail (*bôde*) comes from *bede*. It is possibly true. *Bede* is a Turkish word. Alfalfa – 'žoṇyška' – comes from the Persian language.

---

69 Brehm A., *Zhizn' zhyvotnyh* (*Brehms Tierleben*), Vol. 11, Moscow: Terra, 1992, p. 187.

This bird is very kind-hearted.

In midsummer, female birds can be seen followed by their chicks, in groups of ten to fifteen, or even twenty. Once we saw a quail go under a truck and die. The poor fidgety hen who had been cut in two by the sharp blade of the machine as she rushed to chicks, who were running about. It was sad to see defenceless, abandoned chicks. They are bait for predators, and this tears the heart to pieces.

A few days later, we saw the chicks again. A female quail that lived with her own chicks in a neighbouring paddy field had taken the orphaned chicks under her wing. It was astonishing to see such a little bird that has such generosity and kindness.

These birds do deserve praise. People who leave unwanted children at a rubbish site should learn from them. There is a small number of Kazakhs in this world, yet even so, their orphans are taken abroad. People that send them – officials – don't reason as quails do. A talented poet from Maṇġystau, Sabyr Adaj, says: 'Appreciate every Kazakh as if he/she was the only close person left in the world'. He is right.

The babble of quails can be disregarded by Kazakhs, yet listening to quails singing is a delight for most people of the East, a pleasure.

As a rule, two quails are kept in one house. A pumpkin is cut and covered with a silk cloth. On the first day, the quails are very fidgety. Some inexperienced hunters put them in a box or in a basket without a covering so that the birds can breathe fresh air. This is wrong. When a quail heads outside to free itself, it may hit the basket wall, break its wings, hurt itself or even die. This is why birds should be kept in a pumpkin covered with a cloth in a dark place. A small hole is poked in the side of the pumpkin and a water bowl is attached. Under the silk towel there are a cock bird and a hen bird. They are separated from one another. In the morning when the cock bird starts singing, the hen bird fawns and stretches its neck. So, a morning romance begins. At that time, listening to their sounds in silence is a great pleasure. Now it is clear why they are called after the lovers Farhad and Shirin.[70] The misery of the separated lovers from the Persian romance must sound just like the quail.

There is an old man in the Sajram district of South Kazakhstan who keeps quails. His name is Muhamedsalyk̟. He has plenty of different pumpkins in his yard, with one quail in each of them. Hunters from Andizhan, Namangan, Osh and Dushanbe go there to purchase quails. Sometimes the old man invites his nearest and dearest to listen to 'Farhad and Shirin'. It is similar to the Kazakh tradition of gathering to listen to an epic poem (k̟issa) or bastaṇġy (a gathering organized by youngsters in the absence of older people). The quail starts singing when the owner gives a signal. Although hoarse at the beginning, the bird's voice reveals itself afterwards. The more the audience applauds, the louder the quail. Some laugh, some dance and some people are lost in reverie. One thing that cannot be forgotten is a young married woman who wipes her tears with a tissue, hiding her face and looking down.

---

70 Farhad and Shirin (also known as Khosrow and Shirin) are the main characters of the eponymous tragic romance by the Persian poet Nizami Ganjavi (1141–1209).

The Birds Are Our Friends

The ability to listen to birds singing is a different culture and another world. If you listen closely to songbirds, you will enjoy it like music coming from musical instruments. Birds don't lie.

People who keep quails are a separate community. To an outsider, their behaviour may seem strange. They caress them, scold, laugh, even cry talking to them.

… We had been hunting and didn't notice the sunset. Walking along the Syr Dariâ River we came across a winter camp. After visiting a house with a big yard, our guide said: 'We will stay here.' Being extremely tired we fell down on the floor and fell asleep. I don't know what time it was. We were woken up by the following words:

'We have lost Tahir.'

It was morning. The head of the household, a man over sixty, jumped up in grief: 'Good heavens!'

We all jumped up. We were sad to consider that we had brought bad luck – unlucky visitors. Who had passed away? An old man put his arms akimbo and was going round the yard.

'Poor Tahir, he was so radiant, so brave. Why did you leave us?'

Holding a pumpkin, he said: 'Leila, you are so unfortunate. Oh, beautiful Leila.'

Our guide was a teacher, an experienced, reserved young man. Why wasn't he grieving? He was chuckling.

'Stop it!' he said to the old man at last. 'It's embarrassing. I'm sorry,' he said, turning to us, 'but no one has died. The old man's most treasured cock quail disappeared during the night. Its name is Tahir. Leila is a hen bird. That is why he is upset. It's all right.'

We heaved a sigh of relief.

'Take out the hen bird,' the master said to his son, after composing himself. His son had been sitting in the corner and looking at the floor, as if guilty of something.

'All right, Father.'

The old man took the pumpkin and went to the field of alfalfa with the boy.

We prepared to set off.

'That was embarrassing,' said our guide. 'Don't be offended.'

We reassured him and compared the man's state to that of Aḳan Seri when he lost Ḳu̇lager.[71]

We saw our guide's tiny sliver of a smile. He was laughing at our comparison of Ḳu̇lager and the cock quail.

Soon we set off.

Later we had news that Tahir had been caught in a net that was set in front of his Leila. The old man was very happy and apparently tried to find us, but we were too far away by that time. You live and learn. We neither laughed at the old man's behaviour, nor were we offended. A man who values birds cannot be a bad man.

It is true that some people consider quails a source of income.

Another name for humans is sinners. When a person turns into a sinner, they admire not the singing but the fighting of birds. The laws of the modern world forbid this kind of entertainment. Gambling has always been forbidden, especially in Islam. Any hare-brained game that deludes people is *haram*, not just this.

Players know in advance which quail everyone will bring. Usually fighting quails are

---

71 Ḳu̇lager was the favourite horse of singer, poet and composer Aḳan Seri (1843–1913) that was killed during a horse race; it became a symbol of the cherished talent who falls victim to jealousy.

hunted in the wild. There are different techniques for catching them. When they are caught in a net, first, the white-necked female birds are selected. Then, the thin and badger-legged ones are taken away. It is clear they aren't strong enough. Birds with thick legs, a strong body and a black neck are tamed. Birds are easily domesticated. To become resilient and good at fighting, they have to be hand-fed and be always held close to their master. These birds should not be kept in a cage. In 10–15 days those docile birds become real fighters. Their feed is important as well. Wild birds are generally not plump. These fighting birds are given cannabis seeds among other things. Quails that are used to eating cannabis seeds can recognize their owner in a crowd, and in few days, they become bold. If a man who keeps quails is held to account, the reason will be these cannabis seeds. Despite this, quail fights are still held. In the evening 'quailers' gather together on a street corner. A referee is appointed in advance. A towel is laid in the centre.

One of the players says, 'My warrior will defeat any of your quails. I have placed my bet. My word is good,' then he puts the little quail that is hiding in his coat sleeve into the centre. 'Baluan Šolaķ' walks confidently and circles around, staring threateningly at everybody surrounding it.[72]

Then the second player says: 'My quail will peck the honourable hawker's so-called *Baluan Šolaķ*, and I place my bet.'

The referee makes the owners shake hands, then he counts the money and puts it in a towel. He spreads out his hands and gives his own blessing. The owners then part ways and the quails come forward. Strong quails are usually tall, and have thick legs, a short neck and red eyes. They start attacking at once. The second quail doesn't lose heart, but strikes at its opponent. If it hides or takes evasive action, it is likely to lose the fight. The most privileged ones succeed in pecking their rival even when they have fallen down. If a quail's nib or neck bleeds, it steps back. The owner usually shouts at it and puts the bird back in the centre. Sometimes, inspired by the owner's shouts, the bird will pull itself together and continue fighting. The results differ. Victory and defeat take turns. Frankly speaking, in such cases, as a rule, there is no deceit. The result will be up to the quail itself.

In the East, quail's meat and eggs are among the most valuable foods. Quail soup is given to the most honoured visitors. Eggs are particularly highly valued. Nuṙzaķyp Žaķajuly, a Kazakh from the People's Republic of China, states the following in his book, *Šyŋžaŋnyŋ žabajy ķuśtary (Wild Birds of Xinjiang)*: 'The caloric value of a quail egg's protein is 3% higher than that of a chicken's egg, there is 46.1% more iron, 20% more vitamin B and 188% more vitamin B2.'[73]

Moreover, according to him, quail's meat and blood give energy to the internal parts of a body, sustain normal levels of warmth and cold, regulate blood pressure and cure illnesses such as polyuria. Indeed, in recent years it has been found that the cholesterol content of quail meat and eggs is rather low. This is why on the tables of wealthy Europeans and Asians more and more chicken products are being displaced by quail products. Well, it is now clear why that is happening.

Another effective aspect of quail cultivation for the purpose of gastronomy is that quails grow in six months. Other birds lay eggs during a particular season, but the quail lays eggs intermittently. Between April and the end of September, not only mother birds, but also chicks hatched the previous summer begin laying eggs. Hen quails lay eggs twice a year.

72 Baluan Šolaķ (1864–1919) was a Kazakh composer, singer, poet, *dombyra* player and wrestler.

73 Žaķaju☒ly N., *Šyŋžaŋnyŋ žabajy ķuśtary,* The Publishing House of Xinjiang Youth and Adolescence, 1993.

Russian travellers and hunters have created a number of fairy tales, legends, proverbs and sayings about the quail. Even at the Kremlin New Year's Eve 2001 celebrations, a basket of quail eggs was presented as the largest and most beautiful and delicious dish.

Recently, our Kyrgyz brothers celebrated the 2,500th anniversary of the city of Osh. At a dinner on behalf of the President of the country, guests who had gathered for the meal were served quail. Quail soup is highly valued in Turkey and Greece.

Businessmen are engaged in quail production not only in Russia and China, but also in Almaty. Obviously, this is good for people. However, by using it as an income stream, we must not allow this soft, useful bird to disappear, as their numbers are decreasing from year to year.

Quails have no fault, dear friends.

Quail

Little Owl

*Y*ou know the story of the Prophet David, who was enriched by having thirty sons and then forgot Allah's Qur'anic teaching? The Lord gives, and the Lord takes away. Having lost his beloved thirty sons and recovered from his sorrows, David received a message from Allah once again.

'You are forgiven, my slave. I appreciate you having a new lease on life, tell me your desires – shall I retrieve your thirty sons or shall I bestow you a son to be worth the thirty?'

'Oh, my Lord! I am a slave to your will. I am grateful for whatever you do. Your attention to such a sinner as me is way higher than the world's prestige, and wealth,' says David.

'Do stop wailing, David,' Allah said.

After a year and a day, David's wife gave a birth to a son named Solomon, who was worth thirty times the other sons. Blessed Solomon reigned over ten thousand universes. His father David peacefully left the world.

Is it the devil who tempts a person, or is it man who seduces the devil?

Being well on in years, Solomon married a young woman as lovely as the sun shining above. Once she was annoyed. The Kazakhs say that the anger of a woman can boil a pot. However, they also say that the evil of a woman can be a load for forty donkeys. The young woman was too hard on people.

'What is wrong, my dear?' Solomon asked.

'I want to live in a palace,' she said.

'What kind of palace?' Solomon enquired.

He was astonished since there was no palace like his, embellished with silver lace and white gold, surrounded by a wall engraved with black pearl and clean marble. But here she was – the fury! What was a man to do?

'A king built a palace from ivory, so what? Another erected a house of red wood, it doesn't matter. The apple of my eye, my treasure, my dear king, shall we build a castle for just the two of us to rest? Can it be made of birds' bones?

'Birds' bones you say?'

'Yes, of birds' bones only, my world!'

'Well ...'

Solomon agreed to fulfil his wife's wish. The wife was radiant. Is there anyone who wouldn't tremble in fear if a king sent them a message? Solomon decreed and all the birds from 18,000 worlds gathered in the palace.

That was when Solomon said, 'My servants, I am grateful to you for coming. I summoned you because I dreamt of a grand palace, and Angel Jebrail [Gabriel] visited me and uttered, "It's a palace made of birds' bones".'

The birds clamoured, 'You are our master, we will sacrifice ourselves for your sake.' This was what Solomon expected.

But suddenly a quail advanced before the crowd and said, 'The little owl is missing.'

That was when Solomon's harmonious servants had a falling out. All the birds except the little owl were there. No one knew where it was. The king uttered, 'You, hawk, the acutest creature ever, go and find that contemptible bird.'

'Consider it done!'

The little owl was found drowsing in a maple hole.

'You, get up,' said the hawk. 'You must be unaware of the Great Solomon's order! Otherwise, haven't you heard that in union there is strength?'

'Hey, hawk,' said the little owl, 'go away and don't bother me. I am contemplating, can't you see?'

'Over what?' asked the hawk.

'Whether there are more men than women under the sun. I've been mulling over that for many days. Can you enlighten me?'

'No, I'm not aware of that,' said the hawk. 'Solomon is the one who would know that. Let's ask him.'

'I'll be there when the king calls. First you need to fly and ask him for the answer.'

The hawk flew back to Solomon and told him the riddle that had been puzzling the little owl for so many days.

'He's a fool,' said Solomon. 'Obviously there are more men than women. How come he doesn't know that?'

The hawk flew to the little owl to deliver the answer, yet the latter did not agree with it.

'I doubt it. In my opinion, there are more women than men,' said the little owl.

'Why so?'

'Is a henpecked husband believed to be a man? He is a woman with short haircut, that's the difference, isn't it? Fly and report my words to Solomon. Only then will I comply with whatever he says.'

Solomon, who was told the little owl's words, fell to thinking. He attempted to stand up from his gold throne three times, but he couldn't do it.

'My true-hearted subjects,' Solomon said finally. 'I appreciate you gathering here for me! You are free, my dears! I was such a fool doing my wife's bidding. I am sorry for that. It is the little owl who should be thanked! And I shall never see my rebellious wife again!'

That is an Eastern myth in a nutshell.

The legendary Russian ethnographer and natural historian Grigory Potanin, having heard the myth from the Kazakhs in 1883, translated it into Russian. According to the legend, King Solomon's young wife was called Zuhra. The king, who was set on the right path by the little owl, learned Zuhra's evil, built a metal house, locked her in there and set the house on fire. When the house glowed red, he opened the door. A serpent not a woman squirmed out!

'I'll not only go away, but I'll also turn into a star and will glare at you from the sky!' she said. The little owl had taught Solomon how to protect himself from Zuhra's evil and had rescued the realm one more time.

In the Karakalpak legend, Solomon's wife was called Gulzohra.

The Turks in the Caucasus have the same legend. There was no little owl among the birds brought to Solomon. The hawk went to find it. The holes in the beaks of all the birds were made on the order of Solomon at that time, while the little owl, who did not come, still has no nostrils in his beak.

There are more myths and legends about Solomon than about the other 124 prophets. The legend narrated above is just one of them. However, this legend is mentioned because of the little owl, not because of Solomon. What was the little owl like? Why a little owl, not an eagle owl or a snowy owl? Owls are alike; they all fly at night. That habit has not only been noticed in the East though. In Greek mythology, a little owl traditionally represents or accompanies Athena, the virgin goddess of wisdom.

The name of the Greek capital city, Athens, is similar to the Latin for 'little owl' (*Athene noctua*). Some call Athens 'the City of the Little Owl', which reminds us of positive features such as wisdom, intelligence, knowledge and providence peculiar to the night bird; it bestows our hearts with warmth, humanity and benevolence. Benevolence is the answer. The human heart is the battlefield of black and white; good and evil always come hand in hand. The Greeks revere the little owl, while we Kazakhs avoid it, and even are scared of it, as if it were evil. When we hear a little owl hoot, we try to remove ourselves as far away as possible, superstitious that it foretells misfortune. According to Kazakh ethnographers, if a little owl landed on someone's šaŋyraķ, the yurt used to be moved, whereas the šaŋyraķ would be burned down. Sejtķuĺ Ospanov, a prominent writer, wrote a short story about a little owl which accidentally flew to an *auyl*, but was driven away by the tumultuous children.

Centuries ago, the columns of the Acropolis used to be full of little owls sitting on them. The Greek state protected them, and a Greek army going to war would be in seventh heaven on hearing little owls hoot. That might be the reason why fourth-century BC Greek coins had little owls depicted on them.

Not only the Greeks, but also the Italians used to domesticate little owls, and clipped their wings to prevent them from flying away. They hunted mice, like cats, which was of great benefit to their owners.

A fear of nocturnal birds is found in many cultures of the world. In some cultures, the little owl was called a devilish bird, and some were frightened just by seeing an owl. Probably, such fear was peculiar to people who could not explain natural phenomena.

Who knows, making up another fairy tale might be the only way to save the innocent bird from the fury of frightened people and obsolete superstitions. It has been called 'night beauty', 'an orphan', and 'lost wanderer' as well.

Kazakhs living in Türkistan, Žaŋaķorġan and the lower course of the Syr Dariâ River call the bird 'Murataly'. Why is that?

 The Birds Are Our Friends

Once upon a time there was a powerful rich man who lived in Ķaratau along the Ķara-su River, in the area called Žideli Bajsyn, among the Ķoņyrat people. He had a precocious son who was named Mu̇rataly, which meant 'our dream came true'. A spoiled boy, Mu̇rata-ly grew up into a capricious man, whose bad behaviour disturbed many. At a funeral he laughed aloud, whereas joyful festivals were spoiled by his fistfights. Once he dared to insult Umaj Ana.[74] 'They praise Umaj Ana as though she wasn't just a fucking stupid old woman,' he said. The people who heard this went bright red with shame.

That was how Mu̇rataly was cursed by Umaj and turned into a little owl; he flew away and disappeared into the woods. They say the little owl crying all night is his regret over his past behaviour. People who see an owl sitting on a hut say: 'That is a poor Umaj's bird!' 'Umaj's bird' in Kazakh is *Umaj kusy*, which sounds like *u̇-majķu̇s*, *majķu̇s*, *bajķu̇s* and *ba-jġyz*; that is, little owl. Mu̇rataly is believed to have cursed anyone who called him this, whereas the person who called him Mu̇rataly, and greeted respectfully by saying '*As-sala-mu alaykum*' (peace be upon you), could see the bird dancing joyfully. This legend is only known in the Žaņaķorġan and Tu̇rkistan regions.

In France, a pregnant woman assumed that she would have a girl on hearing the hoot-ing of an owl, or a little owl. In southern India one hoot of an owl signified someone's death; two were a symbol of luck and prosperity; three stood for a long trip; whereas four meant the arrival of guests. The British, having heard the owl's voice, were distressed, as it signified that the weather would deteriorate, they say.

An owl hooting at night still frightens people all over the world. Wandering in the pitch-black night and hearing 'hoo-hoo' would terrify anyone. The point is that wolves and jackals always start howling when an owl hoots. Sometimes they even start barking.

As for Uzbeks, they don't call a little owl 'a rich man's daughter' (*bajġyz*), like the Ka-zakhs do – but 'a rich man's son' (*baiugly*). A long time ago there was a beauty who married a rich man's son in Bukhara. Although the young woman was treated incredibly badly by her husband's stepmother, she bore everything. Nine months and nine days passed and she gave a birth to a child. On recovering consciousness, she saw a black puppy lying in a nap-kin. The stepmother drove her away saying, 'You, unblessed, have dishonoured our blood, our dynasty and given birth to a dog! Take your offspring and burn it!'

Crawling away, the poor woman heard a baby crying 'whooo' in a cemetery outside the town. Despite realizing that her husband's malicious stepmother had deliberately changed her baby for a black dog's puppy, the poor woman could do nothing to confront her, and kept looking for her baby in the cemetery. Her son grew up in a grave. People knew him to be the rich man's son, yet they were too scared of his father's stepmother. It is said that the rich man's son, *baiugly*, was turned into a bird and has been hooting in old sheds and caves since then.

Muslims living in Herzegovina idolize the little owl as 'the Bird King'.

As for Bulgarians and Serbians, they believe the cuckoo and the owl to be sisters. Losing each other accidentally, they have been wailing and longing to see each other ever since. 'They miss each other and howl till they're blue in the face and bleed from the nose,' they say, to make the story even more sorrowful.

Anyway, phenologists deny that owlets bleed from their nose. However, Kazakh, Kyr-gyz and Uzbek myths state the opposite. Nobody knows where this belief stems from.

74 *Umaj Ana* is the Goddess of Fertility in Turkic mythology and Tengriism, and as such is associated with women, mothers and children.

Palestinians still believe the little owl to be the bird of happiness.

Austrians and Dutchmen used little owls to tame falcons. Having clipped a little owl's wings, they leave it on a plain, to wait for a falcon. The falcon is caught with a net when it attacks the helpless bird. This is how the precious bird is caught, as it is sung in the folk song, 'A gyrfalcon brings itself to the net'.

In fact, the little owl is not a frightening bird at all. It's not a predator in the true meaning of the word. Meeting you in the forest, it will not fly away as other birds would. A little owl will 'greet' you by bowing, reaching its head to its feet just like Ancient Chinese slaves used to do!

It is easy to catch a little owl during the day, while it's dozing.

What is frightening about the bird? Kazakhs feel sorry for anyone called *bajǵus* – 'a little owl' or 'a wretched one'. I refuse to believe that it signifies misfortune.

Turlybaj Sultankulov, a vet, wrote the following in the book *Hajuanattar tirśiliginiṇ ġaźajyptary* (*Miracles of the Animal World*):

> … Little owls are unbelievably helpful. We should not believe superstitious people who claim that a little owl's hooting foretells death, and that's why it should be killed. The owl is unbelievably kind, compassionate and shrewd. On noticing a predator eating another animal, a little owl will always wail sorrowfully.
>
> A hunter told a true story about a little owl. Once hunting in the mountains, he heard a little owl hooting. Its voice was incredibly sorrowful. The hunter did not pay attention to it and kept going on his own. However, the little owl's voice became more and more miserable. The hunter, who was keen on wildlife phenomena, couldn't ignore it. As soon as he approached the bird, it flew up as though ordering him to follow it. The little owl directed him to a high rock and disappeared. After a little while, the sun poured down its light and the sky filled with vultures. It turned out that the rock was full of nesting snowcocks. The vultures started to attack the snowcocks, but the hunter frightened the predators away, so that they never came back to that rock again. So, thanks to the kindness of the little owl the snowcocks were rescued.[75]

There is one more myth about a rich man's daughter – *bajǵyz*. Having grown up among brothers, the beauty had many men asking for her hand in marriage. Her father wanted her to marry an old merchant widower, yet she wanted to be the wife of a poor young man who she really loved.

   75 Sultankulov T., *Miracles of the Animal World*, Almaty: Ķajnar, 1977.

The quick-tempered father cursed his daughter and drove her away. The cursed girl was turned into a little owl and has been crying and wailing, missing her home and brothers, ever since. According to the myth, that is why the Kazakhs call the bird *bajǧyz* – 'a rich man's daughter'.

All the myths are permeated with the sorrow of the weak and the sadness of the defenceless who suffer injustice. They are full of tender guiltlessness and pure beauty.

Let us give shelter to the defenceless.

Little Owl

Zejnep's Fairy Tale

A black female dromedary had not mated for three years.

A herdsman tried to cauterize the cow, to treat it for vaginitis, but it continued to give a haughty look. We then took it to the male dromedary, the bull, in the cold winter. Still it did not work. We chopped medicines brought from Žaṇaḳorġan, but they did not work, damn it.

'Leave it alone,' said my grandma, frightened. 'May this be the end of misfortune in our family.'

A single dromedary is very fast and agile and can disappear behind the mountains covered with camel's thorn and kochia grass. If you try to find it, tracking it down in bare terrain, it cannot be found. If you look for it among the prickly reeds and dense thickets, falling and stumbling, it cannot be seen. You crawl along the burning sand, like a lizard looking for a well in the sultry heat, but there is no trace.

Tùrikpenbaj, a man who was a *ḳuda* to our family, said violently in such cases: 'A single woman is like a thimble without lace – she has no home.' Of course, this is an offensive proverb, but he had the right to be angry. I was in the third grade when a large male dromedary belonging to Tùkeṇ drank diesel and died.[76] Its orphaned calf with white eyelashes sobbed loudly with grief. Three years had passed. 'A domesticated camel cannot be called a camel any more' – the white-eyed dromedary of Tùrikpenbaj *ḳuda* still grazed alongside our black dromedary. They were lost and found together. My grandmother put a radial bone on the neck of the black dromedary, and a white ribbon on the white-eyed one. Aḳzer wove the ribbon. Aḳzer was the daughter of Tùkeṇ, four or five years older than me. In the evenings, she and I used to look for our dromedaries that grazed outside the *auyl*, returning home at nightfall.

In the environs of Židelisaj if a little owl screamed, we were not afraid. Among the reeds if a jackal howled, we were not afraid. If an owl flew out of nowhere, we were not afraid. We were not afraid because we had heard the cuckoo singing in the afternoon. We were still impressed. *Cuckoo-koo, koo-koo …*

'A cuckoo,' I said on hearing it.

'Rubbish!' said Aḳzer. 'That's not a cuckoo.'

'Oh, well, what is it then?'

76 Tùkeṇ is a respectful form of address for someone called Tùrikpenbaj.

'That's Zejnep.'

'Whose old wife is Zejnep?'

'Fool,' said Akzer. 'Don't say that.'

I scratched my head and kicked my feet.

'You are still a child,' said Akzer. 'You are a little chick. A long time ago, beautiful Zejnep was in love with a man named Kôkek (Cuckoo) from the Koŋyrat tribe from the Žideliba-jsyn area. Her father was an immensely rich man. Kôkek was a strong and kind-hearted man of large build, tall and dark. But he was poor. The young people swore to be together. The rich man ignored the poor young man and decided to give his daughter to a merchant's son across the river.' Akzer pointed towards Tùrkistan, Šornak and Sauran. 'Zejnep and Kôkek decided to escape quietly from the *auyl*. It was said that Zejnep had distant relatives in the far western side, who had been forced to move close to the Syr Dariâ River for some reason. Their deepest desire was to reach her relatives, at the Swan Sea [Caspian Sea]. But a witch, who was watching the girl, found out their intentions and informed the rich man. The rich man called his daughter and gave her some advice, but the daughter did not listen.

He tried to scare her, but she was not scared. He beat her, but the girl still stood her ground. She insisted that she would only marry Kôkek.

'The hopeless father did not give his blessing and cursed his daughter saying "Damn you to hell!" Zejnep, cursed by her father, turned into a bird. A thousand years have passed since then, and Zejnep is still looking for her Kôkek all over the world – *cuckoo, koo-koo.*

'The witch also turned Kôkek into a bird and sent him far beyond the Swan Sea. He did not sleep at night, calling invariably for his Zejnep. This is the story of two lovers who could not be together. And you are talking about a cuckoo!'

A lump stuck in my throat. I looked at the moon. We were silent all the way home. I didn't want to sleep. I went outside. Behind the camel barn of the old man Tùrikpenbaj were some barely visible silhouettes. One looked like Aķzer, but I didn't recognize the second – someone lanky. The sky was covered with clouds. Probably, they wanted to collect dung before it started to rain. I was approaching to help, when suddenly that lanky slob jumped over the fence and disappeared into the dark. Aķzer leaned against the wall petrified. 'Uh, it's you. You scared me,' she said after a while, recovering herself. 'Go to sleep. We need to get up early tomorrow.'

I looked forward to the morning with impatience. I hoped Aķzer would not repeat the fate of Zejnep. I wished Aķzer happiness. They say that Kôkek is now far beyond the sea. I had never seen the sea. What was the sea like? Oh, I wished I could go hand in hand to the sea with Aķzer. Perhaps the sea was bliss. I wanted to grow up faster. There were four more years until graduation. A terribly long time!

The next day we returned by the same road. The cuckoo was screaming again.

'That is a cuckoo. No, no, that is Zejnep,' I said. It seemed to me that Aķzer would be offended if I did not correct my mistake. And if offended, she would no longer call on me to look for the dromedaries in the evenings.

'Quiet,' said Aķzer, covering my mouth with her hand. She had hot palms. A warm breeze blew from head to toe. I had never experienced such a feeling before. If only she could stand like that forever. The cuckoo kept calling. I noticed that Aķzer counted how many times it cried *cuckoo.* I also started to count. Please continue. I didn't want the cuckoo song to end. Cuckoo, *koo-koo.* One, two, three. One, two, three. One, two, three …

'Only three months,' said Aķzer, hugging me. Only three months till what? School would start in three months. But what did Aķzer, who had graduated last year, have to do with it?

'You don't go to school,' I said in bewilderment.

'You are still a child, my dear boy,' said Aķzer, smiling. 'You are still a little chick.'

I did not like her laugh. My heart sensed something bad. I was silent.

School would start in three months.

After three months, both the black and the white-eyed dromedaries had got used to their fetters and stayed near the *auyl* the whole time.

Grandma said: 'I had a dream recently. If God wishes, the two dromedaries will mate this year.' Grandma's dreams used to come true.

After three months, despite her father's objections, Aķzer fled with a lanky tractor driver named Balta, who lived near the dance hall. They were planning to go to the Swan Sea in the west.

So, the seventh year of school started sadly for me. After school, I used to go outside the *auyl*, pretending that I was looking for the black and the white-eyed dromedaries. They lay in a bare place nearby. I kept going. It was raining. My face was covered with raindrops. Yes, raindrops. Sour drops. Not sour, but poisonous drops. But I did not cry. The clouds were crying.

Where is Aķzer now? Wherever she is, I hope she's alright. Does she remember a skinny blond kid who loved to listen to fairy tales? I left the *auyl* too. When Aķzer got married, I said that I would not stay in the *auyl* for a single day after graduation. It seems that the angels heard my words, I was destined to live the rest of my life elsewhere. But as you can see, I have not forgotten either the *auyl*, or Aķzer, or the fairy tale of Zejnep, or even the black and the white-eyed dromedaries. And I have not forgotten the cuckoo.

Every spring I remember the fairy tale about Zejnep. The cuckoo arrives in early summer. This is a blissful time when the rain and the piercing winds stop, and nature takes on a beautiful form. A red moon rises like the sun over the Kelintôbe *auyl*, just like those nights when Aķzer and I looked for the dromedaries. Morning also descends gently. The cuckoo screams. *Cuckoo, koo-koo*. I do not believe the rumours that it is a bad bird.

After Aķzer's lovely fairy tale that warm summer, I started to question the deep-seated prejudices shared by the majority about the cuckoo. I think it affected my way of thinking in general, and my tendency to query any longstanding, widely held beliefs started that very summer. Who knows, maybe if I had not listened to fairy tales, would my life have been different? Afterwards, I read a lot of books and listened to many legends about the cuckoo, but the cuckoo was not praised in any of them. Praise aside, from these stories one did not feel a drop of pity for the cuckoo. Listening to these tales, it seemed as if this little bird

were to blame for all the disasters and tragedies made by human hand in this sinful world.

I heard a lot of songs where people cursed the cuckoo, but I didn't believe in any of them, because I remembered that old story of Aķzer.

'Well, let it be,' said my childhood imagination. 'Let people slander the cuckoo, but in the end, someone will prove that it is a good bird.'

The poet and singer Biržan Sal had a song called 'Kôkek' ('The Cuckoo'). Despite its somewhat negative tone, one can feel the love for this bird in the song. It says, 'Instead of just

83

jumping pointlessly around and repeating "*cuc-koo, cuckoo*", fly away and bring me a message from my beloved, and I will sing about you until my death.'

I want to draw your attention to one thing. In some areas, the cuckoo and the hoopoe are confused. Kazakhs sometime call the hoopoe *sasyk kôkek*, that is, 'stinking cuckoo'; it has a pinkish-brown crest, and often hangs about barns and storage rooms. Its voice is very similar to that of the cuckoo. According to a Ukrainian legend, hoopoes fly with cuckoos on their back. In fact, they are two entirely different birds. The cuckoo looks more like a hawk than a hoopoe. People who are not into birds often confuse the cuckoo with the falcon because of the stripe on its chest and long tail. Kazakhs from China sometimes call it *sakau kôkek* or 'dumb cuckoo'.

The second feature is that the cuckoo is very rarely seen. It lives alone in forests, on the coast, in dense thickets. It is the size of a pigeon and a migrant. At the end of May and the beginning of June it arrives at the foot of the mountains, rivers and lakes in Almaty; more precisely, at Butakovka, on the bank of the Esentaj River, in the Alma-Arasan Gorge. It lives in these localities, as it feeds on pine caterpillars and the larvae of hawk moths. Scientists have found that the cuckoo eats about forty grasshoppers, fifty tree beetles, five May flies, four spiders and fifty fleas a day.

I was very pleased with this news from biologists. I repeat, I have been sure it is a useful bird. In a few years, perhaps, people will begin to tell pleasant stories about the cuckoo.

Unfortunately, I could not find any other evidence to justify the bird. In all countries, the cuckoo is spoken of as a parasitic bird that does not make a nest and lays its eggs in the nests of other birds. In addition, in ancient stories the cuckoo is associated with magic, mysteries and evil.

For example, in one of the legends of the Ukrainian people, the cuckoo is described as a girl who married a snake. According to another legend, a frivolous and wanton girl started screaming 'cuckoo, cuckoo' to scare her mother. Her frightened mother cursed her so that she would wander all her life. They say the girl turned into a cuckoo.

The French believe that if the cuckoo arrives before the trees start to bud, then the spring will be dry, the summer will be cold and the people will suffer misfortune. Travelling peoples believe that if a person who is sitting or lying has heard the voice of the cuckoo before the Easter holiday, they will be unwell all year. To avoid unhappiness, a person needs to go round the tree where the cuckoo sits nine times, and then eat the bark of that tree.

During the Russian Tsar's rule, young men were taken to the army for twenty-five years. Ukrainians cried when they saw the cuckoo in front of their houses and thought that a long road was waiting for their sons, that their sons were about to be taken for military service.

Slavs believed that however many times the cuckoo called, they would live for the same number of years. In Russian villages, people often grieved, thinking that death was approaching, if the cuckoo only sounded a couple of times then flew away as if frightened by something. According to another superstition, when the cuckoo screamed, you needed to grab any money and coins in your pocket firmly, and then all year round you would have money, a rich table and a festive mood. But if at that moment there was no money in your pocket, then failure awaited you. Of course, the cuckoo was to blame.

Irish people call the last two weeks of April and the first two weeks of May 'the rough month of the cuckoo' from the phrase *garbh mi na gcuach*. Kazakhs also call April 'Kôkek', the cuckoo.

Biržan Sal's aforementioned song was as follows:

Who does not like the month of cuckoo, when the flowers blossom?

My beloved is like the summer, all in bloom.

What is my sweetheart doing? Is she sitting or resting?

Cuckoo, fly and find out how she's doing.

I was very surprised when I learned that only two peoples refer to 'the month of the cuckoo'.

The legend of the cuckoo originated in Ancient Greece. The god Zeus fell in love with beautiful Hera and lost his peace and sleep. Zeus's household could not eat and were lost as well. The proud girl did not show any kindness to anyone and did not want to acknowledge Zeus. Zeus reflected for a long time, then he turned into a cuckoo, flew to beautiful Hera and chirped pitifully under her window. Hera heard the bitter voice of the bird and felt sorry for it. She let it into her house, took it in her hands and cuddled it. At this moment the dishevelled bird turned into the excited mighty Zeus and ravished her. Soon, Hera felt in love with Zeus too. Since then, the cuckoo has turned into the sacred bird of the beautiful Hera. To this day, the Greeks associate the bird with early signs of spring.

The Polish considered a man who kills a cuckoo a real criminal. A Polish girl instructed others before her death, 'Plant a viburnum on my grave. The cuckoo will fly to the tree. I will rest in peace if I hear its voice.'

According to German mythology, this bird ran errands for the god of thunderstorms, Donar. Donar sent the cuckoo to the earth as a harbinger of spring. Farmers in Salzburg have popular expressions such as 'If the cuckoo arrives, it's time for love', just like the Kazakhs, who say 'The cuckoo flies in; the summer comes'.

Finns, like the Germans, consider it a symbol of love.

According to another German legend, God singled out all the birds so that they would make nests for themselves: the stork would take the roofs of houses; the lapwing took the valleys and the lark, the steppes. As the saying goes, 'A fussy girl will end up with a bald man', but the cuckoo, which did not like the mountains, the steppes or the valleys, ended up without shelter. Therefore, it does not have its own nest.

You see, we have returned to fact that the cuckoo does not make a nest and uses other birds to incubate its eggs. There are about 150 birds in the world that are parasites, but not everybody knows this. Ornithologists say there are about 127–130 species of cuckoo, only 80 of which are parasitic. Obviously, the remaining fifty species that incubate eggs them-

selves will not save all cuckoos from the terrible cliché that appeared a long time ago. It is easy to be denigrated, but it is difficult to get rid of slander.

By the will of God, I spent my youth in Uzbekistan. I returned from the army and tried myself in various areas. Once I went to Myrzašôl. The local newspaper was published in the Kazakh language. I, who had never seen cotton, was hired by the Agriculture Department of the newspaper. The late writer Sajymžan Erkebaev said, 'A person who does not sit in his place will sit on his shame.' I accidentally found a job – *korni* (Persians and Uzbeks use this term) – and in order not to feel a burden to the rest and to learn the work, I often took business trips.

Uzbekistan's territory is not as big as Kazakhstan's, and the territory of a whole district in Uzbekistan is like of a tiniest state farm in Arķa. If I set off early in the morning, I could visit several state farms in one day.

One day I stumbled upon some silk farmers in a mulberry tree garden. It was not far from the main road. The Uzbeks call the silkworm *pilla*. They are incubated in a dark room until they grow and begin to make silk. They feed on mulberry leaves. No one is allowed to peep through the door. During the *šildelik*, the first forty days, no one is allowed to approach or see them, so as not to jinx them. This word is likely to come from the Persian word *chil* (forty).

Let me remind you that in Bukhara and Samarkand, the newly married bride is not let out of the house and not shown to anyone for forty days. This is also called *šildelik*. Unlike the Kazakhs, the Uzbeks and Tajiks are very superstitious. Moreover, all traditions and customs are strictly observed.

The silk farmers were sad because pests had appeared on the mulberry trees and eaten all the leaves. They could not spray pesticide, as the silkworms would die from the smell. They dreamed of flying *kakku*. Uzbeks call the cuckoo *kakku*. There are two birds whose names sound similar in almost all languages and one of them is the cuckoo. For example, in the Balkar, Karachay, Gaguz and Kyrgyz languages it is *kukuk*; in Bashkir *kekuk*; in Azerbaijani, *gugu gushi*; in Nogai it is *kokek*; in Turkish, *guguk*; in Khakass, *koyak*; in Teleut it is *kook*; and in Shor it is *keyek*. These names probably appeared because of the song of the cuckoo, 'who calls itself', as Kazakhs say (that is, *cuckoo, koo-koo*). It turned out that only cuckoos eat the worms that live on mulberry trees.

When I went there another time, I heard the cuckoo's voice.

It was lunchtime and really hot. We sipped green tea in the shade. There were dense thickets around. On a thick branch of a tree there was a house sparrow's nest, which the Uzbeks call a 'farmer sparrow'. The leader of the silk farmers said, 'Yesterday the cuckoo left its eggs in this nest'. As soon as he said those words, a huge cuckoo with a short, grey neck flew in and began to break eggs with its beak and swallow them in a hurry. Then a second cuckoo arrived hastily and began to drive it off in a very pitiful voice. It had a bitter voice that gave me goosebumps. The Uzbek, who was pouring tea, rose abruptly from his seat and drove the two birds away. He wiped sweat from his forehead and said, 'The male eats its eggs, and the poor female desperately tries to protect them.'

Since then, I do not believe the slander about the cuckoo. In newspapers, women who leave their children in orphanages are often compared to the cuckoo. The same is true for women who hire nannies for their children. This is a common expression in the Kazakh, and quite an unfair one, as you see. Perhaps the poor bird will not get rid of its undeserved bad reputation any time soon.

I think that the cuckoo lays its eggs in others' nests not because it is trying to run away from its maternal burden, but because it is trying to save its child from its cruel father. The poor mother is ready to do anything for her child. Imagine mothers who age prematurely because of husbands who are drunks and drug addicts, who are unable to support their family.

People say in vain that the cuckoo disappears after it lays eggs in others' nests. After the female secretly lays its eggs, both the female and the male do not stray far from this nest. The male tries to eat all the eggs, while the female tries to save future chicks from its wicked father. When children are sometimes abandoned in the courtyards of hospitals and then shown on TV, it seems to me that their poor young, but old-beyond-their-years mothers watch secretly from a corner.

The cuckoo has a spotted chest, but it also has problems with its chest. Its breast is very large and disproportionate to its size, and this prevents it from incubating eggs. In other words, if the cuckoo tried to incubate its eggs it would break them. Almighty God probably enabled the cuckoo to understand this danger, as it lays eggs, but never hatches them itself. This conclusion was made by scientists who studied cuckoos' bones. I think we must admire the cuckoo, for finding a way to save its chicks from apparent danger.

Who would argue with the fact that mothers who cannot have children for various reasons, or cannot provide for them, but still fully realize their maternal duty, are worthy of respect?

The cuckoo flies separately from other birds to Africa and the Arabian Peninsula in the autumn. No one waits for it to return. It is regarded as an uninvited guest. We don't even notice it. Perhaps the birds confuse it with a hawk or are afraid that it will break their eggs; at the sight of a cuckoo, birds begin to chirp loudly and flap their wings. The call of the female cuckoo is unpleasant for other birds, as is the chirping of the male cuckoo. A cuckoo, submitting sadly to its fate, flies into dense thickets knowing that its chicks are alive and well. But in this life there is nothing superfluous; everything was created by Allah for a reason.

Some scientists have calculated that one cuckoo prevents twenty to thirty other birds from being born. It must be true. When a cuckoo lays eggs in a nest, it breaks the eggs of the nest owner. However, as we said, cuckoos exterminate caterpillars and hairy worms on mulberry trees, which is beyond the power of other birds.

Am I the only one who is trying to justify the cuckoo? What about Akzer? She may remember the fairy tale of Zejnep when she is bored, sad and lonely in her homeland on the shore of the Swan Sea. Probably, the cuckoo's voice will remind her of a small *auyl* on the bank of the Syr Dariâ. I believe that she still considers the cuckoo a good bird.

Thank you, Akzer. Thank you for the little joy you gave me. When I think of my life spent in struggle, in which faith and doubt, joy and sorrow, good and bad fought continuously with each other, I realize that they have been my destiny. This has been my fate, Akzer.

Cuc-koo, koo-koo … I am counting. I want to know how long I am going to live.

Starling and Thrush

Your stone heart melts when the thrush sings at dawn ...

Ùkili Ybyraj[77]

The starling will arrive soon.

The clouds are stubbornly covering the sky; they won't disperse before the starling arrives.

What is the power of this little bird? There is not a single poet who would not compose a verse about it. Look through the Kazakh folk songs; there are more than sixty songs about birds, many of which are dedicated to starlings. The ancient *seri* loved to call their steeds, golden eagles, frisky hounds, even their favourite shotguns *Ķaratorġaj* (starling/thrush).[78]

How many birds are there in the world? Science says no fewer than 100 billion. How powerful is the science that calculates every moving creature on the earth. These 100 billion birds are divided into 8,600 (according to some sources 10,000) species. Why do Kazakhs love the starling so much out of these 8,600 species of birds?

Who does not know the starling? In childhood I often saw its pictures in books, and besides, I was interested in the song of this black bird with a yellow beak, which arrives with the onset of March. Starlings can parody exactly the old songs of grandmothers, who card wool in the shade in summer, as well as barking dogs, cawing crows and neighbourhood girls' laughter. The starling loves people. It's sweet. There is no need to build all sorts of traps, construct cages, arrange nets or a 'sticky hand' – a favourite method of falconers. If you feed it from your hand, it will fly to you itself. The tamed starling blooms and glitters, as if it had been brushed with oil.

It feels so comfortable at home that it could be mistaken for a domesticated fowl. It frolics like a married girl who comes to visit her relatives. Is there a Kazakh who has not heard the song by Aķan Seri called 'Ķaratorġaj' ('The Starling')?

---

77 Ùkili Ybyraj Sandybajųly (1860–1930) was a Kazakh folk composer, *aķyn* (improvisational poet of song-like recitations, usually accompanied by *dombyra*) and singer (tenor).

78 *Seri* – traditionally a sophisticated group of artists skilled in singing, composing, poetry, hunting, eagle hunting. They used to wear striking costumes. Nowadays, *seri* is a synonym for a 'refined young man' or a 'lover of women'.

Ḳaratorġaj flies, flapping its wings,

It has pearls under its wings.

You were a childhood friend.

How did I lose you?

Ḳaratorġaj, you fly with difficulty.

You cry, poor thing, not able to land on the ground.

Sorry, dear readers, but from now on I want to stop praising the starling (*ḳaratorġaj*), because I doubt that the starling, about whom the ancient old men sang and composed verses, is actually this same bird. These doubts did not appear casually. For a long time, I have been bothered by the thought that we still cannot distinguish the starling that old Kazakh songs sing about.

Where do the doubts come from?

Firstly, the song of the much-praised bird called the starling in large and small textbooks, in useful and useless dictionaries, in worthy and worthless literary works, in encyclopedias and educational TV and radio programmes, is honestly not so inspiring.

Given the fact that our people greatly appreciate music, this doubt is amplified.

The melody that inspired such a sophisticated person as the poet, singer and wrestler Ùkili Ybyraj, who created such masterpiece songs like 'Gákku', 'Žajmaḳoṇyr', 'Ḳarakôz', 'Ḳaldyrġan', 'Šalḳyma' and 'Ḳyzyl asyḳ', should be far more pleasant, more beautiful.

It seems that the starling rides on another bird's coattails. No, this is not its fault. *We* are to blame for confusing it with another bird.

In one Hadith of the Prophet Muhammad al-Mustafa it is said that 'Even the birds fly according to the will of Allah'. Allah created us all.

By the way, it must not be forgotten that the starling's song and imitative abilities are not like those of any other bird. This talent stems from its uniqueness.

According to ornithologists, it is very difficult to tell the exact time when a starling will sing. There is one bird that sings at dawn, but none of the reference sources (books, newspapers and magazines, radio, television, etc.) consider this to be the starling. Let us leave the name alone. Let us define its colour. It is a black bird, completely black. The aforementioned song by Aķan Seri starts as follows:

> There is a deep ravine beyond the Ertis River,
> There is a grey horse dragging its silk rope.
> Sitting on a tree branch, high above the ground,
> *Ķaratorğaj* sings at dawn incessantly.

If in the autumn the back, neck and chest of the starling (*ķaratorğaj*) are streaked with dark spots, then the bird referred to in the song above as *ķaratorğaj* is entirely black. Okay, the problem is not its colour. Outwardly, this bird is not much different from the starling. It is smaller than a rook, but bigger than a starling. Russians call this bird *drozd*; that is, 'thrush'. I think that this is the bird that the Ancient Kazakhs celebrated as the *ķaratorğaj*. In Kazakh dictionaries published in recent years, the bird was listed as *sajraķ* – literally 'songbird', *ķara sajraķ* – 'black songbird' and *siyrķujryķ* – 'cow's tail'. Well, 'songbird', and 'black songbird' both describe the bird more or less accurately. But why on earth do we call it a 'cow's tail?' I do not understand the connection between the bird and the cow's tail. If someone is able to explain this, then I am ready to listen.

When the thrush sings inspirationally at dawn, your body will tremble as if it is being electrocuted, because you do not expect such a beautiful melody. Then you don't even notice how you are still frozen in place. A beautiful melody slowly emerges from the depths and approaches you.

This is not *chirping*; it is a single continuous and beautiful melody, not an intermittent one. A gentle melody that begins with a single rhythm takes you far into the sky after a while, as if tearing out your heart, then it lightly soars in the air, like poplar wool in May. In this very moment it makes young men dismount from horses, and girls stand still in awe. At that moment you involuntarily recall Ùkili Ybyraj's lines: 'Your stone heart melts when the thrush sings at dawn …'

At a certain point, the song ends suddenly. You hold your breath. Usually while listening to good music, you get nervous – this is because you wish deep down that the song will not end. Like all good things in the world, the song of the thrush also ends suddenly.

When you get up from your place, sighing, suddenly the beautiful melody continues, as if a very thirsty person had taken a sip of pure spring water. You lose your mind.

I don't know about you, but I have no doubt that the real *ķaratorğaj* (as Kazakhs call both the starling and the thrush) is the thrush.

Such a bird must be treasured.

Those who have not heard, or cannot hear, this song are just unfortunate creatures.

The singer who found his or her own song is happy. Sometimes I pity those lovely girls who sing on TV, but have failed to find their song. Oh, if they managed to find their song, they would be great singers, but now their talents are wasted. Sometimes I feel sorry for the song. There are so many who seek to create artificially a talent that Allah did not bestow on them. There is no authority to stop them. The authorities today are like a helpless old man who can manage nothing and keeps repeating, 'Oh, I don't know. Times have changed …' In particular, when older singers (they themselves know who I am talking about) force their voice, you are surprised at people who will do anything to become famous. The beautiful song does not choose a composer or performer for fame, money or authority. It is a mystery. When you are annoyed by talentless composers, shameless singers, unscrupulous poets and unfaithful advertisers, you want to share your sorrow with the bird. But that bird is not here. Instead, there are many tits, crows, rooks and so on.

There is no thrush.

However, it will come. Not long to wait.

We know that other nations love to listen to the thrush's song. The poet Robert Burns composed 'Sonnet Written on the Author's Birthday, on Hearing a Thrush Sing in his Morning Walk'. You might wonder why the author gave such a long title to a poem that only consists of fourteen lines. You can feel that the author wanted to fully convey the double joy of his heart, so perhaps that is the answer.

In the USA, an annual meeting is held to support the development of science. During the meeting, music researchers and ornithologists concluded that the thrush had a great influence on Wolfgang Amadeus Mozart in writing his immortal works. You can clearly hear the thrush singing in his *divertimento*, 'A Musical Joke, K.522'.

Ornithologist Luis Baptis, who lives in San Francisco, tells another story. One day Mozart bought a thrush in the bazaar for four pennies. They say that he loved this bird so much that he carried it in his arms all the time. The thrush died suddenly. Saddened, Mozart wore black clothes, buried his bird in a white tomb and cried for a long time, as if saying goodbye to a loved one.

The Germans have always revered the thrush. To the question 'What is the thrush's song?' they respond with Caesar's saying: 'I came. I saw. I conquered.' Brehm admitted that the thrush has a wonderful song. By the way, the Latin name of the thrush is *turdus musicus*.

In Eastern countries, a pumpkin is divided in half and covered with a cloth to make a quail's nest. Guests drink tea while listening to the birds sing, to relax nerves and relieve fatigue. In addition, during various holidays, craftsmen parody the voices of birds according to the numerous requests of people. Musical instruments that mimic the voice of birds are called *kerki*. Hunters often use them.

If we want to know what instrument can imitate the thrush's voice, we must first recall the flute.

Russians have written a lot about the thrush as well. Turgenev penned several stories about it. Maxim Gorky and Fyodor Chaliapin used to go to the taverns solely to listen to the thrush singing. Rich Russian men tamed thrushes and had people to look after them. It is said that these bird keepers were skillful artists who could imitate the exact melody of various songs by whistling. In Russian bazaars, the price of a thrush reached 200 roubles – the price of a horse. But why should we be surprised?

Thrush, my dear,

I was waiting for you,

looking impatiently at the road.

In this folk song, a man compares his beloved to a thrush. In the song, 'Syrdyņ ķara-torġajy' ('The Thrush of Syr'), a girlfriend is compared to a bird:

If you were a bird, I would decorate you with a lace of silk,

I would make you a silver perch.

I would have hung a golden necklace around your neck

and gently cherished you, taking you in hand.

If we are talking about the ability to appreciate a song, then there is not a single song that could match the two lines of Ükili Ybyraj: 'Your stone heart melts when the thrush sings at dawn ...'

Of course, the conversation about the song will never end, like life itself.

The thrush will arrive soon.

January has begun. This month will pass very quickly. February comes next. It's not worth considering short February. Then March will come. When March comes, the thrush will come too.

If only it would come soon ...

The Birds Are Our Friends

Rosefinch

*M*ajra was my neighbour's daughter. She was the oldest child; brave and gregarious. She was about five or six years old. Even though she had only recently moved from the *auyl*, she had already learned Russian. She had a friend of the same age named Lena. They were friends, but they were children, so there were moments when they fought.

'Majra, who upset you?' we asked, to make her talk.

'No one.'

'I think someone's upset you!'

'No.'

However, she soon cheered up. Whenever you looked around, they were playing together in the garden. I was going home at noon.

'Uncle, this is a *bipyl-bipyl*,' Majra said, jumping out in front of me. I did not understand what she meant at first.

'What did you say, Majra?' I asked. Lena seemed to be waiting for this moment.

'You see, no one says this. She means, "Have you seen Vitya?" Do you understand?' she said, as if she had defeated Majra and was enjoying it.

Majra looked at me fiercely, without taking her eyes off me, then turned and ran away. Oh dear, she was annoyed. Lena pointed to a large red-breasted bird that sat at the very top of the pear tree.

'There. "Have you seen Vitya?"' she said.

She was right. If you listened to the cry of the rosefinch, it seemed that a very slow-speaking person was asking "*Vityu videl*?" – 'Have you seen Vitya?' It cannot be confused with other birds.

What about the *bipyl* of our Majra? It turned out that Majra had heard '*Vityu videl*?' (Russian) as '*bipyl-bipyl*' (Kazakh). I realized this too late. I had to apologize to my little neighbour. Later, on speaking to her, I learned that little Majra's mother sang the folk song 'Bipyl' beautifully. When her mother was singing the chorus, Majra sang with her:

... Kůldi–kůldi, my sunshine,
my house is like a festival every day,
Bipyl, Bipyl, Bipyl–aj,
come on, friend, play one kůj.

Since then, for us, another name for a rosefinch has been *bipyl*.

Rosefinches arrive late. Their *bipyl-bipyl* can only be heard by the end of May. When the apple trees bloom and the garden flowers, if you hear a familiar song, then the rosefinches have already arrived. It is a red-breasted bird and as small as a sparrow. Its wings, tail and flanks are grey, streaked with brown. But if you look closely, you can see red areas under its grey plumage. The female is very difficult to distinguish from the common sparrow. The only striking difference is its song. Its song is not like any other song. When you find out that this little bird flies to India to spend the winter, you will understand why the Ancient Kazakhs dreamed of wings. Another difference is its name. Kazakhs call it *ķuralaj*, meaning both the saiga calf and the rosefinch. Russians call it *chechevitsa*, which means both lentil and rosefinch.

Kazakhs call the five or six extremely windy days of spring *Ķuralajdyŋ salķyny* (the cold of the *ķuralaj*). They say that at this time the saiga antelope allows its calf to graze. Kazakhs also compare a beautiful girl to a *ķuralaj*. There is a folk song 'Eyes like those of a *ķuralaj*'. Who are they talking about? The bird or the saiga calf?

When Kazakhs talk about a skilled marksman, we say 'The one who shoots *ķuralaj* in the eye'. What kind of *ķuralaj* is it? The bird or the saiga calf?

The saiga, along with the argali (mountain ram), deer and the Siberian ibex, is considered a sacred creature by Kazakhs, or *koŋyr aŋ* (literally: a brown animal). Kazakhs do not shoot them unless times are desperate. Kazakhs' sophisticated sense of right and wrong does not allow them to consume more than necessary. Shooting a saiga calf is unthinkable; only heartless people are capable of it. In the ancient Kazakh epic romance *Ķozy Kôrpeš – Baân Sulu*, the antagonist, cruel and relentless Ķarabaj, is described hunting deer. He is so greedy that he leaves his companion, Sarybaj, and gallops to the fallen deer. He cuts the

belly of the deer when it is still alive and sees two baby fawns. He slaughters the fawns as well, takes the carcass of the deer and its two fawns, and heads home, whistling carelessly.

This is an unthinkable cruelty. Ancient poets were very eloquent when describing unpleasant characters. The stanzas that introduce Ķarabaj's hunting scene occur at the very beginning of the poem, foretelling the character's cruelty regarding his daughter, beautiful Baân, who eventually falls victim to his avarice.

It turns out that the phrase to 'shoot ķuŕalaj in the eye' is not related to the saiga calf.

If we are to assume that this phrase is about the rosefinch, we have already said that it is smaller than a sparrow (only 19–26 grams). Is it brave to shoot such a tiny bird? Probably, this is a figure of speech meaning to shoot at a small target. Otherwise, it is unthinkable for a real marksman to show his skills by shooting a small bird in the eyes.

Rosefinch

Crow Loves Its Chick

The famous Russian poet Vyacheslav Kiktenko wrote a book, *Gorod* (*The City*), in honour of his hometown of Almaty. He described the city poetically and said that in Almaty there were two native trees: the elm and the poplar. It seems to be true. But lately, the inhabitants of our city, which resembles an anthill, have begun to cut down these two 'aborigines' and have planted exotic trees brought from afar, even from overseas, for the sake of beauty. Our new neighbour at the summer house wanted to chop down a large elm in Almaty, and plant Japanese cherry trees instead. We had not noticed that the crows made their nest at the very top of this elm tree. Their chicks were just getting stronger. When the loud sound of the saw approached the tree, the crows began to caw noisily. Nobody paid attention to them, and the tree was immediately cut down. The nest also fell. At that moment, crows, like black clouds, surrounded the fallen tree. They did not let anyone near. Our neighbour did not want to go himself and sent a large bull terrier, but the loud crows drove the dog into the barn. My neighbour ran at them with a stick. He stumbled along the way and fell to the ground. The crows immediately flew up to him and began to flap their wings and peck. We all ran up and just managed to rescue him.

This hurt our neighbour's pride, or he was embarrassed in front of everyone. In any case, he stood there for a while and then began to throw stones at the crows. At this point, the crows were divided into two groups: one group rescued the fallen chicks and headed for the forest; the other group went on the attack. As a result, our neighbour's shirt was torn to shreds. The crows not only pooped all over the soon-to-be planted cherry trees, but also circled over the house for a long time.

Our neighbour came back after a while, dressed in another shirt. We thought that the winged 'assault force' would attack him again, but no, they paid no attention to the *enemy* in the new shirt, just made some noise and flew away. Does this mean that the crows have eyesight problems? It is said that many animals cannot distinguish colours. But it was clear that it is nothing to do with the crows. We witnessed this event with our own eyes, and it remains an ornithological mystery to this day.

Since biblical times, if any two birds have been subjected to slander, one of them is usually the crow.

As if this bird is to blame for the fact that the human lifespan is limited, we hate it because it lives for a long time. Muḵaġali Maḵataev, in his poem 'Žazylar estelikter men turaly' ('There will be memoirs about me') denigrated the crows:

I know that in some centuries, in distant future,

a worthless crow will be alive for a hundred years.

Until recently, some scientists believed that crows lived for as long as 250–300 years, if not 1,000 years. This is rubbish. Birds do not live that long. As for the crow, it is clear in ornithology that they may live for 70–75 years maximum, but only for 30–35 years on average. Besides, even if crows really live for a long time, how can the bird itself be blamed for this?

We fail to appreciate that the crow is one of those birds that is loyal to its family and ready to protect its chicks from any danger by any means. No wonder the Ancient Kazakhs said that 'A crow affectionately calls its baby bird *white*'. Its second likeable feature is that the crow does not leave its homeland even during fire, plague or famine. It does not leave its homeland, even if there is unbearable heat or a terrible storm. Indeed, we must learn a lot from nature.

We accuse crows of stealing. Actually, the crow is a very alert bird. It does not lose sight of anything. Such qualities as apathy, lethargy and negligence are alien to it.

Let's say that these things are all true. Would you believe that the crow is a very intelligent and smart bird? You wouldn't? In fact, crows, unlike songbirds, quickly learn the human language.

On the outskirts of Almaty there is a small district called Ul'žan. The travellers of Central Asia live there. They call themselves *mu-cap*, the Persian-speaking people. They are peculiar, intricate people. Children are actively engaged in taming birds. They tame not only the chicks of sparrows, quails and tits, but also the nestlings of the crow. When they say '*ab*' ('water' in Persian), the chicks perch on a bucket full of water.

If the children shout '*pou*' ('leg'), the chicks fly noisily and land on their knee.

Then they give the command '*dast*' ('hand') and the chicks sit on their arm.

After playing this game in the square, the children say '*raftan*' ('let's go'). The chick sits on its master's shoulder and returns home. It does not fly away. And it does not croak, but is an obedient, sweet and neat bird.

Not only can crow chicks learn 20–30 words in 20–30 days, but they can also repeat these words without error.

The crows' mating season begins in February and is a thrill to witness. You may be surprised to see two black dots in the February sky. They resemble true lovers. There is nobody in the sky except them. They fly at the speed of light and then freeze and start dancing and somersaulting. They hover in the sky like parachutists, locking their toes together. These are real sky acrobats. They dance and eat from each other's beak. This is how they caress one another. The fact that they are dancing in the sky, and not on mountains or in ravines is fascinating. In addition, they are dancing not in the bountiful summer, but in winter, in the severe cold of -50 to -60°C. Isn't that brave? By the way, its newborn chicks do not freeze at -20 to -30°C of cold – that's what endurance and resilience looks like.

We are talking about crows. Ravens, rooks and grey crows of the *Corvus* genus are a separate topic.

In fact, the poet Bajbota Serikbaev was right.

> *Is the crow guilty of staying in the autumn?*
> *After all, it remained in its native land.*
> *Let's not curse and badmouth the bird,*
> *What's its fault?*

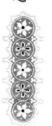

Dipper

*I*n summer 1998, the writer Aʹbdiżamil Nuʹrpejisov and I were resting on the shore of Lake Alakôl. Apparently, the Maķansy lakeside of the Semej region was a popular place.

I was sitting on the shore staring at the far island; not at the island itself, but at a girl swimming towards it. Approaching the lake, I had noticed her, a little girl of eleven or twelve years sitting on the beach, hugging her knees, looking at the island and not paying any attention to the children playing around. I had decided not to disturb her and went on.

In the 1970s, Ernar Aʹuezov discovered relict gulls on the island, which became popular after the short film *Appaķ ķuʹstar araly* (*The Island of White Birds*).[79] I knew that the island had been given the status of a relict gull reserve. I was wondering what the situation was these days.

In the morning the coast was crowded with gulls. The dignified lake doesn't allow the filth to remain in its body, but drives away all the rubbish to the shore, which is where the gulls flocked. The little girl swam in the lake, then she swam away. I was still not paying proper attention – kids are just kids. But she was swimming further and further away. Only a white bow on top of her head could be seen from time to time. And there I was, still sitting, assuming that she was about to float back.

Clean air, pure nature and healing water. Astronauts returning from a space flight come to rest on this coast. In *Batyrlar Žyry* (*Heroic Epics*), Lake Alakôl is called 'the water from which the dog cannot be bothered to drink'. Just think how healthy and sacred the water in Kazakh lands would be if the lakes that dogs were scornful of drinking from had such healing powers.

'Let's wait a bit and then call the rescuers!'

I raised my head. Aʹbeṇ was standing nearby.[80] He did not take his eyes off the brave girl who was swimming far away and about to reach the island.

'My goodness, what a swimmer. I noticed her yesterday. She was floating out there,' he said in surprise. Honestly, I hadn't noticed. There were many children playing in the sand and having swimming competitions. It was difficult to discern anyone in the crowd.

---

79 Ernar Aʹuezov (1943–95), outstanding ornithologist, son of the prominent Kazakh writer Mu htar Aʹuezov.

80 Aʹbeṇ (or Aʹbe) is a respectful form of address for Aʹbdiżamil Nuʹrpejisov, or for someone called Abdijamil in general.

But now I was getting really scared. The little girl looked like a white gull chick, diving and swimming out on the water. At some point, the white chick disappeared completely.

'Don't worry,' said the local teacher, approaching us. 'She's a real *suŝylḳara*.[81] She sometimes even reaches the island. She'll be back soon, don't worry.'

It was as though he saw it in a crystal ball: first, a white bow appeared, then the girl herself. We waited with bated breath. Enough time passed to boil milk; she still wasn't there. Then enough time to milk a mare also passed; she still wasn't there. We got up, then sat down, then walked along the shore. We couldn't keep still. But she was still swimming.

'Let's go inside, A'ben,' I said.

'No, boy,' said A'ben, 'We will wait. Stop dragging me inside.'

I didn't object. What could I say? It made no sense to argue when our respected A'beṇ dug his heels in. The only thing to do was wait.

And there she was, a white chick. She did not pay any attention to us, just came out of the water, shook herself off, sat down on the sand and hugged her knees: frozen just like a little stone sculpture.

100   81 *Suŝylḳara*, literally 'water lover' or 'aquaphile'; also a dipper.

'Come here, dear,' said A'beṇ to the girl. The conversation began. The girl's and her parents' names, her school, *auyl* and district were all carefully written down. I only learned why A'beṇ had done that the next day.

After breakfast A'beṇ, having thought a little, said: 'We need to talk to Kôŝerbaev.' Ķyrymbek Kôŝerbaev was then the Minister of Culture, Education and Health.

We immediately found the minister's phone number.

'Mr Minister, sorry to bother you,' said A'beṇ at once. 'I have a favour to ask.'

Then he recounted the story of the little swimmer from Alakôl. He said that children like her, if given proper training, might become successful swimmers, the pride of the country one day.

Ķyrymbek Kôŝerbaev was the most decisive minister I'd ever known. They say his late father Eleu had been the same. Like all determined people, Ķyrymbek Kôŝerbaev made decisions having carefully weighed up everything, which was obviously better than constantly changing his mind.

A couple of days passed. Soon the minister himself called back. He had given a special task to the regional and district Departments of Education to supervise the swimmer girl. A'beṇ and I thanked the minister sincerely.

Where is this girl today? She has surely finished school. If she is safe and sound I'm sure we will hear about her soon.

Perhaps on reading this article she will contact the editors and tell them about her life. Unfortunately, I have forgotten her name. The only thing I remember is her nickname, *Suŝylkara*, which not only stands for a person that enjoys swimming, but is also the name of a bird – a dipper – and a game. Forty days of scorching heat usually enable all the children to do nothing but play on the beach. They run along the shore, scare birds and splash around all day long. There are many games such as *Žalaķ*, *Žaryspaķ*, *Maržan ilu* and *Suŝylķara* (in some areas that game is called *Sùṇgime-sùṇgi* as well).[82] So, what is the game *Suŝylķara* like?

Children compete for how long they can stay under the water. Supporters begin counting as soon as the participants dive: one, two, three, four … Some children do not stay down for long, while others remain under water for ages. The latter are respectfully called *suŝylkara*. The second competition is about swimming a long way. How far can a child float downstream or upstream? A metre, two or five, or perhaps fifteen or twenty? Those who are called 'real *suŝylķara*' – 'real dippers' – are the ones who can swim the furthest.

Where does the word *suŝylkara* come from? The word *suŝyl* (water-lover) is clear enough, but why *ķara* (black)? The word *kara* has always had a positive meaning in Kazakh; for instance, *ķara domalaķ bala* (dark, moon-faced boy), *ķara nar* (the strongest camel), *ķara šaṇyraķ* (lit. black šaṇyraķ; the black wooden circle at the top of the yurt, in

---

82 Children's games: *Žalaķ*, catching smooth stones with one hand; *Žaryspaķ*, a game of tag; *Maržan ilu*, fishing for pearls; *Suŝylķara* – diving game.

Dipper

vernacular use means ' the grand home where parents live'), ķarajǧan ķara orman (thick forest), and so on. But these names are not related to this game.

Suŝylķara is the name for a dipper. The Latin family name is Cinclidae. It's a dark brown creature with a white breast. Its nest can be found somewhere unreachable; for example, among stones, under bridges or on branches. It is ball-shaped with a barely visible hole for an entrance. You can find about 4–8 eggs there. Nestlings hatch in about two weeks. Like a hummingbird, the dipper has chicks twice in the summer. The most exciting thing is how the bird finds its food.

> There is a bird tweeting unceasingly
> On the riverside, that is as slim as a girl's waist.
> Oh, sprinkling dust of snow, hold on.
> Let us enjoy the song till dawn.

The chanting bird in this verse is definitely the dipper. A few people in November can hear the bird singing while they walk along the frozen river in the cold. This is the time when all our feathered friends have already flown away to warm countries. In general, it is difficult to imagine birds singing in the winter. However, once you hear a bird elegantly singing on a mountain river, you know it's a dipper. As the Kazakhs say: 'Summer is for the needy, winter is for the strong.' Isn't it courageous of dippers? That is one of the dipper's peculiarities.

The other amazing feature is the way it finds food.

A person who first sees a dipper gathering its wings and dipping its head into the water may feel sorry for the bird, thinking that it has been injured. However, the dipper does this to catch a worm or a dace in the water. Its wing feathers are very close together and no water can penetrate between them; the water flows off its oily wings.

The dipper is the only bird in the world with valves in its ears and eyes that close as soon as it dives into the water. It dives to a depth of 1–1.5 metres, sometimes 2 metres, and can even swim at a depth of 20 metres, in search of food. Having found food, it gathers its wings and curls into a ball so that the river current can bring it up to the surface.

We have mentioned that the courageous girl was called 'a dipper' by her folks, so why don't we call the dipper brave?

Have you ever seen the River Aķbulǧaķ in Altaj?

The prominent poet Iliâs Žansùgirov wrote about the River Ile in the Žetisu region:

> Brave, self-willed and untamed,
> The Ile neighs and hugs the mighty hills.
> … It makes noise on the slopes of Alatau,
> It snorts, and stamps like a bull.
> The Ile breaks through the stones, rams the hills,
> And embraces the desert, resembling the stallion's mane.

And what about Aķsu-Žabaǧly nature reserve's foaming waters?

A bit nearer the rivers Talǧar and Butaķty flow close to Almaty.

Have you seen the Esentaj and the Kimasar rivers break their banks in the summer? They say that these rivers used to run even faster in the past. In particular, the Esentaj and Talǧar rivers could even wash away a horseman.

The Birds Are Our Friends

The River Kimasar is notorious for being a wilful river (even its name makes a statement: Kimasar – 'who will dare to exceed?'). Human beings are scared of the threatening stream, let alone unintelligent animals. It is the tiny, fearless dipper that dives into its waters.

Nowadays Norwegians, whose Viking ancestors crossed the Atlantic on sailing boats, consider the dipper their 'national bird'. When choosing a symbol, the Norwegians associated the dipper with their ancestors, as they lived on the seashore, fighting the element of water, and were unbelievably courageous, just like the little heroic bird.

There are many other swimming and diving birds, such as the penguin who can dive at a depth of 265 metres and swim for 120–130 metres under the water, or loons who can dive up to 50 metres and swim for up to 300 metres. There are plenty of such examples. At the twelfth conference of the International Bird Conservation Forum held in Tokyo, in 1960, states elected their national birds: the Japanese chose the pheasant; South Africans took up the nightingale; the Belgians preferred the red-footed falcon; the Austrians voted for the heron; the Germans opted for the crane; Iceland chose the white falcon; the British chose the robin; Portugal elected the magpie; the USA took up the bald eagle; and the Netherlands preferred the spoonbill – each to their own taste. And so the Norwegians elected the dipper.

Anyway, we haven't revealed all of the dipper's secrets. Birds have their own eternal universe full of mystery. Let us proceed to the kingfisher that also dives deep into the water. It's definitely the most unique creature ever.

Kingfisher

Do you remember how shotguns are riddled in verbal folklore? It is said:

> There's a bird named the kingfisher.
> It has leaden spherical eggs.

If walking alongside mountain rivers, one can't help noticing a pretty bird sitting quietly on low-hanging branches. It's because our fauna contains few birds as strikingly colourful as the kingfisher. Its bright blue back and tail, its purple beak, its metallic copper breast, white throat and red legs are unmistakeable. Anyone who sees it can be amazed, thinking, *How come all the colours of the rainbow are combined into one?*

The kingfisher is full of mismatched glory and an inharmonious shape presented via its long beak and short tail. It may seem that a colourful cloth got hooked on a branch, or a tiny jewel. Middle Eastern countries liken the kingfisher to a diamond left in a tree by an angel. A riddle originated there would sound the following way:

A diamond dropped from a tree limb,
And jumped into the water.
I watch in a state of awe
How the fish is caught in its claw.

Our Balkar and Karachai brothers call it *balykchy chymchyk* (a fisher robin), whereas the Bashkirs call it *balyksy torǥaj* (a fisher sparrow). Each country names it differently, which is understandable. There are eighty-seven kinds of kingfisher. Seeming not to care about anything, the quiet 'diamond' bird suddenly dives into the water, like a bullet from a gun. Who would have thought that a bird with such a long beak and short tail could be so agile? It is no coincidence that the Kazakhs call it *zymyran* ('swift' or 'rocket').

You cannot even spot how quickly this bird can rush headlong from the branch it's sitting on to catch an unconcerned small fish swimming close to the surface. Gulls cannot be compared with the kingfisher. The kingfisher's main food is fish. Even in the deepest mountain water it can catch a fish and carry it to its nest on the sheer riverbank. This is a burrow rather than a nest. The kingfisher excavates it just like the European roller does, in soft riverbanks, usually just below the top of a vertical bank with no vegetation on it. The burrow is about 1–1.5 metres deep, which is also convenient to protect the chicks. Another means of protection is the smell, which scares animals and people passing by. No other bird has such a stinky nest. The bones and fins of fish eaten by the kingfisher roll around the nest; it can't be bothered to clean the nest and the air there is not ventilated. As Kazakhs say 'Powerful in the field, poor at home' or 'If anyone acts like an aristocrat, see him at home', which mean if someone tries to give the impression of refinement, see how they behave at home. This definitely reflects the nest of a bird that poets have equated to diamonds, rubies and gold cloth in looks. However, this bird is still admirable.

The kingfisher is one of the few birds praised as a symbol of beauty in the literature of many countries. Ovid narrates an Ancient Greek myth about Alcyone in his *Metamorphoses*.

Metamorphoses – considered 'the Poets' Bible' – was written more than 1200 years ago. Publius Ovidius Naso burned this poem comprising more than 250 Greek and Roman myths out of spite, after getting into trouble with Augustus and going into banishment beyond the Black Sea. (Have poets and rulers ever found a common language?) The world of literature would have lost one more treasure but for Ovid's loyal friends, who had learned the poem and recorded it on paper. It reminds us of the immortal phrase 'Manuscripts don't burn', in Bulgakov's *Master and Margarita*.

Unfortunately, Ovid passed away and didn't see his work rise up out of the fire like a phoenix. The poem vividly describes the process of turning one phenomenon into another. The cursed owners of black magic turn into bogeymen, while innocent victims become incredibly happy. What is left for the

poor poet to do? Probably poets and birds are the most vulnerable creatures in the world. A defenceless poet pitied a defenceless beauty, and that was how the legend of the beautiful Alcyone was born.

According to the legend, the beautiful Alcyone was the wife of King Ceyx, who died at sea. The Aegean Sea's strong tides cast his body on the shore. Alcyone, waiting for her husband on a high cliff, could not bear it and jumped off the cliff. God's grace turned her into a kingfisher.

Ovid also said: 'In the midst of winter, it will suddenly become warmer and a week without frost will come. At this time, the kingfisher will lay eggs.' Pliny, as if confirming Ovid, also wrote: 'When the kingfisher plants his eggs, the Sicilian shores splash in the rays of the sun'. It may be so. But, as the ornithologists say, they have chicks three times a year. One of these periods could be in the winter months.

In Ancient China, the kingfisher's blue feathers were placed in the headdresses of the imperial palace princesses.

In the Middle Ages, the Europeans hung kingfishers by the beak above the door to protect a house from 'danger, threats and the evil eye'. In general, there are many rituals and superstitions in the world whose victims are birds.

Each kingfisher owns his own piece of land, where other birds are not allowed. He chases magpies, dippers and sparrows out of his territory. Ernest Thompson Seton wrote about a kingfisher confronting a hawk in one of his short stories.

As a result of recent activities there are many kingfishers on the rivers near Almaty, and their chicks can even be found on the lower mouths of the Esentaj and the Talġar rivers.

There is a lot to tell about waterfowl. In ancient times, poets sang: 'Some are like sugar and others like honey; some are like birch and others like willow', presumably about girls; so among the birds there are those who are distinguished by beauty, elegance, bravery and strength, and those who give joy or sadness. But there are some birds that we should be afraid of; for example, the bittern.

The Birds Are Our Friends

Bittern

*S*teppe Kazakhs call a damp area overgrown with reeds, cat tails, and grass *tomar*. The Kazakh writer and playwright Bejimbet Majlin, in his story 'Šuǵanyŋ Belgisi' ('Shuga's Memorial'), wrote: 'Before us you can see Lake Ḳamysaḳty. Its surroundings are full of *tomar*.' His contemporary, the poet and writer Sáken Sejfullin, in his novel *Tar žol tajǵaḳ kešu* (*Thorny Path*), described it as follows: '*Šubyra* is a watery *tomar*. It is surrounded by flowering meadows.' The rest of the Kazakhs use the word *tomar* for the thick root or stump of the saxaul tree or tamarisk (salt cedar). For example, until recently, for the residents of Ḳyzylḳu'm or Maŋǵystau, the best fuel was the stump of the saxaul.

The spring of 1954 was more severe than the winter for the locality of Saryarḳa. An indispensable feather grass steppe, especially for sheep and horse pasture, was ploughed up. People came from everywhere to develop the virgin land, in the Virgin Land Campaign. There were different people among them. Some destroyed ancient graves and used the locals' wooden grave markers as fuel. Hooligans, mainly tractor drivers, settled on a lake that was overgrown with reeds, in a deserted area. On the sides of the lake there was a *tomar*, and at the foot of the *tomar* was an old cemetery. They ousted the inhabitants of this prosperous region and things descended into lawlessness there.

An old man, Aldan, an elderly retiree and a winner of several awards and medals, told a story that had happened on the shore of one of these *tomars*.

As they say, 'You reap what you sow', and by the evening those would-be-heroes-cum-tractor drivers were frightened, closed their tents and did not dare look out. Some even slept in their tractor cab. There was one main reason. Before midnight, their rest was broken by mosquitoes. After midnight, the voice of a wild bull wafting from the side of the *tomar* made their hair stand up on the back of their heads. The wild bull sometimes stomped back and forth in the reeds. At such a moment, the frog, which usually croaked incessantly, ceased to make a sound, the mole cricket quietened down immediately and silence reigned. What was the secret of this *tomar*?

Why wasn't a wild bull seen during the day?

The mystery of this hotly debated lake was not solved for two to three years.

Some recalled the stories of a group of Englishmen who had travelled to conquer the New World and had been trampled by one-eyed bison bulls in the State of Nebraska, and then the local residents abandoned the area. Others repeated incredible legends of the mys-

terious monster in Loch Ness. No wonder they say 'fear has big eyes'. Such a rumour spread among the tractor drivers, according to which the wild bull lay at the bottom of the lake during the day and went ashore at night, in search of food. Thus, the bold mechanic Ivan Ivanovich, who spent half of his life in jail and feared nothing, decided to bet a bottle of vodka on shooting the bull with his friends. Having not listened to the people, he got drunk, took a gun and went to the *tomar* in the night. By noon the next day, Ivan was found dead on the shores of that lake. Specialists from Tselinograd Regional Hospital, who studied the body, came to the conclusion that his heart had 'exploded'.

This conclusion added fuel to the fire. The priest from Tselinograd's Russian Orthodox Church refused to come and perform the funeral service. The opinion of the mullah was obvious, but nobody needed it.

'We were silent about it, waiting for the final outcome,' said the elder, Aldan, who was then an accountant in the nearby *auyl*. 'To those who asked, we answered "we do not know"

and nothing more. On the Astrakhan side, there was one Nogai mullah who said: "Do not disturb the locals' graves any more. Fix the ones that were destroyed, and then the wild bull will not harm you". The same hero-tractor drivers who had destroyed everything in their path were now subdued. Soon they left Ķamysty for good.'

In fact, there was no wild bull. It was the bittern that roared like a cow at night. The bittern is a water bird. 'Ignorance makes one drink poison,' they say. For a person who has not heard it before, it is very frightening to hear the bittern's cry. Imagine you are walking along the shore of a lake on a very dark night, and are already frightened. Suddenly you hear a loud bull's cry. How can you not believe that the drunk Ivan Ivanovich died that night of fright? Experts in the field of 'musical ornithology' (its conventional name), which has appeared in recent years, emphasize the difficulty of recording the bittern's voice. This bird is rarely seen. If they stick to the reeds and stretch their neck to the sky, even somebody nearby may not notice it. Since it is rarely seen, this bird is the reason for a variety of stories.

One legend says that a bittern is the guardian of Solomon, the King of the Water (according to Kazakh legends). Solomon instructed the bittern to safeguard the entire universe and protect it from enemies. Since then the bird has guarded the lake at night and screamed.

The legend is like that, and scientists who have seen it for themselves say the following. A bittern collects water in its mouth and breathes in such a way that we hear frighteningly loud sounds. The bird is also irritated by mosquitoes at night and beats on the water with its long beak. Others say that the sounds of the bull come from the bird when the bittern first lifts its head to the sky and remains in this position for a while. It fills its stomach with air, its chin swells, its throat dries out and then the bird sharply lowers its head. The frightening sound, referred to above, then comes out. This last story seems to be true.

Another story says: 'There is a bird called a bittern whose voice is booming, but if you come closer it's as small as a sparrow.' What does it mean? As depicted in the painting by the young artist A'liâ A'bilova, the bittern is not as small as a sparrow. In fact, ornithologists qualify the bittern as the largest species of bird. It should be not about the body but about the voice of the bird. It is not for nothing that the Ancient Kazakhs called it *kôlbuķa* (a lake bull).

In his story *A' upildek* (*The Bittern*), Sáken Sejfullin described the voice of the bird as follows:

An unpleasant sound comes from the lake. This sound belongs to the bittern bird. The voice of this bird booms, as if someone choking on water is crying out for help.

The bittern's voice makes the following sound: 'A̋up! A̋-a̋-u-u-u-i-p-p! A̋-a̋-u-u-i-p-p!'. The deep water suffocates the bittern. The bird is weighed down.

Making the sound 'A̋-a̋-u-u-i-p-p! A̋-a̋-u-u-i-r-r!' the bird tries to cope with the weight.

Its voice is distinctive. Its frightening, gasping, oppressed voice drives a person to deep fear and unutterable sadness.

> A bittern chokes under water,
> A grieving voice comes from the lake.
> When will the sun come up and clear
> The dark and strangling mist?

> The bittern lives in the abyss,
> It could destroy the lake.
> Human fate is a relentless beast,
> Why is there no help for the suffocating bird?

The bittern is found in Saryarḳa, on the shores of the Syr Dariâ River, on Lake Balḳaš. There is another fascinating bird that doesn't look like the bittern – the penduline tit.

Penduline's Nest

*T*he penduline is a tiny bird. Put it in your hands – it is smaller than your palm. If it is as big as a *sùjem* – a measure of length, roughly equivalent to the distance between an outstretched thumb and the index finger – it means you are lucky and you have caught a large penduline. Its weight is slightly more than that of a box of matches. It is very difficult to distinguish between a female and a male. They both wear a brownish grey plumage in the winter and summer; only around their eyes are they black, as if smeared with kohl. It is a very modest bird, not distinguished either by beauty or by song. It is very hardworking. Like all hard workers, it minds its own business: it is not after fun, unlike other birds that jump aimlessly from one branch to another. In spring, the male arrives first and starts to make a nest. More precisely, it does not build a nest, but weaves it. He is 'the wisest of men who creates coherence from complexity' (Abaj).[83] Its elaborate domed nest, made of thistledown and reed, and poplar and willow twigs, resembles a single mitten in which there is a hole for the thumb.

It sings unceasingly when building its nest, a very pathetic song too. If you listen, you can hear 'I am sad and dreary. Who will support me?' It is the bitter sob of a creature longing for its distant beloved. Many Middle Eastern poetic forms, including *ruba'i, ghazal, mustazat,* and *tarji-band,* can be brilliant examples of love poetry. If you listen carefully to birdsong, you can hear the same motif. Of course, Kazakh poetry didn't embrace these aforementioned poetic forms. Probably, it never will because it has its own elaborate traditions. It is said that art with an authentic voice does not imitate or absorb another. But art with its particularly strong traditions will cling to these customs. It cannot be compared with anything else. Personally, the penduline's pitiful summer song reminds me of *muhamas. Muhamas* are an age-old genre. Each stanza consists of five lines. There is not a single Persian poet who did not use them. Saadi, Fizuli, Hafiz, Jami, Bedil, Ogahi and Navoiy created different examples of *muhamas.*

Tsy, tsy, tsy, tsy. This is the song of the penduline. Would this be a *muhamas* if you translate it into human language? I think it would not be surprising. As our respected writer Sábit Muḵanov used to say, 'back to the topic'. It is impossible not to return. The penduline's nest is not like those of the other 10,000 birds. What could be better than uniqueness?

Birds' nests are a whole architectural world and included in *Guinness World Records,*

---

83 The quote is from Abaj Ḵunanbajuly's poem 'Ôleŋ Sôzdiŋ Patšasy, Sôz Sarasy' ('Poetry the King of Literature').

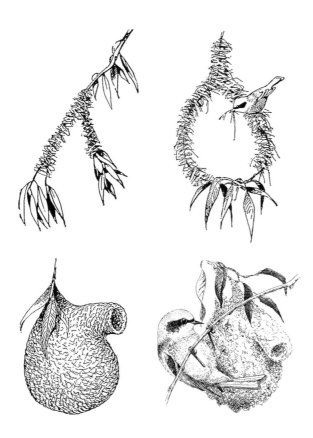

starting from the world's largest golden eagle's nest (width, 2.9 metres; depth, 6 metres; weight, 3 tons – this nest was discovered in 1963 in St Petersburg, Florida, USA) and ending with the smallest nest of the kinglet that is slightly larger than a dragonfly.

Birds like the oak goose, the woodpecker and the owl make nests in the holes of tall trees. The pheasant, in contrast, makes its nest on the ground. The sandpiper also does this: it finds a sandy shore and usually lays four eggs. The nightjar is not fussy either: it spreads leaves under a tree and that's the nest for you. But you should not think that it is very easy for birds to lay eggs. For example, take the chiffchaff, which builds its nest in bushes or in wall-creeping plants using dead vegetation, and glues it together with a thick feather lining.

The magpie's nest resembles a ball and has two entrances. A crow's nest resembles a large shallow plate. The grebe's nest floats on the water. The kingfisher does not make a nest, but digs a burrow in the riverbank, just like the European roller.

The black grouse and partridge make their nests in the summer in a treetop, but believe it or not, in the winter they sleep buried under the snow. The swallow makes a nest on outbuildings.

In the Museum of Art, in Tashkent, there are different snuffboxes for *nasvai* (snuff) made in past centuries.[84] Uzbeks call them *noskavak*. The snuffboxes are made from *naskabak*, a type of pumpkin specially grown in Samarkand. Craftsmen put newly grown pumpkins in special containers, and decorate the outside with different ornaments. As a result, snuffboxes different in form and decoration are grown that can be carried in a pocket, in bootlegs of high boots or attached to a belt. The tit's nest resembles the same ornate round snuffbox: it sheathes its round nest with henna, then covers it with down, and decorates the inner walls with feathers, down and wool, as if hanging carpets. But still the best nest belongs to the penduline.

Normally, pendulines make nests far apart from one another. They probably do not want to fight for food for their chicks and want to live peacefully in their own territory. This is peculiar to pendulines living in the forests of the Edil-Žajyk̦ and Elek-Ķobda rivers, as well as those living in the lower part of the Syr Dariâ River.

84 *Nasvai* or *nasybai* – tobacco snuff mixed with dried plants (archa, saxaul, meadowsweet, birch tree) believed to be a mental and physical stimulant.

A highly debated topic in ornithology is the fact that sometimes ten or more pendulines nest close to one another. There is a stream in the Žamaty Valley, in the Žambyl district of the Almaty region. On the bank of this stream there is a place where many pendulines' nests are located. There are such nest groupings on the banks of the Šelek and Bartoġaj rivers in the Ujġyr and Kegen districts. At first glance, it may seem that a woman hung up her children's wet mittens to dry.

In Kazakh there is a phrase 'ķuŕḳyltajdyŋ uäsy', that is, 'penduline's nest'. This expression is used to describe cramped homes. Sometimes it means cosiness and comfort. But the miniature nest is not at all small for two tiny birds. The penduline make nests large enough for the two of them to fit. Heat, wind or rain are not a threat to such a nest. It remains tied to a branch, swaying gently in any hurricane. Another surprising fact is that predators that destroy the nests of other birds cannot reach the penduline's nest. The goshawk flies around the 'mitten', then flies away, realizing that it cannot

do anything. The same with sparrowhawks. Red foxes, corsac foxes, and stoats can't reach it, and snakes can do nothing. It is a real fortress. In a sturdy nest wrapped exquisitely in various herbs mixed with saliva, the penduline lays eggs twice a year and hatches 6–10 chicks. That's what fertility means.

People consider the penduline sacred. There is a legend among the Kazakhs of Turkmenistan that all the female camels of one rich man miscarried because he shot a penduline.

Another legend tells of the poor wife of a beekeeper, who believed that pendulines feed on bees. God revived the penduline that had been killed by the beekeeper, and it came to the young woman every night and asked for honey. The beekeeper, who felt sorry for his wife running around the house shouting, 'Give honey to the penduline. Give honey to penduline', abandoned his craft and moved out of the forest. This place is still called Penduline Beekeeper.

There is a belief that the meat and soup of a penduline, even its bones (its dried, ground bones are added to the soup), can cure people with broken legs, dislocated shoulders, and so on.

Nests not only have healing qualities, but are also edible in some cultures. For example, people living in South-East Asia make a soup called *solangan* from an edible swiftlet's nest and serve it to their most respected guests. These swiftlets make their nests at the very top of a mountain using their solidified saliva – a source of protein. Malaysian, Filipino and Indonesian men who climb the mountains for these tiny nests believe that this business is worth the risk.

We mentioned before that the penduline also plasters its nest with various herbs using its saliva. Despite the fact that modern botany is advancing quickly, there are many things in phytotherapy that are still incomprehensible to us. For example, Kazakhs have long used pendulines' nests to cure illnesses associated with the lower back, joints, the bladder and the urinary tract. Many say they are very helpful. Probably one of the herbs that pendulines use is particularly helpful for such diseases. Maybe it's all about faith. We cannot say; the conclusion must be drawn by medical specialists.

A word is born from a word; nothing is born from silence.

> Cattle graze in Mukyrtaj of Sauyr,
> The penduline's nest is considered a remedy.
> Call the boastful poet here,
> I'll disgrace him with my verses.

These lines from folk poetry may be the basis for another story. For example:

Let's read a folk legend. On the bank of the Šelek River in the Almaty region there is the Žamanùjdiṇ Šaty Gorge. A long time ago, the only brother of a rich man butchered the skin of a rabid wolf with his bare hands, then accidentally injured his arm and went mad. At that time, rabies was not treatable. The people did not know how to cure him and mourned. Why wouldn't they mourn? The young man was not a dog they could kill, or carrion they could burn. Once, when his rabies retreated, the young man said: 'It is the will of God. Do not cry. Build a stone house without windows and doors in the gorge and lock me up in there. To feed me, you can wrap the food in a handkerchief and put it in the slot using only a pole. Do not pity or come near me.' The people cried and carried out their master's order. Every time they brought him food, the rabid young man chewed the end of the pole. People noticed that he was stretching for the pole rather than the food, and asked for advice from the elders of the *auyl*. They suggested that the pole must have touched many different herbs, and one of them must have had healing properties. And so it happened that one day the young man was completely cured of his illness, after chewing the end of the pole. This stone house is still called the Žamanùjdiṇ Šaty Gorge. Of course, this is a legend. But Kazakhs have always lived in harmony with nature and learned from it. There are many stories about the healing properties of herbs; therefore, when speaking of the penduline's nest's power, we have to mention them.

However that may be, we must wish the little bird well that has earned so much respect. Who knows, maybe it cares about the Kazakhs too. They say that the bird is an angel.

P.S. By the way, there is another word, *surkyltaj*, which rhymes with *kurkyltaj* (penduline), and is the name of a bird, but also means 'an unscrupulous poet' or 'flatterer of the authorities'.

Where does this term originate?

There is nothing new in this world. Everything was before us, and after us everything will be the same. But man doesn't, or doesn't want to, learn from the past. For example, people have always fought for power, and killed their dearest people, not to mention strangers. Those who came to power in a dishonest way and were cruel did not die a natural death. And if a righteous and just ruler ever sought eternal power, then luck would leave him.

They say that once a bird called a *surkyltaj* flew to an unlucky ruler. Nobody saw the ghost-like bird everafter. The people did not see it but they were afraid, because it could appear out of blue at any time. The brutal vizier (*bi*, judge, foreman, false oppositionist, guard, court, mercenary, etc.), who opressed the people was compared to this bird.

Therefore, it was said that 'Every khan has a *surkyltaj* at his side'.

Another story says that a new khan always tried to surpass the previous khan in power and wealth. He started his rule with a change, in other words, with *perestroika*. The house for songbirds was renovated and rebuilt. A long time ago, a special kind of parrot was called *surkyltaj*, who shouted and informed the khan at the sight of a stranger or when the guards fell asleep. The new khan brought his bird to his palace, and the bird not only decorated the palace, but also guarded it. It is true that each ruler thinks about his own security first of all.

According to another legend, *surkyltaj* is not a bird, but a grass. As they say, 'Hero until the first bullet; rich until the first drought' – one of the most terrible misfortunes is drought. At this time, all the grass fed to livestock dried out. However, *surkyltaj* (grass) grew very thick during the drought, but unfortunately, the cattle did not eat it.

These are folk stories passed down the generations without ever being written down. If other versions of them can be found, we will be happy. But for now, this story is over.

Great Tit

*I*n the past, Kazakh children played counting games. There are many types of them, one of which is called 'The Tit'. Children are divided into two teams of five or six and stand in line, opposite each other. Sometimes they can stand in a group and choose one as *khan*. The khan follows the line and starts to count each child: 'One, two, get ready to go. Three and four, five, six, seven is here. Eight is in a hollow; nine is partying. Where is ten? If I hit him, will he cry? Yelp, yelp, yelp, where is ten?' The *khan* then hustles around and looks for number ten, distracting the attention of children. The children hold their breath and do not move. The khan suddenly points to one kid: 'Ten is you, tit. Well, take off!' At this moment, the *tit* should hide quickly behind the *khan*, and while he is doing so, the rest of the children should try to catch him. If the *tit* flies away, then their closest neighbour must pay a fine. If the *tit* is caught, then he must sing or dance, or else he will be hit on the head. Alternatively, to avoid punishment, he can twitter like a tit and make the rest laugh. This game teaches children agility, speed and quick-wittedness.

Sometimes we do not notice the little bird the size of our fist that flies before us when we walk through the woods, the park, or along the road. If you look closely, the great tit is a very beautiful bird. Its yellow underparts immediately catch the eye. Anyone who has not seen this bird before may think that it had been sitting in a bowl of yellow paint. This tiny colourful bird does not sit still all day long. Starting from the beak to its little head, it is a strikingly glossy black with white cheek feathers; its upperparts are bluish-grey. When it flies, you can see a white stripe in the wings and a brown stripe stretching from its throat to its tail.

If you notice how the children feed birds by hand in the winter, you can be sure that these are great tits. The bird is very fond of people and, therefore, popular.

As they say, 'A beloved son has many names.' In some areas it is called a 'blue tit' or 'beautiful tit', and in other areas a 'yellow chest'.

In cold winters it is hard for great tits. If you see a bird falling from a branch in the morning frost, do not pass by. Perhaps it is still alive. Its legs or wings may be frozen or broken. If you take it with you to the house, warm it and feed it for a couple of days, you will do a good deed. It is a cavity nester and usually nests in a hole in a tree. Its nest is clean, tidy, and spacious enough for 8–9 eggs. They put dry branches on top of the nest, then cover it with feathers and fluff so that snow, rain and frost do not fall into it. If your house is as cosy

as a tit's nest, it will be good for a wounded bird. Keep in mind that great tits' favourite foods are insects, worms, sunflower seeds and millet. If you are lucky and the bird recovers, then it will begin to sing. This is how it asks for freedom.

Sometimes its attachment to people hurts it. Some people, admiring its beauty, take advantage of its naivety and keep it in a cage. The tit is not poultry; it is very difficult to tame it. The right thing to do is to release it. Oh, if only you knew what a pleasant sight it is when a bird soars high in the sky, gaining its freedom.

Ivan Turgenev wrote many texts of romances for singer and composer Pauline Viardot, whom he loved madly. One of them is called 'Sinitsa' ('The Tit'):

> I hear a tit ring,
> Amid the yellowing branches.
> Hello, little bird,
> The messenger of the autumn.

Of all Russian writers, Turgenev especially loved nature. Even the writer Mikhail Prishvin himself, who left the popular expression 'to protect nature is to protect the Motherland', respected Turgenev very much and considered himself his pupil. The great writer spoke of the tit as the 'herald of autumn'. Great tits live in the mountains and forests surrounding Almaty in the summer, and in the autumn, they return to the city.

This is reminiscent of the Ancient Kazakhs, who moved to the mountains in the summer and returned to autumn and winter pastures in lowlands with the onset of cold weather. Great tits, like our ancestors, usually group together and live in certain areas, despite the expression 'birds have no borders'. If young tits suddenly break the rules, entering foreign territory and are *beaten* by *local* tits, their *brothers* do not protect them. If they suffer innocently, they get up and fight to the death.

They, like the Ancient Kazakhs, live with their elders in a group and obey them. If we speak in modern terms, this is a society in which hierarchy is very strictly observed. In the social life of this *society*, territorial and hierarchical elements are intertwined.

The American writer Ernest Thompson Seton wrote a fairy tale entitled 'Why the Chickadee Goes Crazy Once a Year?' The chickedee, is North American for tit.

According to the story, long ago, beautiful tits lived freely in a bountiful forest in North America, where there were a lot of berries and cereals and it was summer all year round. One day, Mother Nature informed all the animals and birds of a coming disaster. She said, 'Beware and be careful, there has been a catastrophe. An old matchmaker with a white beard in white clothes called "Winter" is coming to our land' (Abaj). [85]

'Who is Winter?'

'Is this really a formidable old man?'

'He is covered with frost, is very cold and breathes through the cold, frost and snow.'

'What is frost, cold frost? What is snow like?'

While the other birds fussed, the tits continued to have fun and didn't worry. They were not concerned even when the other birds flew to warm countries. 'Let them fly away. We are not going to die even if others say "We are dying".' The trouble came suddenly, for one day their paradise with dense green herbs and pure ponds was covered with snow. The beautiful tits didn't know what to do. They flew fussily to and fro; fell into large holes in the ground; lost their way, cried, but couldn't leave the ravine; froze, but couldn't find shelter. For nearly a week they wandered about. As the saying goes, 'In three days you can get used to hell', and so they began to get used to it.

What else could they do? They slowly learned to find food under the snow, find seeds of fruit trees, and thus began to move away from people. They gathered their strength, and no longer feared either a severe frost or a piercing wind, and flew freely.

But you should pay attention to one thing. Thompson Seton writes in this fairy tale that out of habit, tits lose their wit and begin to hide in the crevices of windows, doors, roofs and balconies when the first snow falls.

According to a Middle Eastern tale, Hazrat Ali was a mighty warrior who had the power of five men at once. The Prophet Muhammad (peace be upon him) was pleased with his fight on the path of Islam and gave his daughter Fatima to him as a wife. What was Fatima like?

She had big eyes, a small nose,
beautiful forehead,
and a slim and delicate waist.
She had thick, long braids;
People admired her beauty.
She served her man and was faithful.
She went to bed late and got up before anyone else.

But Fatima was often worried that she would not get up on time and would miss morning prayer. By the will of God, this never happened. She went to bed late and got up early, even when her husband Hazrat Ali was away for a trip. The people started to gossip about the fact that she had begun to lose weight since marrying. Some said to the Prophet: 'Oh, the Messenger of Allah, your daughter looks emaciated and as if sick. Take her away from her husband. She is your daughter, after all.' The Prophet warned them that marriage was a sacred unbreakable oath and forbade gossip.

---

85 The quotation is from the poem 'Kys' ('Winter'} by Abaj Kunanbajuly.

'How do you wake up early?' neighbours asked Fatima.

'All by the will of Allah,' answered Fatima.

In fact, she had a favourite bird. At dawn, it set about singing in front of her door. Fatima woke up and began to prepare breakfast for her husband.

At this time, a drought began in the Arabian land. People began to exterminate the birds, fearing that they would eat an already scant crop.

Fatima's tit hid in the roof of Hazrat Ali and survived.

In the spring the ice melted and it seemed that thunder was rattling. Hazrat Ali saw the tit and laughed. When he laughed, it seemed like a thunderstorm. 'Ah, Fatima, you have shown that you are the true daughter of the Prophet. Even the tits are looking for salvation from you. How can I not be happy? From now on this bird will be your bird. Good people, do not touch Fatima's bird, let it live and multiply, then you will also live and multiply.'

Since then, the Tajiks called the tit 'Fatima's Tit'. According to another legend, however, Fatima's Tit is another bird. This was the story of Fatima, who our mothers reverently call 'Bibi Fatima'.

Yes, it is good when everyone has their own bird!

Wood Grouse

nother lovely bird of Arḳa (central and southern Kazakhstan) is the wood grouse, known as the 'deaf grouse' in Kazakh. Why deaf? It is also dumb, but no one calls it the 'dumb grouse'. I read in Alexey Kuprin's story, 'Na glukharei' ('To the Grouse'): 'The grouse is one of the birds that has no tongue. If it has no tongue, then it is nothing less than dumb.'

In nature, there are many surprising things. The penguin cannot fly, but it has wings. The ostrich too. But how can a kiwi be called a bird?

Some scientists say that birds fly depending on the density of their feathers. The swan has 25,216 feathers, but even a tit that has only 1,000 feathers can fly. So the problem is something else.

There are birds that live only in the water and can't survive on land.

And the wings of the bustard, in contrast, stick together after a heavy shower.

I have long been disturbed by Kuprin's story. Everyone has their own opinion. In particular, do not argue with hunters. Today, my guide was a hunter named Ivan Prokopovich. He didn't have a particularly high opinion of Alexey Kuprin.

'Nonsense! I don't care that he is a writer. There are no birds without a tongue!' he said. Then he looked at me and continued: 'You will see when the time comes.'

I hoped that today was the day I'd have a chance to study the wood grouse. Later I confirmed it did, in fact, have a tongue, but it was so short and small that it was not completely visible, so the author was also right.

Pine forest. Mid-April. At this time, cotton was planted in southern Kazakhstan, weeds were pulled out, and rice was planted in Syr (a common name for the Ḳyzylorda region) and prepared for irrigation. Sheep began to lamb. But Arḳa remained in the winter's grasp; the lake was still covered with a solid layer of ice. But the snow was already beginning to fall less frequently and it would soon melt. This is how April looked in those parts.

Local Kazakhs call the lee of a thick forest *šubar* – spotty; it is abundant in nutrient-rich plants. They are probably called that because of their colour. Ġabeṇ, Ġabit Mùsirepov, wrote in his novel *Ulpan*:

> The wealth of the Kazakhs is horses. If you do not keep a horse close to the
> lee of the forest in winter, you will lose your horse. As they say, 'Hero until

121

the first bullet, rich until the first disaster.' Is a horseless man a man? Is he a Kazakh?

We left behind the aforementioned lee of the forest.

We had already been watching the grouse for two days. We couldn't catch it yet. My guide, Ivan Prokopovich, laughed at my light clothing and how I held a gun. Let him laugh. I was ready to endure any humiliation to see the courtship rituals of the grouse, so vividly described in literature.

We arrived at the pine forest yesterday morning. As soon as we entered the forest, Ivan raised his index finger to his lips and made it clear that we should be quiet. We were after the mating rituals of the wood grouse. This bird breeds once a year in mid-April. As long as some unskilled hunter such as myself didn't scatter them, they would perform their court-

ship rituals at the same site as they had done every year. So said my guide. I believed him. Russians are not like us; they love order. They know how to obey and subdue. It is very difficult for Kazakhs to obey anyone. We always want to do things our own way. We do not want any masters above us. One out of every two Russians loves military life, which teaches strict discipline. Even a wandering wino or a barefaced liar boasted that he had fought in Afghanistan if he had done so. What is there to brag about? They hang their uniforms in the most prominent place at home after returning from the army, and the photo album is kept in a chest. When Kazakhs return from the army, we give our belt to our brother, our boots to our nephew, our trousers to our neighbour, our jacket to our older brother, and we celebrate our return. And today I had no choice but to follow a skinny Ivan, who trotted awkwardly ahead of me.

Suddenly, Ivan stopped and reached for the gun on his shoulder. I stopped too.

At this moment a canvas tent collapsed. Either the tree fell on it, or it could not bear the weight of snow, but the tent broke. Then Ivan loudly shouted 'Shoot! Shoot!' Shoot what? At that moment, three or four black chickens jumped out from under a pine tree, out of the snow, and flew away into the forest.

I thought that the tent had broken, but in fact it was the sound of flying grouse, which resembled black chickens.

I did not shoot, but froze in surprise. Ivan was angry and threw a fit. It seems that he, too, couldn't shoot. He probably trusted me. And here I am …

After that, Ivan Prokopovich was angry with me. He did not speak, his brows were furrowed. Russians usually cannot resist vodka, but this ghoul did not even look at it. What could I do? I had to accept it. It seemed he would not forgive himself for having shown the grouse's refuge to such a clumsy individual as me. A real hunter would not tell such to just anyone. He was jealous. He wanted to enjoy wood-grouse hunting himself. He didn't like to share the joy, which was understandable. If someone said that they knew a place where there were many birds, it was a reason to take notice. He was either lying, or trying to send you to a place with no birds whatsoever.

Perhaps Ivan Prokopovich could not really find this place.

Another great Russian writer, Yuri Kazakov, wrote in his diary about his trip to the north: 'To find the place where wood grouse are hiding is just like finding a military airfield underground.' It is a mistake to assume that any clearing in a forest is the mating site of the wood grouse. In the forest there are different clearings. For example, there were areas where the reeds lay torn up by their roots, which meant wild boar had been looking for food. If there were cavities on the white snow, it meant that roe deer had slept there. Their footprints in the snow were clear. We did not stop in several places where wood grouse could hide. Our guide shook his head and we moved on. When we passed through an open area, we noticed a single mitten. A white mitten. A baby's mitten. So there must be a dwelling nearby.

I decided to hang it on a branch so that the parents of the child could find it easily. When I was about to reach the branch of the nearest tree, something dropped to the ground, and then second something followed. It was as if a solid ball had fallen from a tree onto a flat board and quickly rebounded – *tik, tik, tik, tik …*

The wood grouse eats seeds. Unlike other birds, it feeds on stones as well. Why? Nobody knows. I thought about it after hearing these sounds.

We walked for almost half a kilometre and heard the sounds of those balls again, very close to us. We looked at our guide, but he pretended not to hear. Another strange sound was heard, as if someone was sharpening a knife. My guide stood still for a bit, then began swearing in Russian. Still air. Lonely forest. Pure, white snow. I recalled a scene from an Eastern fairy tale, when the sister-in-law reproached a girl for gossiping in the apple orchard: 'How can your beautiful mouth, which eats such a beautiful apple, utter such a bad word?'

It began to get cold in the morning. We crossed the stream and walked to the side of the forest. It was quiet everywhere; open terrain. Thick grass tangled our feet as we walked through the snow. Not only the drifts, where no one had walked, but also the roads on which cars had not driven revealed that there were no longer enough cattle these days in the country. The tops of the trees moved with the wind and resembled the swaying tail of a sturgeon that had just been pulled out of the water. Probably, old people had this picture before their eyes when they described the end of the world as 'the time when the pike will reach the top of a pine tree'.

I had heard that a person starts to walk in circles in the forest when lost. It seemed this place was familiar to me. Probably, we had walked in a circle and returned to the same place. My guide shushed me again to be quiet. I fell silent. He whispered that no one but us had ever come here, probably to dispel my doubts. I pretended to believe him. I might have believed him if I had not seen the mitten that I had hung earlier on the branch. It was visible from afar. I silently noted the trick of my guide – he wanted me to get lost if I came here again without him. Okay, I put up with it.

So I was told to remain silent. We sat without talking, close to each other. Ivan raised his head. On top of the tree was sitting that 'black chicken', raising its tail, which resembled a huge Chinese fan. It looked more like a turkey than a black chicken. Its eyes were red. I remembered that bulls' eyes turned red during the breeding season, and assumed that this was a mating habit of the wood grouse. It turned out that this was the case. The wood grouse's eyes usually turn red in spring time, during the pre-mating and mating seasons. This is why ill-informed people sometimes call it 'red-eyed', although the redness disappears during the rest of the year.

On top of the branch was sitting another wood grouse. It seemed alarmed and very cautious. It watched all that ran, flew and crawled, as if ready to run away if it heard another sound.

In the east, the sun began to redden. There were clear lines in the snow, as if someone had drawn a knife through it. If we looked closely, we could see that these were traces from the tail of the grouse. These lines indicated that this was like the Great Wall of China and if someone stepped over it, they would find trouble.

As soon as I thought about it, in that very moment, the black cock jumped from the tree and rushed towards another male. They began to move in our direction, pushing one another and twitching. Ivan took a gun and loaded two bullets. I put my index finger to my

lips and shook my head so that he would not touch them. Ivan thought that I wanted to shoot them myself and just smirked. It was an ironic smirk, which meant 'Shoot! You still won't hit it!' He laughed bitterly.

The two males grabbed each other and carried on. I did not shoot and did not allow Ivan to shoot. They went on two different sides, raising and lowering their tails. We Kazakhs rightly swore, saying, 'No brains, just like a chicken.' It seemed that it was not a smart and cunning bird.

The male grouse is striking. Its head, neck, back and sides seem black from a distance, but if you come closer, you can see that they are buffy yellow and shine like a gem; its neck, beard and folding tail are especially beautiful. Looking at the latter, one could guess that wood grouse is a distant relative of the peacock.

When the two *heroes* both dispersed, the rest of the cocks began to descend from the tree. Then came the hens, as if out of the ground. I say 'out of the ground' because they are usually found in dark places and do not come close to the males. They make a barely audible sound and are barely visible. It is at this time that the males begin to run amok, as the females' barely audible sound excites the sensitive lovers.

According to Alfred Brehm, females are so fond of baby birds that they do not move from their nest when the eggs hatch. They will not fly away even if you lift them by their nape and relocate them. They will sit as if saying, 'Kill me if you want, but do not touch my chicks.'

The mating rituals had begun. This was the *show* that I was after. A male with a straightened tail lifted its beak. At that moment, another *ball* fell from the tree and bounced immediately. Actually, there was no ball. It was a grouse song that we learned about later.

In this particular song, the sound resembled the roar of cartridges scattered across the floor. Then there was a sound as if sharpening a knife. After some time, there was a sound like someone rustling in the snow, and sometimes it sounded like the cawing of magpies. According to ornithologists, this moment of rustling is very dangerous for the grouse. At this point they may become deaf, because the small cochlea inside their ears is filled with blood, swells and closes their hearing channel. They hear neither the tramp of people's and animals' feet, nor the firing of a shotgun. Kazakhs therefore called the wood grouse *saŋyrau ķuř*; that is, the 'deaf grouse'.

In one of the Kyrgyz folk epics, a young man says to his beloved, 'Let my dead body be pulled out of your arms.' I read a lot of poetry, but have not met such a striking phrase before or since. I saw a lot of birds and read about even more birds, but never heard of another bird that was deafened for a period of time.

Some writers compare grouse mating dances with the extravagant religious festivities in some countries. No, the grouse dances are not anything like that – there is no need to look for comparisons.

Our talented writer Aʹlibek Aşķarov has recently become a nature singer. His essays on Altaj read like poems. Indeed, one cannot help becoming a poet when born in such an amazing land as Altaj. In his story *Ẓazatyr oķiğasy (An Event in Ẓazatyr)*, he describes inspiringly not only the mating rituals of the wood grouse, but also the order of observance of hierarchy in the life of these birds. The meticulous care of the author revealed by his essay is exemplary. No one in Kazakh prose except Aʹlibek has yet conveyed the courtship rituals of wood grouse so beautifully and accurately:

The grouse's dance is a magnificent example of the eternal creativity of nature. In this case, it is unforgivable for a hunter to miss the annual mating rituals of the gracious grouse, the noblest of birds.

… Ķaraman [the main character in the story] particularly admired the male wood grouse distinguished by its size, dexterity of movements and mastery of the method.

It ensured that the young males did not fight and played by the rules. Here, one of the young cocks, who wanted to compete in strength, rushed at it. It acted agilely and hit the young upstart. The latter rolled over, flapping its wings. The male could not maintain its rage and moved to the other end of the site. Then it raised its head and its bright red eyes, like a patch of black smallpox, and turned to the site. It noticed how another two young males clung to each other under a pine tree. It seemed to wonder to itself, 'Did their competition really turn into a battle?' Then it ran at them, and pushed two *suckers*, who didn't know what the grouse competition meant, and separated them, demonstrating its power and anger.

Ķaraman had already seen the cock teach the young males to sing, play, compete and defend themselves. But he had never seen such a sensitive bird that could display such vigilance and concern for others.

Speaking of the males, one highly disputable proverb says that 'A man with a gentle voice has no energy, and a woman with a male voice has no shame'. In 1991, the Tashkent edition of *Ezuchchi* released '*Kitab-u-lazzat un-nisa*' in Russian and Uzbek. This erotic anecdote, published originally in Persian, first appeared in Ancient India and then spread all over the Eastern countries. According to Aķseleu Sejdimbekov, in this book of erotic pleasures, there are similar conclusions to the Kazakh proverb.

The hawk recognizes a weak wood grouse by its voice. If the male makes a weak sound during the dance, it means that it is not strong enough. The all-seeing hawk attacks

it immediately. In the blink of an eye, the hawk ruffles its feathers and 'lowers it from the red hollow,' as they say. In contrast, hawks, vultures, even large falcons do not come close to the male wood grouse if it shouts loudly and shakes its beard. Females often choose loud and red-eyed males as their mates. God is powerful, and strength means strength in everything.

Turgenev, Bunin, Kuprin, Leskov, Prishvin, Paustovsky, Kazakov, Treypkin, Rubtsov and Bianchi – there are few classic Russian authors who have not written about the wood grouse. Russians love these birds. In Russia there are many companies, shops and restaurants called 'The wood grouse', 'The wood grouse's nest', 'The dance of the wood grouse', and so on. *Rossiyskaya ohotnichiya gazeta* (*The Russian Hunting Gazette*) often features a picture of this bird on the front page. Any Russian who considers themself a hunter is able to tell you a beautiful story about the wood grouse. Yet, they hunt them ruthlessly. At the end of the nineteenth century, 65,000 wood grouse were hunted each year. Today, there are two or three times more hunters in Russia. The fate of the poor bird is pitiful.

The Xinjiang Kazakhs have a *kùj* called 'Ķurojnaķ' ('Grouse's Courtship'). It is performed on a *dombyra*. Occasionally the strings of the instrument are tweaked to convey how the grouse runs. What could be better than a *kùj* to describe a sudden move or speedy action? The famous poet Žaŕken Bôdeš knows by heart the words of the folk song that might be accompanied by the aforementioned *kùj*:

Play, play, uncle, 'The Grouse's Courtship',
Who else could play it so well?
Even the arrogant daughter of the khan
Fell for this mighty kùj once played.

The Altaj Kazakhs call the wood grouse *sausyldaķ*. According to the book *Šyṇžaṇnyṇ žabajy ķuśtary* (*Wild Birds of Xinjiang*):

> The male grouse is typically 60 centimetres in length, its weight is 5–6 kilograms, the weight of the female is 2 kilograms, its wings have white spots, but are more reddish-brown if viewed from the side, then it has a long tail and feathered legs. They inhabit pine, spruce and coniferous woods. They sleep under snow in sub-zero temperatures of -40 to -45°C.

It is believed that the wood grouse is found in eastern regions of Kazakhstan. *The National Encyclopedia of Kazakhstan* [86] and *The Kazakh Soviet Encyclopedia*, published during the Soviet Era state the same.[87] Is this bird only found in East Kazakhstan though? Here we'd like to clarify something.

The wood grouse is a settled game bird, living in the same place in winter and summer. It does not look for warm countries to winter. In winter, it sleeps under the snow. Perhaps

---

86 *The National Encyclopedia of Kazakhstan,* Vol. 6, Almaty: Ķazaķ ènciklopediâsy, 2004, p. 471.
87 *The Kazakh Soviet Encyclopedia,* Vol. 7, Almaty: Ķazaķ ènciklopediâsy, 1975, p. 41.

that is why scientists did not believe for a long time that it could migrate and get used to new places. Tôlegen Ajbergenov wrote about the mother camel's devotion to its native land:

> The mother camel chewed to death her calf
> If it was caught by enemies, and never turned back.
> She rushed to her homeland. Tears rolled down her face.
> Inside was a longing![88]

Camel and wood grouse don't usually get used to new places. Many of the experiments conducted by Soviet ornithologists to resettle the bird failed. International ornithologists followed the experiments closely, when in 1965–68, a group of wood grouse was brought from Siberia to northern Kazakhstan; more precisely, to the forests of the Borovskoy district of the Ķostanaj region for acclimatization. They did not comment until the end of the experiment. Many remember that in 1950, squirrels were introduced successfully to Meņdiķara and Uzynkôl. But let's leave the squirrels. What happened to the grouse?

Some believed that they would die out soon, others that they would return to Siberia, whereas a third group assumed that they would pair with local grouse and a new species would appear. Interbreeding was indeed a possibility. The breeding season for the wood grouse and the grouse coincided. The bird that appeared as a result of interbreeding was more like a wood grouse. They grew strong and robust in contrast to others, and fought to the death. At first, scientists thought the bird was unable to reproduce. (A mule is born from a mare and donkey, but cannot procreate.) In contrast, it turned out to be very prolific. To date, the Scots have profusely raised this particular breed. There are very few wood grouse in Europe and it is said that even in Russia there are very few of them left. Therefore, we must be doubly careful of these gorgeous birds that adorn our forests. At the end of the day, we don't have many forests.

Five to six years have passed since then. Scientists who saw the dance of twenty-five male grouse in the village of Borovskoe, in the spring of 1973, reported happily to Moscow about the successful introduction. So it turned into a local bird. But unfortunately, before and after this incident, the acclimatization of the wood grouse was not that successful. It is surprising that our encyclopedias do not know about such an important event.

---

88 Tôlegen Ajbergenov (1937–67) was a prominent Kazakh poet. The citation is from his poem 'Aruana bauyr dùnie' ('The World of the Longing Female Camel').

Probably next time it would be worth transporting them from the Altaj and Arḳa to the Žetisu forests. After all, we have brought Altaj deer to Alatau successfully. Remember the squirrels? Perhaps the grouse will get used to the Alatau as well. Of course, it is up to the experts. Our task is to propose the idea.

My guide, Ivan Prokopovich, left me alone in the middle of the forest without saying goodbye. Good luck to him.

Sometimes loneliness is bliss. I walked in silence.

It seemed I needed to say something. I needed to say something to this forest, this sky, these fading stars, these heavy clouds on the horizon, myself …

The voice of the wood grouse was heard from afar. The poet Tôlegen Ajbergenov wrote:

> What could be better than shooting birds in the moonlit night,
> Or even if you are not shooting, at least pretending to shoot? [89]

How do I translate this for Ivan?

The wood grouse breeding season came to an end. It was over in the blink of an eye. The fog dissipated. Dawn. It was quiet. As the saying goes: 'After the girl's departure, the *auyl* seems dull.' Everything was gloomy, somehow pathetic, like the empty streets of the city during the long holidays. But why did I feel sorry?

The life of a human being is just a fleeting moment after all, like the grouse's merriment.

89 The quote is from Tôlegen Ajbergenov's poem 'Ḳazaḳstan kôktemderi' ('Springs of Kazakhstan').

Pheasant

If you walked before me once again,
You would remain forever in my heart,
My pheasant dream.

Tôlegen Ajbergenov

The winter was favourable that year throughout the Syr Dariâ region. The snow melted early. Every year these places saw floods that the locals referred to as 'hearth-smashers' or 'boat-wreckers'. As soon as the sun started warming up, the ice broke into pieces like glass, and rushed down, making crunching noise from calved chunks. The ground quickly turned green, and the jida trees bloomed, announcing the arrival of the spring. When the jida trees bloomed, the River Syr burst its banks again. The older people used to call this process a 'flood of flowers'. It meant the summer had arrived.

On the east side of the Kelintôbe *auyl*, birds gathered in such countless numbers that it seemed all the birds from the Upper Baltakôl, Šošḳakôl and Ḳašḳansu lakes had come to this lake and the whole region clamoured, shrieked from morning till night, creating a noisy market of birds. Densely grown spiny reeds stretched from Kelintôbe towards the ravine and reached the thick berry woods, on the other side of which a red tamarisk was blazing. There is a saying, 'My blooming sister will sing her song among the red tamarisk', popular not only in these Syr regions. By 'blooming sister' they certainly meant the pheasant. As an example of wealth and abundance, common pheasants flew back and forth from dusk till down. That spring the land of Syr was full of plenty and excess.

Only, the old man, Ḳalmyrza, whose family lived alone near the river, was unnerved and sad. He sent a message to the collective farm leaders warning them that the next winter would be very severe, and people should gather everything they could, beginning with reeds, reed thickets, even the dull leaves, camel thorns, bollards, white quinoa. He expected *žuṫ*, the famine.

The old men were angry at this prediction. 'May snakes lay eggs in his jaw,' they responded furiously.

'How on earth is there going to be a famine, when there is a bloom of abundance?' smirked the younger generation.

In the end, nobody listened to the old man's forecast. We were children then, playing games, getting up early to search for birds' eggs in the deep ravines. One day we saw Ķaleke in the nearby woods.[90] He was leaning forward and walking among the thick spiny reeds, which looked like a green tunnel. Although he noticed us, he didn't stand upright, but continued bending and looking down. He halted.

Then he shouted to us, 'Come here, little brats!' When we were there, he pointed at some eggs and said, 'These are pheasants' eggs. Don't touch them. Taking them is sinful.'

Only two or three eggs lay in a shallow hoof print probably made by a horse. In those years, pheasants in the Syr Dariâ were too many to be counted. We stood and wondered how there could be so many pheasants, if each laid only two or three eggs.

---

90 Ķaleke is a respectful form of address to someone called Ķalmyrza.

'If the next winter is warm and favourable, pheasants will lay between ten and fifteen eggs, perhaps even twenty,' continued Ķaleke, as if he had the ability to read our minds. 'But this number of eggs you see is not a good sign. I have inspected everywhere, beginning from Lake Baltakôl to Lake Sausakôl, but everywhere they have only laid two or three eggs, no more,' commented the old man, wiping his sweating forehead. In the past, there was a similar situation in the *žuț* in the Year of the Dog. That was 1969. In that year, as soon as December arrived it snowed heavily and the temperature went down to -16°C and then to -20 °C. A severe frost stayed from December, right through January, February and March, until April, when the frost seemed to surrender its throne, but the cold still remained. Schools closed. Transport stopped. The number of sheep that died was immeasurable. Shepherds remained with only their crooks before them. The ice on the Syr Dariâ River was so thick that cars and tractors carrying hay could cross the river easily.

We witnessed in that winter that saigas from the Ķaratau mountain range fled to the *auyls* and found shelter in the cattle sheds. We also remember the frozen dead bodies of cattle gathered in layered rows outside the *auyl* and, when it became warm, the remains were burned. Helicopters were sent specially from the centre of the district to Kelintôbe *auyl*. They flew above the *auyl* and threw sacks of newspapers and magazines from the sky. In the woods and on the little islands, the *auyl* dogs carried the frozen bodies of pheasants back and forth, which was tough for their teeth. In the end, unable to eat those remains, the dogs left them to one side. The older people said that such a severe winter had also happened at the end of the war in 1944–45, and again in 1952.

Every astrologer or stargazer, as well as the modern science of ornithology, does not deny the fact that among all the existing birds, common pheasants have extraordinary abilities to predict the weather. In some countries, people say that meteorological stations keep pheasants and breed them in special aviaries to observe their behaviour, and with their help forecast weather and climate change.

Moreover, legends say that the Emir of Bukhara, Sayyd Alimkhan, before the Russian Conquest, sent 300 peasants and soldiers to a place called Sitorai Mokhi-Khossa to build a palace. The Emir ordered them first to dry the place. Two years later, he built an artificial reservoir there and a garden. That garden still exists. Sitorai Mokhi-Khossa still stands too. One of the wonders of the palace for Asian and European travellers is the garden filled with various types of singing birds. By the order of the Emir, pheasants were let into that garden, along with other birds. In the science of ornithology, this type of bird is known as the 'Bukhara pheasant', which lives along the lower reaches of the Syr Dariâ River.

'Emir Alimkhan appreciated pheasants very much,' wrote the historian, 'because one of the particular characteristics of this bird was that pheasants could predict earthquakes. These birds started beating their wings with great strength. Screeching and frustrated, they flew back and forth before the White Palace, sending a *message* to the Emir. The pheasants saved sacred Bukhara many times from disaster.'

By the way, we should not assume from the above example that Emir Alimkhan kept his pheasants purely for their *seismological* sense. Another reason was that pheasant's meat is

The Birds Are Our Friends

very tasty, as the lines from *The Baburna-ma* testify: 'There is abundance of bird in Mawara an-Nahr. A man cannot imagine that pheasants are so fat in this place that four men cannot finish one pheasant.'[91]

Many Kazakhs might be familiar with the late Kazakhstani writer and nature expert Maxim Zverev, who often wrote on the topic of 'The pheasant-seismologist'.

This feature of pheasants is interesting. However, modern science has not unveiled its secret yet. It is still an enigma how pheasants that you and I see every day are able to predict changes in the weather, as well as earthquakes.

In Kazakhstan, common pheasants mostly inhabit the region of the Syr Dariâ River, and their second common dwelling is the territory of the River Ile.

The ring-necked Žetisu pheasant lives along the River Ile. The male Syr pheasant is green, whereas the plumage of the male Ile pheasant is violet. The difference between the male and female pheasants is not great. Ornithologists consider there to be two types of ring-necked pheasants in Eurasia, and forty-two types of them in the world. The Syr pheasants feed mainly on the plants in the woods, as well as the insects on the riverbanks, rice, rice millet and garden fruits and vegetables. The Žetisu pheasants eat sea buckthorn, jida berries, wild apples, berries, blackberries, raspberries, sorrel, hawthorn and other vegetable-type foods rich in vitamins. The mountain pheasant is much heavier and its meat is tastier than that of the lowland pheasant.

Pheasants were introduced to England in the sixteenth century. They were domesticated and some research was done to improve their breeding success. In particular, the English aristocracy drove pheasants before hunting parties, when they chased their prey.

With the idea of domesticating these birds in nature reserves, such as Ķaraşeŋgel and Talġar in the Almaty region, Kazakhs started to breed pheasants. Such experiments exist in the neighbouring Kyrgyz territory, the city of Kopolshite in the Czech Republic and in Bulgaria. Achievements in this field differ in these regions, but experiments are helpful to increase the quantity of birds. Pheasants from Ķaraşeŋgel aviaries were sent to the woods of the Zhongar and Ile Alatau Mountains, Lake Balķaš, the Žarkent, and Alakôl regions and the Aķsu River shores.

In the beginning, the introduction was not very successful. However, recently, the outcome has shown better results. Nowadays, pheasants brought from the pheasant aviary in Tokmak city, Kyrgyzstan, acclimatize completely to the local climate in the mountainous south-eastern part of Almaty. In particular, there is an abundance of these species in the nature reserve of Ile Alatau, places like Remizovka, the Alma-Arasan ravines and the Kamensk Plateau. And in Butakovka's summer cottage regions pheasants almost walk into the gardens. In general, if they are cared for properly, pheasants grow very quickly in number. In recent years, many hunting organizations have appeared in Almaty, and it makes us alert. According to some statistics, recorded since the 1860s, about eighty species of birds have disappeared from the earth.

91 *The Baburnama*, the events of the year 899, or 1494 AC.

Ornithologists have always been fascinated by the male pheasant. It is usually larger than the hen and differs not only in its bright colours, but also in its size and gaudiness. The golden pheasant, silver pheasant, imperial pheasant, white-eared pheasant and brown-eared pheasant are all colourful, highly decorated birds, with a white ring on their neck to catch one's eyes from a distance. (The latter two do not inhabit Kazakhstan; they are said to inhabit Tibet and the Mongolian Mountains.)

The poet Amanhan A'limov described the pheasant as 'a kettle breast pheasant' in one of his poems. Definitely a true description. When pheasants grow fat, their breasts become large, reminiscent of the body of a kettle. Presumably, beauty and intelligence do not exist equally in one object, as male pheasants do not play any role in building nests or rearing the young, and have nothing to do with helping the chicks to fledge. They are, according to Abaj, 'after fun the whole summer', and so frivolous that a male pheasant entered *The Guinness Book of Records*.[92] The book says: 'The most careless fathers are the roosters of the hummingbird and the golden pheasant whose females hatch the eggs by themselves during the entire incubation period.'[93]

It is not difficult to believe this previous reference, if we observe the Žetisu pheasant's behaviour before the egg-laying season. As soon as the spring arrives, a long-tailed, colourful red cock becomes more attractive than before with its showy appearance. It shines and jumps, decorated with bright colours. Female pheasants surround the cock day after day, and the cock fights off other males, and so enlarges its *harem*. Sometimes the number of female pheasants in the group grows to 20–25 birds.

Female pheasants remove themselves from the group and lay eggs. Three and half weeks later chicks start to appear. Meanwhile, left with only two or three female pheasants at its side, the male is exhausted. At the end of May, the cock pheasant, with its head down, barely dragging its bones, stops mating and its main concern becomes food. It has nothing to do with rearing the young. As they say, 'Male dogs are all alike.'

'Bukhara pheasants reproduce in the same way,' wrote ornithologists about the Syr pheasants. But the question arises: Why should it be called a *Bukhara* pheasant?

We usually look up at someone's silver object while sitting on a golden chest. It is believed that Moses, mentioned in the Old Testament and the Qur'an, in order to free his people from slavery, removed them from the world and wandered in the desert for forty years. It is clear that enslavement of one's mind is not erased easily.

The Argonaut leader, Jason, the hero from Colchis (in modern Georgia) in the Ancient Greek myth, saw a golden fleece hanging on a tree along the Phase River. When he came closer to the tree, he noticed a beautiful bird grazing nearby. With the help of the magician Medea, the hero Jason took both the golden fleece and the beautiful, colourful bird, and returned to Greece. The beautiful bird was a pheasant. Since then, experts have believed that it is the most beautiful bird to inhabit Europe.

'What's the name of this bird?' asked the Europeans.

'They caught it along the Phase River in the mountains of Qaf,' explained the Greeks. Pheasants spread in Europe from the lands of Greece. Other birds have different names in every country, but the pheasant is called by the same name throughout the whole Europe – *phasanius*. Until now, historians, literature experts and ornithologists, when talking about pheasants, have started from this myth and hold that Mount Qaf was the place where the bird originated.

---

92 This quote is from Abaj Ķunanbajuļy's translation of Krylov's fable, 'The Dragonfly and the Ant'.

93 *The Guinness Book of Records*, 'Natural World', 1989, p. 36. (Since 1999, renamed *Guinness World Records*.)

The Birds Are Our Friends

In our opinion, the pheasant is not a mountain bird. It also did not exist on the rocks or foothills, nor in the canyons of Qaf, nor along wild mountain rivers, but inhabited fertile and seeded land, the flat woods and grassland plains. It was clear that during the scorching summers of drought years, it would have moved towards the slopes. Even if we say that a bird from a particular species does not choose borders, it would be fair to conclude that the pheasant is a bird from our lands. We think its first homeland was Central Asia, Syr Dariâ, Aẗmu Dariâ (Seikhun, Zheikhun), and rivers like Ile and their banks.

If we refer to some old scientific works that researched climate change in different territories, you will definitely believe this theory. The pheasant is not a migratory bird; it lives in our lands all year round. It does not leave its native parts. Every Kazakh fairy tale starts with, 'Erte, erte, erte eken, eški žùni bôrte eken, ķyrġauyly ķyzyl eken, ķujryķ žùni uẓyn eken …' That is, 'Long, long, long ago, when the goat had grey fluff, when pheasants were red and their tails were long …' Where does the word ķyrġauyl (pheasant) come from? We do not know this. But we do know that this word does not derive from Arabic or Persian, as many Turkic words do. Such tales and legends emerged in pre-Islamic times; they might even have existed since before Christ.

Anyhow, hunting the pheasant is a traditional activity that has existed since ancient times, although nobody clearly says when. In the aforementioned book, Babur wrote about Sultan Ahmad Mirza: 'He loved the birds, and even when he was too old, he used to shoot pheasants and quails dead with a slingshot.'[94] This means that the best hunters not only used bows and rifles, but also slingshots. As they did not have rifles yet, nomadic Kazakhs seemed to have used special arrows referred to as tiz oķ instead. The third method of hunting was setting traps and throwing nets to catch birds. There are many ways of doing this. The fourth method is to hunt with the birds of prey. It is a highly regarded experience for Kazakh and Kyrgyz hunters. If we listen to our Kyrgyz brothers, they say: 'Peregrine falcons, hawks and ordinary eagles may hunt 20–25 pheasants a day,' and that such types of hunting 'leave an unforgettable impression'.[95]

Gyrfalcons and grey goshawks diving steeply from a height cut their prey's throat or back, whereas peregrine falcons, sparrowhawks and northern goshawks kill their prey by chasing after them and kicking. Usually, when other birds hear the rustle of a northern goshawk's wings, they tremble with fear. For this reason, Russians call northern goshawks 'winged wolves'. When they hunt, even the eagle does not interfere in their business, people say. A driver called Krivonosov, a resident of the auyl of Novoalekseevka, near Almaty, reported that a bird had fled into his car through the open window to hide from a northern goshawk. 'I did not know what to do, but was able to press the brake quickly. When I at last came to myself, I saw a northern goshawk flying not far from us and there was a fainted pheasant in the car,' he wrote.[96]

It is particularly interesting when a peregrine falcon catches a pheasant or a duck. At a great speed, the falcon strikes with a clenched foot from below the whirring pheasant or the noisily flying duck. It swings and turns down again, then immediately catches its prey, falling awkwardly, without letting it drop.

Yes, falconers say that pheasants are easy quarry for birds of prey. Is it true? No. As they say, 'The fox's beautiful fur is its misfortune.' It is because of their tasty meat and healthy

94 *The Baburnama*, regarding events of the year 899, or 1493 AC.
95 *Kyrgyz National Games*, Frunze, 1978, p. 84.
96 *Yunyi Naturalist*, Vol. 12, 1982.

broth that pheasants are attacked in the air or on land, but they can be efficient in self-defence. If hit unexpectedly, a cock pheasant can drop in mid-flight and cut the breast of its enemy with its sharp claws. On its leg, it has spikes, a *callus*, the size of a rose thorn. Once cut by this spike the falcon does not attack again.

However, this is a rare case. Anyway, 'There is God in a shabby house,' so the heavens defend these insecure pheasants. Now, let us look at this situation. Pheasants do not nest in the top of trees they just hide their eggs on the ground under bushes. Foxes, wolves, the wild spotted cat and steppe foxes roam day and night for food, but do not notice the drab female pheasant under the bush, incubating her eggs. We know that predators' sense of smell is perfectly developed. In spite of this fact, the fox, usually a cunning animal, passes by, so the pheasant nests safely. So, what is the secret? The secret is that before its eggs hatch, female pheasants lose the scent from their body. Now shouldn't we believe in the power of the Creator?

Another interesting fact is that when pheasants are wounded, they never lie in the place where they have been shot, but fly away about five or six metres further on, to hide themselves. Where does it get the power that gives it this strength before it dies?

Usually, the pheasant has its own survival method. If you walk after it, you rush forward to catch it. When you have almost reached it, suddenly it flies away noisily then lands again. You try again. It is in front of you. It drags its wing and hides in the undergrowth. You think you've caught it, but unluckily you fail again. However, the pheasant does not go on too long. Next time you try to chase it, you catch its tail and your heart is thumping. Your other hand reaches towards it. At this moment, the *wounded* pheasant flies away. You are left with its fluffy tail feathers in your hands. Escaping by 'losing its tail' is not only common for lizards; the pheasant also has this feature.

The pheasant leads you far away from the place you met it first, because it has its chicks there. The female pheasant has to play such tricks to save its newly hatched, soft and weak wingless chicks.

In Kazakh folklore, samples selected by Vasily Radlov provide lines that remind us of this situation. 'Asyŋ, asyŋ, asyŋa, bereke bersin basyŋa, bôdenedej žorǧalap, ķyrǧauyldaj ķorǧalap, Ķydyr kelsin ķasyŋa', that is, 'May the food you eat be blessed and may you prosper. Running like a quail, cautious like a pheasant, may Ķydyr visit you'.[97] It means that pheasants have had defensive features for a long time.

If you look carefully at pictures depicting the Firebird in Russian fairy tales and poems, they resemble the image of a pheasant.[98] It is an imaginary bird. Who knows if there was a bird like it in the world. Nevertheless, let us hope that people do not repeat the Firebird's fate. May pheasants, 'the pheasant dream', run in front of our eyes, but not in our fantasies!

---

97 Ķydyr: legendary saint who brings luck, happiness and prosperity; he also grants people's wishes and helps those in distress.

98 The Firebird, or *Zhar-ptitsa*: a magical bird in Russian folklore and fairy tales.

Hoopoe

Rumours spread quickly in the *auyl*.

'These Chinese played dirty tricks,' said the headmaster.

'As they say, "Excess fat is not a burden only for a sheep." They became wealthy in a couple of years by growing rice, and now they want to do anything they like,' commented our neighbour.

'The mullah doesn't want to stop it. He's writing a letter of complaint to the regional committee, demanding that those Chinese men should be convicted,' added his sister-in-law, who was a teacher.

'No need to write a statement. Just let me cut his head and point him towards *Qibla*,' burst out Jabo, the only Chechen in the *auyl*.[99]

Usually, conflicts begin from nothing. However, this conflict in fact started in an abandoned old barn in the *auyl*, 'a deserted dugout' which was situated a distance from the *auyl*. No, it didn't exactly start in the old barn, it began with a hoopoe that built its nest in the ruins of an old sheepfold. Actually, nobody paid any attention to that damned hoopoe until that event, as there were many birds in the *auyl* in springtime, and nobody even knew when the birds flew away and when they returned.

In the past year, two or three scruffy Chinese men had arrived in our *auyl* and nobody had any idea where they had come from. They were penniless. Initially, they didn't even have a dog in their yard, but soon after they suddenly became well off. They planted onions and rice, grew various smelly herbs and salads, looked after them, stacked them up, mowed and then harvested all of them. They didn't speak Kazakh and their Russian wasn't good. The *auyl* dwellers called the oldest one Kolya.[100] One day the mullah was suspicious about Kolya, who was visiting 'the deserted dugout', so the mullah pretended he was looking after the cattle grazing nearby and began to observe the Chinese man. Guess what Kolya was doing there?

He was sneaking to the hoopoe's nest and was feeding its chicks with insects that he brought with him. The mullah was startled. He whispered to himself: 'Oh my God, what's he doing?' He got closer to the nest. He saw how Kolya had clipped the wings of the baby

---

99 *Qibla* – the direction in which Muslims should face when they pray, towards the Ka'aba in Mecca.

100 Kolya, originally a Russian name (shortened form of Nikolai), probably an appropriation by the villagers of his real (Chinese) name.

hoopoes and tied them to the nest by their legs. The baby hoopoes ate two portions of food daily: one brought by the Chinese man; and the other by the mother hoopoe. The chicks were so fat that they were not able to think about flying. *I need to wait till the end*, thought the mullah and left the place without being noticed and said nothing to anyone. When he turned up the next day, the nest was empty.

As soon as he discovered the chicks had gone, he decided to visit the Chinese 'wall'. (By the 'wall' we mean that the Chinese had surrounded their dwellings with prickly fences in a way that was unusual for the neighbourhood.) When the mullah arrived at their house, a group of four or five Chinese people had plucked the chicks and were adding various vegetables and herbs, to stir-fry a spicy meal with the hoopoe chicks' meat. The mullah was on time to witness the 'crime', raised hell, and began beating each of them.

Having heard the sudden noise, people in the *auyl* gathered. What happened after that was described at the beginning of this chapter. The *auyl* was not quiet.

'What a horrible thing! Who eats hoopoe meat?'

'It will be better if they leave. We need a peaceful life.'

'The hoopoe [the mullah called this bird *babisek*, not *sasyk kôkek* – smelly hoopoe; both terms are used in Kazakh] is a bird that has been blessed by prophets. Killing them is a big sin,' the mullah said.

The other person, after the mullah, who knew religious conventions well, was Jabo, the Chechen, and he became even more furious about the event. He was saying something in his own language (probably he was cursing), gritting his teeth and repeating 'I'll kill them'. To our surprise his father, an old man called Ali, never told his son to 'cut it', nor did his mother seem to care about these things.

After the people's involvement, the Chinese left the *auyl*. I don't remember where they went, but they did not come back. Several years later, I reflected on that story again when, by chance, I found a book called *The Traditions of North Caucasus People*.

Before they adopted Islam, Chechens associated the arrival of spring with the hoopoe. As soon as the hoopoe arrived and sang its usual '*hoop-hoop*' song they believed it was a sacred bird – 'Tu-sholi's hen' – and celebrated the Spring Festival.[101] And so I understood why Jabo the Chechen had been so concerned and so angry with those Chinese.

Times have changed and the law has changed too. I am not sure if Kazakhs have been fully modernized, although, in general, people have changed. Nowadays we are allowed to read the Holy Qur'an, and have even translated it into Kazakh. The following are *ayahs* (verses) of the *surahs* (chapters), taken from the Qur'an:

And Solomon succeeded David. He said, 'O people, we have been taught the language of birds, and we have been given from all things. Indeed, this is evident bounty.' (27:16) And gathered for Solomon were his soldiers of the jinn and men and birds, and they were [marching] in rows. (27:17) Until, when they came upon the valley of the ants, an ant said, 'O ants, enter your dwellings that you not be crushed by Solomon and his soldiers while they perceive not.' (27:18) So [Solomon] smiled, amused at her speech, and said, 'My Lord, enable me to be grateful for Your favour which You have bestowed upon me and upon my parents and to do righteousness of which You approve. And admit me by Your mercy into [the ranks of] Your righteous servants.' (27:19) And he took attendance of the birds and said, 'Why do I not see the hoopoe – or is he among the absent? (27:20) I will surely punish him with a severe punishment or slaughter him unless he brings me clear authorization.' (27:21) But the hoopoe stayed not long and said, 'I have encompassed [in knowledge] that which you have not encompassed, and I have come to you from Sheba with certain news. (27:22) Indeed, I found [there] a woman ruling them, and she has been given of all things, and she has a great throne. (27:23) I found her and her people prostrating to the sun instead of Allah, and Satan has made their deeds pleasing to them and averted them from [His] way, so they are not

---

101 Tusholi's hen (Chechen) – according to Chechen and Ingush beliefs, Tusholi was a pre-Islam Goddess of Fertility.

guided. (27:24) [And] so they do not prostrate to Allah, who brings forth what is hidden within the heavens and the earth and knows what you conceal and what you declare – (27:25) Allah – there is no deity except Him, Lord of the Great Throne.' (27:26) [Solomon] said, 'We will see whether you were truthful or were of the liars. Take this letter of mine and deliver it to them. Then leave them and see what [answer] they will return.' (27:27-28) She said, 'O eminent ones, indeed, to me has been delivered a noble letter. Indeed, it is from Solomon, and indeed, it reads: 'In the name of Allah, the Entirely Merciful, the Especially Merciful, Be not haughty with me but come to me in submission [as Muslims].' (27:29-31) She said, 'O eminent ones, advise me in my affair. I would not decide a matter until you witness [for] me.' (27:32) They said, 'We are men of strength and of great military might, but the command is yours, so see what you will command.' (27:33) She said, 'Indeed kings, when they enter a city, they ruin it and render the honoured of its people humbled. And thus do they do. (27:34) But indeed, I will send to them a gift and see with what the messengers will return.' (27:35) So when they came to Solomon, he said, 'Do you provide me with wealth? But what Allah has given me is better than what He has given you. Rather, it is you who rejoice in your gift. (27:36) Return to them, for we will surely come to them with soldiers that they will be powerless to encounter, and we will surely expel them therefrom in humiliation, and they will be debased.' (27:37) [Solomon] said, 'O assembly [of jinn], which of you will bring me her throne before they come to me in submission?' (27:38) A powerful one from among the jinn said, 'I will bring it to you before you rise from your place, and indeed, I am for this [task] strong and trustworthy.' (27:39)

Said one who had knowledge from the Scripture, 'I will bring it to you before your glance returns to you.' And when [Solomon] saw it placed before him, he said, 'This is from the favour of my Lord to test me whether I will be grateful or ungrateful. And whoever is grateful – his gratitude is only for [the benefit of] himself. And whoever is ungrateful, then indeed, my Lord is Free of need and Generous.' (27:40)

He said, 'Disguise for her her throne; we will see whether she will be guided [to truth] or will be of those who is not guided.' (27:41) So when she arrived, it was said [to her], 'Is your throne like this?' She said, '[It is] as though it was it.' [Solomon said], 'And we were given knowledge before her, and we have been Muslims [in submission to Allah]. (27:42) And that which she was worshipping other than Allah had averted her [from submission to Him]. Indeed, she was from a disbelieving people.' (27:43)

She was told, 'Enter the palace.' But when she saw it, she thought it was a body of water and uncovered her shins [to wade through]. He said, 'Indeed, it is a palace [whose floor is] made smooth with glass.' She said, 'My Lord, indeed I have wronged myself, and I submit with Solomon to Allah, Lord of the worlds.' (27:44)[102]

102 Qur'an, Verse 27 (16–44), available at: https://quran.com/27.

There are a few birds that are mentioned in the Qur'an. One of them is the hoopoe. According to some zoologists there is only one type of hoopoe. Maybe for this reason people want to learn more about this bird. The second notable feature is its appearance, especially its crest and of course its colourful (white, black, yellow and blue) plumage. It is called 'a young woman in a colourful jacket' or 'a guard in a motley robe' in some Eastern countries.

In summer, it is hard for either people or animals to pass close to a hoopoe's nest. First-ly, if the bird hears any kind of strange sound, it squirts its faeces right at the stranger's face. Secondly, it hisses at intruders like a snake. These two qualities are not found in any other bird species. Another interesting detail is that they tirelessly make sounds like 'hoop-hoop' when sitting on a tree branch or on the roof of a house. This sound may continue 20–30 times. Some people confused its voice with that of the cuckoo. In fact, they are quite dif-ferent birds.

A hoopoe doesn't tidy its nest, just like the kingfisher. In other words, it is a sloppy bird. Caucasian Turks also call this bird 'the careless cuckoo' (salaḳ kôkek) or 'devil chicken' (šajtan tauyḳ).

So, why is this bird mentioned in the Holy Qur'an? The first thing that comes to mind is that there is another kind of hoopoe in our Prophet's (peace be upon him) homeland called an African hoopoe and this may be a significant bird. It lives in the African forests and groves and is a stately beautiful and neat bird. Sometimes it is called the white-headed hoopoe (aḳbas baᵇisek). Another type is the cuckoo-tailed hoopoe (kôkekḳuȷ̌ryḳ baᵇisek). The hoopoe can also be found in South Africa, Angola and Sudan, and is a beautiful bird, like the pheasant.

But all of the above turned out to be just a groundless assumption. The bird that was in the service of the Prophet Solomon is the hoopoe (sasyḳ kôkek – lit. 'smelly hoopoe'). Maybe, Allah, whose prophets differ from people by their kindness and graciousness, considered and said, 'If we don't render honours to this poor creature, called *smelly* from olden times, no one will.' Anyway, there are lots of stories about hoopoes in ancient East-ern literature. This reminds us of our own ancestors, who often treated defenceless and maltreated outsiders with the greatest respect, and even allowed them to rule over the people.

The Persian poet Farid ud-Din Attar's book, *Mantiq-ut-Tayr*, was translated into some Turkic languages.[103] The word *Tayr* means 'bird' in Arabic. Therefore, the name of the book can be translated as *The Conference of the Birds*. Undoubtedly, you might have read Max-im Gorky's poem named 'The Song of the Stormy Petrel' (*Burevestnik*).[104] If you remem-ber, it is about a giant storm petrel that became the leader of all birds and incited them to Great Deeds (Revolution). In Farid ud-Din Attar's fable, which existed before Gorky, it is described how the hoopoe, the sage among birds, tells all the winged creatures that they should look for the legendary Simurgh bird, and leads them.[105] Later, Alisher Navai, taking inspiration from Attar, wrote a book called *Lison-ut-Tayr* (*The Language of the Birds*), which was translated into several languages, except Kazakh.[106]

---

103 Farid ud-Din Attar (*c.*1145–*c.*1221), a Persian poet and Sufi theoretician.

104 Maxim Gorky (1868–1936), Russian poet and writer.

105 Simurgh – a gigantic, powerful, generally benevolent mythical bird in Eastern folklore, which acts as a mediator among the three worlds: celestial (gods); Earth (man); and the underworld (the dead).

106 Alisher Navai (1441–1501), a Chagatai Turkic poet, writer, politician, linguist, mystic and painter.

The plot of Navai's epic poem is close to Attar's fable. It is about how the birds all over the world gathered together and started arguing: 'Who should rule?' At that very moment the wisest bird, the hoopoe (*hudhud* in Persian), said: 'O brothers, this is a meaningless quarrel and nothing good will come out of it if we shout "I am the strongest, No, I am," at each other. Let's find the Simurgh bird together and he will judge fairly.' Thus, singing and carolling they began their journey. They couldn't find the Simurgh, but they reached six places: Aspiration, Affection, Enlightenment, Imitation, Forgiveness and Will.

Navai listed all the famous epic poems written before Attar, and said:

> As all of these masterpieces are worthy of sincerity, respect and praise, so the *Mantiq-ut-Tayr* deserves the praise that equals to all of them combined. To understand this, you need to know mysterious languages. Perhaps, the mysterious language is that of the Prophet Solomon himself. Obviously, it is a difficult task to transform the languages of hundreds of birds in a special way. But this book describes the particular song, flight and arrival of each bird. With the divine support and praying for the soul of the Sheikh [meaning Attar], I am intended to write such a book, to pay him homage.

Dear reader, of course you know that this is Sufi literature. To know Almighty God (Simurgh), firstly you need aspiration and diligence, then a warm heart.

The poems of Attar and Navai both deserve assiduous attention, and one day we will have a generation that will study Eastern literature, not superficially as it is done today, but

in depth and thoroughly. We leave it to them to present these aforementioned masterpieces of world literature to the Kazakh people. Our task is to focus on the role of the hoopoe in both works. The hoopoe is the guide and the sage. Others follow and obey it.

In the chapter titled 'The Words of the Hoopoe about Simurgh When the Birds Were Looking for a Shakh to Rule over Them', it is said that 'the hoopoe was an eloquent sage, a powerful bird leader. God created it with an exceptional mind, and there is a crest at the top of its head, signifying its *royal* status. It knows thousands of secrets like the Angel Gabriel.' In the end, the hoopoe leads birds (the people) to the truth – to God. Yet we Kazakhs underestimate it and say, 'Oh, is this the same old smelly hoopoe [*sasyk̦ kôkek*]?'

As we say, 'Don't judge a book by its cover'. Should we not look for greatness among ordinary people, and simplicity among great people? Aren't we the same old people who called the wisest and most powerful Abylaj Khan *Sabalak̦* (Shabby)?[107]

Indeed, did the prophets, the best of mankind, figure that this beautiful bird has been mistreated for a long time and favour it because of this?

107 Abylaj Khan was a Kazakh khan who headed the national liberation struggle against the Dzhungar conquerors during the seventeenth and eighteenth centuries; the liberator of Kazakh lands and unifier of the three zhuz (tribal unions headed by their own khan). He was orphaned at an early age and was a servant to Tôle *bi* (judge), who gave the boy a nickname, *Sabalak̦* (Shabby), because of the latter's looks, until his true identity was revealed.

Crossbill

K anatbergen is a Kazakh who moved from Karakalpakstan to his fatherland. 'Our forebears were originally from Ķarmaķšy,' he used to say.[108] He was nimble, generous and very hospitable. During my usual trip to the mountains, on the slope of 'Üšen' Hill (Triplets), the name we had given to the neighbouring three hills, we noticed a tiny house with a white roof. Spring water streamed under the thick plants. Its water was freezing. There was a thick grove of beech trees. Ferns grew everywhere. A person who had not seen it for himself would not believe that ferns could grow in the suburbs of Almaty.

As soon as the ferns ripened, people took them to the market to sell. But there weren't any Kazakhs among them. There was a legend saying that 'the blue stone of Samarkand will melt once a year and the one who sees it will be happy'. There is a similar legend about ferns. First, people say, 'Ferns bloom only once a year in moonlight.' The second saying is, 'The one who sees the fern bloom will be wealthy and lucky.' Near to the spring there are maple woods, and further into the woods thick white birch trees can be found. These birch

trees become red in the autumn, catching one's eye, and furthermore, there is a steep hill full of pine trees, where it is impossible to go, not only for vehicles, but also for people.

The three hills resemble a row of three steps. That is why we call them 'Üšen' (Triplets). People do not live in this area. Earlier, shepherds from the Talġar district used to stay there for four or five days when moving to *žajlau* (summer pastures). Today there are neither shepherds nor sheep. That was the reason we headed

108 Ķarmaķšy is a district in the Ķyzylorda region of Kazakhstan.

straight to the white-roofed house, which seemed to us as if it had landed straight from the sky. A man of about fifty in jackboots greeted us blankly:

'Welcome,' he said. 'Come in, into the house.'

It turned out one of the nouveau riche Kazakhs, who had bought the whole 'Ušen' forest, had hired Ķanatbergen as a guard. He had built him a house, with land to farm and cattle to breed. The cattle belonged to the owner, but the calves belonged to Ķanatbergen. Ķanatbergen was happy with this deal. He liked saying 'Okay!' and 'Good, I'll do that'. He called the owner 'žasuly', which means 'older brother'. Calling and naming the manager or your boss 'aġa' – older brother – even he is younger than you, is a traditional form of address in Asian cultures.[109]

Before the New Year's Eve celebrations, he sent me a letter via his 'žasuly', which read, 'Visit me, brother. We will have a great day! Best regards, Ķaķabaj.' Therefore, I went. Ķaķan was delighted to see me.[110]

'There is one bird, brother, a very interesting one. So interesting that if I tell you about it, you won't believe me,' he said. 'I haven't seen it before,' he continued. 'Such a bird has never lived in Karakalpakstan, brother.'

He was right. It is possible that animals that dwell in Karakalpakstan, near the Aral Sea, in Khorezm ravines do not live in our Alatau territories. In addition, mountain birds do not inhabit the steppes. I noticed that an amazing bird which had confused Ķaķan, was not the same as described in a student's textbook.

It was so quiet there. In winter, hawthorns were black with the cold. In the flood plains or the bottom lands, high trees soared to the skies and became thick woods because of hops and wolfberries that shrouded them and prevented anyone from accessing the forest. Dried hops looked like a carpet of motley threads hanging over the forest. It was difficult to distinguish between the barberry and wolfberry shrubs. Among the maples, one could hear the blue tits singing their usual song, 'tsit-tsit'. A magpie chattered. As we passed through the thick woods and went up towards the third coniferous forest, a hawfinch flew horizontally before us. In the distance, we heard a crow cawing. On the ground were the prints of a roe deer, a trail that led to the water and back. The deer might have seen the plastic bag hanging on a bush and turned to look at it. Deer suffer from excessive curiosity.

It is hard to believe that enormous fir trees in the Alatau Mountains grew up only from button-like seeds. Nobody planted these seeds in these steep hills. Probably, they were carried by the wind or dropped from the mouth of a bird onto the black soil. Then the roots knotted together, tied themselves to the earth, lived and grew. For many years, these trees were able to survive wind, landslide, storm and flood. But over the passage of time, that handful of soil became too small. The trees' thick roots broke the stones, searching for a source of life. In the end, the tree found that source – the spring water. That is the power of the Almighty.

We were tackling heavy snow. My companion, who had never seen the mountains before moving to Kazakhstan, had become a skilled mountaineer.

As Kazakhs say, 'Man gets used to hell in three days.' It was hard at first to walk from slope to slope, but now I jump in the mountains like a deer,' my friend explained and laughed cheerfully. I was curious about the bird Ķaķan had mentioned before. It definitely wasn't a dove. Perhaps a snowcock? No, it was impossible. Snowcocks lived higher than these places, at an altitude of 3,500–4,000 metres.

109 Aġa is a polite way to address an elderly man.

110 Ķaķabaj and Ķaķan – affectionate and respectful forms of address for Ķanatbergen.

Suddenly, a crossbill flew overhead. Ķaķaṇ did not pay any attention to it. We were walking. All the way, we saw broken cottonwoods, birches split in half, and ruined maple trees. An ash tree was also lying in two pieces – straight beautiful lines, as if someone had painted on its trunk. My heart ached seeing this insane damage to such beauty. If this ash tree trunk had been given to the hands of a master, they would have turned it into valuable furniture. European masters liken the ash tree to gold. Kazakhs used broken trees as firewood or timber, or just left them to decay, paying no attention to them. Previously, ash bark had been used for blue, black and brown dyes, and its leaves were fed to cattle. Nobody's interested in these traditions nowadays.

'Here it is,' said Ķaķaṇ, pointing at a red-breasted crossbill sitting on top of a tree. 'Have you seen such a bird before? No, you haven't. Please, tell me you haven't seen it before.'

'That is a crossbill, Ķaķaṇ.'

'Is that the cursed bird which emigrated from China?'

'Not China. This is our common, local crossbill. We've seen it along the way.'

'I showed it to *žasuly*, and he explained in Russian that it might have emigrated from China.'

'Oh, ignore this *žasuly*!'

I understood later why Ķaķaṇ spoke about the bird as a 'cursed bird'. As soon as someone saw a crossbill, the first thing they would notice was its beak.

The crossbill looks like a sparrow, but is a bit bigger than a tit. A male crossbill is very distinct among the white fir trees with its reddish plumage. The female crossbill's back is brown and its underparts are yellow. It is easy to distinguish male and female birds from each other.

At first, you will question why such a little bird needs such a big beak. When observed closely, one may be surprised by its distinctive mandibles, crossed at the tip. This is the reason why Kazakhs call it 'the bird with a scissors beak'. When flying it sings '*chip-chip*', then changes to '*kle-kle*'. May be that is why Russians call it a '*klest*'. Crossbills only breed in certain parts of Kazakhstan. Their main territory is coniferous forests full of spruce, fir and pine trees.

Ķaķaṇ and I viewed the area using binoculars. On the top of a giant fir tree, probably at least 300 years old, sat a brownish female crossbill. It was not moving. A red-breasted male crossbill flew before it at speed. The female gave no reaction. A clump of snow fell down from the treetop. We were walking under the trees; however, she remained motionless, like a statue. Usually crossbills are sensitive to every whisper, to rustling leaves, but this one surprised us by her stillness that could be interpreted as both courage and indifference.

'Maybe it's frozen,' said Ķanatbergen, looking at it carefully.

'When did you see it last time?'

'Yesterday and the day before yesterday it was sitting like this, but on Thursday it wasn't here.'

'Then, that means it's been sitting for three days?'

'Yes.'

I reflected on this. The way the female was sitting suggested that it was sitting on eggs. The red-breasted male flew down and started extracting seeds from cones as if it were picking out sunflower seeds. Then it flew up with the seeds in its mouth. When the male was closer to the female, the yellow-breasted crossbill quickly opened her mouth. It seemed as if the male were a humble sparrow that was feeding a cuckoo chick.

'Hey, it seems alive,' Ķaķaṇ said, startled.

'Let's go,' I suggested.

I threw the seeds I had brought with me under the fir tree. They say that 'The poor have seven winters', so I understood that the snow was thick in the mountains, and it would be difficult to go any further. I was sure that the red-breasted crossbill would take care of its mate.

One thing bothered me about them. I had never read or heard before of birds breeding during a severe winter. Eagles are a different story. They usually nest on rocks on the high summits of mountains unreachable by humans. They often breed when it's stormy and windy, so their chicks face the harshest conditions from the very beginning. This is why they are considered the Lord of Birds.

But what about these little crossbills? Were they brave or were they crazy? As they say, 'A man on foot who tries to keep pace with a horseman will tear his groin.' Crossbills were no match for eagles, and trying to imitate one of the strongest birds could end badly.

I might have been wrong about the female crossbill sitting on the eggs; it might have broken its leg or its wing. It is a common fate for small birds like the crossbill to be injured and become prey for predators.

I went back to the city very late. It started snowing as soon as I arrived at the junction of the Butakovka River and the Šybyndysaj spring, which meant that it must have started to snow in the mountains even earlier. I felt pity for the couple living at the top of the tree, devotedly taking care of each other.

I decided to visit them the following weekend. However, I was not able to. Ķaķaṇ also kept quiet. Anyway, one day I left work earlier than before and made my way to the mountains. It was impossible to get to Ûšen, even to the *auyls* under the slopes of the mountains. So, I went home and waited for the next weekend. Thank God, the day was clear. I started for the mountains at dawn.

'It has flown, my brother,' Ķaķaṇ told me at once.

I did not ask what had flown, as I knew he was talking about the crossbill we had seen. According to our calculations, the crossbill had been sitting on its eggs for about 15–16 days. Ķaķaṇ had visited the crossbill when he was descending from the hills with some wood. When he viewed them through his binoculars, he had seen 5–6 chicks in the nest.

My God, thought a puzzled Ķaķaṇ in surprise. The colour of the chicks was greyish and their beaks were straight. What was the answer? Was it possible that the female crossbill had been confused and had been incubating the chicks of a different bird?

Ķaķaṇ was muttering, so no one could understand him.

Suddenly several crows gathered and started to croak noisily. We wished for neither snow nor strong winds …

The case with the crossbill chicks was not a surprise to me. I had read somewhere that, in the beginning, the chicks' beaks were straight, then over time, when crossbills started to extract pine kernels from the cones, after a few months their beaks became crossed at the tip.

After that, time passed. I still remembered a tale that Ķanatbergen had told me. Although it was a bit difficult to understand it in his particular language (Karakalpak mixed with Kazakh), I comprehended the tale. The Kazakh version was as follows.

Long, long, long ago when the goat's tail was short, the Great King Solomon, who governed 18,000 worlds, had a bird named Anha. The bird laughed like a man, could speak like a man and lived with the people. Animals were animals, a horse was considered one of people's treasures, and yet could kick people one day. A dog also had the same fame as a horse, and yet could bite people when the time comes. Only Anha was beyond reproach.

King Solomon used to say: 'Oh my people, the light of my eyes, the song of my soul. The Almighty granted me everything that I asked for but eternal life. I know there is death. My Anha bird can speak, dance, sing and play a musical instrument, but it never cries. You should pray for it to not to cry. The day when Anha cries, I'll die.'

Therefore, the people and animals of the 18,000 worlds tried to make the Anha bird happy.

Long, long, long ago, King Solomon's guard was a wolf, his cook and tea-maker was a fox, his gardener was a crane, his watcher was a stork, his announcer was a magpie, his messenger was a crow, the guard in his garden was a goshawk and his guard in the mountains was a red eagle. Therefore, let us discuss the red eagle. The red eagle grew and lived in the mountains, away from other birds, and looked down on them. When it visited King Solomon at his palace, it only greeted the king, but ignored the Anha bird. Once, King Solomon grew bored and created a black camel out of a dark cloud and sat on it, created herds of horses and flocks of sheep out of white clouds, an umbrella out of a blue cloud, made a raindrop from the rain, a whip from the wind, a lash from the fire and a bat from the storm, and travelled to different worlds for several months. When he returned to his palace from his exciting trip, the king met his favourite bird Anha. It was almost in tears.

'The red eagle offended me,' said the Anha bird.

'What's the matter?' asked the king.

'The eagle said: "You are so close to King Solomon that you could kill him and become king instead of him. Why don't you? What's the matter with you? How long are you going to remain his plaything? If you cry and shed your tears, the world will crack into two, won't it? Shall we both become kings of those lands and govern those worlds separately?"'

When Solomon heard this, he became furious. When King Solomon was angry the milk turned into yoghurt, the butter curdled, the mountain turned into soil, the ground turned into leaves, sugar into salt and water turned into ice. When King Solomon shouted there was an earthquake on the land, the land under the sky croaked like frogs, the yellow sea turned into a black sea, the black mountain shifted the white mountain, the world crashed and seemed to end.

Then the violent king hit the land three times with his right hand, three times with his left hand, then turned his hands back and cursed the red eagle with the following words: 'Whenever you eat, may the food be tough, may your enemy be superior. May you eat insects, and live far away and all alone. May you become as tiny as millet, as insignificant as a spot, as frail as a sparrow. May your beak be curled, curse you, traitor!'

As they say, 'The cursed will never be well', and the red eagle became extinct over time, and disappeared from the land. Further than the Qaf Mountains, closer than Ķaraspan, in the middle of nowhere, facing fierce winds, a small number of red eagles was left.[111] After that the red eagle diminished, became weak and as thin as a sparrow, and its beak curled. It did not want to be seen anywhere by anyone, but lived at the top of a tall tree, in the rocky cliffs of the mountain.

Was this crossbill now nesting on the top of a tree with its curled beak the same bird that had been cursed by King Solomon?

And so, the list of 'cursed birds' now added one more – a crossbill – to the cuckoo, the hoopoe and the crow.

However, I do not want to accept this version, because birds can't be cursed. People might create tales where they wish to hide their sins or misbehaviour, but why should birds be blamed for humans' shortcomings? Usually, when a person that turns to Islam at some point (even if it's too late) and starts to pray five times a day, posts alms prescribed by Sharia in favour of the poor, starts reading the holy book – the Qur'an – they are at first introduced to comparatively easy *surahs*. For instance, the *surah* Al-Fil (the *surah* of 'The Elephant'). This was a Meccan *surah* consisting of five verses which reads in the following way:

> Have you not considered, [O Muhammad], how your Lord dealt with the companions of the elephant? (105:1)
>
> Did He not make their plan into misguidance? (105:2)
>
> And He sent against them birds in flocks, (105:3)
>
> Striking them with stones of hard clay, (105:4)
>
> And He made them like eaten straw. (105:5)[112]

You know that Islam is a highly developed discipline and there is no lack of interpretation or explanation. There are different theories how and why the *surah* of Al-Fil originated. Let us discuss the meaning of this *surah*.

The Prophet Muhammad al-Mustafa (peace be upon him) played a tremendous role in building holy Mecca as a sacred place with the Kaaba, fighting against his enemies in battle; a crowd that was not able to accept the considerations of Islam, *surahs* and Hadith. Certainly, it would have been better if non-believers had left Mecca without any battle; however, those opponents of Islam tried to destroy the Kaaba.

When the Prophet Ibrahim and his son Ismail started building the walls of the Kaaba, the Prophet uttered: 'Oh, Allah, the Merciful, please, accept this from us, as you are the One in whom we believe and pray for.' Therefore, the Kaaba really became a blessed holy place, but it had enemies too.

---

111 The phrase 'Further than the Qaf Mountains, closer than Ķaraspan, in the middle of nowhere, facing fierce winds' means 'no-man's-land.'

112 The *surah* Al-Fil, available at: https://quran.com/105

A representative of Habashstan in Yemen (now in Ethiopia), a man named Abraha, marched upon the Kaaba to demolish it. He organized a large army with weapons and used elephants for transport. Elephants were the most dangerous and hazardous type of transport in the war. It is known from history that to fight an army of elephants was impossible. There are many poems, epic stories, legends and fairy tales about elephants in Eastern literature. When people heard that Abraha's army was close to Mecca, the citizens were frightened to death. Some wanted to flee, others wanted to surrender to save their lives. Only real mujahidin praying to Allah stayed to fight the enemy. They prayed to Allah and asked the Almighty for help and support.

Meanwhile, the elephants, which were making their way forward to destroy Kaaba, started to retreat and escape. Abraha shouted and urged them towards Mecca, but the elephants were out of control. He looked fearfully at the sky and noticed little birds carrying stones in their mouths. 'That was the green Ababil, whose beak was yellow,' says the holy book.[113]

Suddenly, stones dropped onto the elephants. At first, the first row of the army was destroyed, and then the middle row was killed. The thirteen elephants started to flee, trampling their masters and roaring on the battlefield. In this way a powerful army of intruders began to fail and disappear from the field. The enemies became stalks and straw on the battlefield, as the Qur'an tells us.

It was the manifestation of the power of Almighty, wasn't it? Otherwise, how could we compare the power of elephants with that of small birds? To sum up, hard power is not the key to success.

I like this story and do not believe at all that the crossbill is a damned bird. God blessed all birds from the beginning. The Ababil and the crossbill are blessed too.

Take care, friends!

113 *Ababil* refers to the miraculous birds in Islamic belief (identified as swallows) mentioned in *Surah* 105 of the Qur'an that protected the Kaaba in Mecca from the Aksumite elephant army of Abraha.

Blackbird

*I*n one of the TV food shows, a singer who was more ambitious than shameful, who had more connections than talent, was showing how to cook his favourite salad. It was Sunday. We were at home. My guest was an Uzbek poet.

'O my god! O dear, what are you doing?' exclaimed my guest, suddenly approaching the TV screen as if he were going to step into it.

'What's wrong?' I asked.

'You see? It seems that this fellow doesn't know anything about the poison.'

My Uzbek friend was worried about the singer, as if he were going to die right there. When I looked, the singer was arranging celery leaves on the edge of the plate and decorating them with different snacks. In fact, my friend knew that Kazakh men do not know much about the kitchen, and so my knowledge about the topic was limited. So, my guest began explaining everything:

'Only celery stems should be used for food; its leaves are poisonous.'

Earlier, I had seen a music video, where a singer was singing among pink flowers on the mountain slopes. The flower was called fraxinella. If you touch it, it will burn your hands. Many people are aware that the wounds from fraxinella will not heal quickly. That is why they don't go near it and don't feed animals with it. In spite of this, our scantily dressed singer was playing and singing joyfully among the fraxinella flowers. It seemed to me that the poisonous plant itself was frightened of the ambitious singer girl.

Obviously, both of these stories should be treated as two different topics. Let us wish health to both singers. Almost everyone can be poisoned after all. Only on rare occasions might there be a person on whom the poison will have no effect. Have you ever heard about the bird that can't eat or fly without adding poison to its food? This bird is called a blackbird.

Yew berries grow among the forest trees and are remarkable for their exceptional beauty. They are also poisonous, like fraxinella. So, ornithologists of the world are surprised by the addiction of blackbirds to yew berries (*taxus baccata*). The seeds of the yew

berries are toxic. The power of its poison is equal to that of plants such as thermopsis, henbane, fraxinella and hemlock. Cattle do not eat these plants. People who live in mountainous areas do not allow their children to go near them. Don't be surprised if you see a black bird with a yellow beak, which is slightly larger than a starling. This bird is called a blackbird. You can find blackbirds in all the recreational parks of Almaty, especially along Dostyķ Avenue and Gornaya Street near the Medeu ice rink.

In recent years, they have stayed there for the winter when other songbirds have flown away to warm countries. When autumn comes, sadness arrives with it. 'Just as birds fall dead when they are shot, so the yellow leaves fall from the trees' (Prishvin).[114]

Cold rain, muddy roads, quiet forests, mute mountains … What a pity that the painter Isaac Levitan did not visit the mountains near our city of Almaty. If he had visited this place, more breathtaking landscapes would have been added to his portfolio.

It is a joy when the sun appears from time to time in the cloudy sky in gloomy, cool autumn. You also appreciate the moment when you suddenly hear the singing voice of a bird in the grey and dull forest. This is the voice of the blackbird.

It seems like Mother Nature specifically left this bird so that we would not be sad in this grey season. If you read the lines in Tôlegen Ajbergenov's poem about this time of the year, then you'll immediately remember the blackbird, which is also left in the wood: 'I'm deserted, alone at home as a lookout left to guard the snipers' camp.'[115]

The water thrush is in the water and the blackbird in the forest. Both are like another power of nature that can even make stone thrive. The voices of these two birds may alleviate the deepest winter. They are like ambassadors of the summer, held hostage in a foreign country.

The blackbird is also a messenger of spring. This is a fact. It manages to build its nest before other birds arrive from warm lands. In particular, it builds its nest in a maple grove located near the water. By mentioning water, I have remembered one story. Last winter we met a group of film-makers that were carrying their equipment and coming down from the head of the Esentaj River. After conversing with each other, they told us how they had seen two blue birds in this area. A blue bird, 'the bird of happiness', builds its nest on the banks of the mountain river. However, the blue bird could not have been where the film-makers had walked. It was impossible, as that noble bird lives in a quiet, safe place, away from any noise. While we were talking, we noticed a blackbird, which flew under the bridge in the direction of the bushy woods on the other side of the ravine.

The film-makers ran after it carrying their equipment, chasing it. It turned out that they had been looking at an ordinary blackbird when they had been describing the blue bird. At first sight, these birds look similar and both of them appear black. When they fly towards the sun, their backs shine and attract attention. The blue bird changes its colour to blue. Everyone pays attention to this beautiful bird that comes and disappears from sight. However, we know that the main features of the blackbird are not only its appearance but also its voice. It is an interesting fact that nature does not give each bird equal beauty and ability. Many beautiful birds are not singers. On the contrary, there are many singing birds among small, plain-looking and thin birds; for example, the kingfisher and nightingale, or compare a goldfinch with a whitethroat. What does a robin look like and what is the voice of a starling? There are lots of similar examples.

114 Mikhail Prishvin (1873–1954), a Soviet writer.
115 The quote is from Ajbergenov's poem 'Apalarym' ('My Sisters').

The Birds Are Our Friends

If the blackbird is scared of something, it flies away tweeting and whistling. A person who hears its strange *'tweeting'* for the first time will be surprised to learn that the owner of the most beautiful singing voice at dusk is the same blackbird.

Yes, it sings mostly at dusk. The nightingale has a rest at this time. As if Mother Nature wishes that 'Every day and even every moment of spring should not pass without music', when the nightingale is having a rest, it is the blackbird's turn to sing.

Then the blackbird sings for one or two hours without stopping. We have talked about this before, and we'd like to repeat the words by Ùkili Ybyraj that he used in his song:

When the blackbird sings at dusk
your stone heart will melt.

Although the original lines mention a thrush, I think it is talking about a blackbird that sings at dusk.

The sophisticated singer Ùkili Ybyraj, who, according to his song, 'visited many places and hunted birds that drummed on the lakes', would not have been surprised by the tweeting of the thrush that lived in the khan's palace. Usually, owing to the 'law' of the bird keepers, we may rate birds according to their singing talents in this way:

1. Nightingale. No one doubts its first place;
2. Common whitethroat;
3. Blackbird;
4. Song thrush;
5. Redwing;
6. Robin;
7. Common redstart.

The list goes on. Apparently, this is not a document approved by any official or competent authority. This is just a subjective assessment that is given to songbirds recognized by the general public.

The Darwin Moscow State Museum, in cooperation with the Avanta publishing house, recorded the voices of ninety-eight birds. They didn't just record their voices, but also mixed and remastered them, and put them on a CD which they attached to the *Children's Encyclopedia*. It is an indispensable audible aid for ornithologists, bird lovers, and also for children. This application is more comprehensive than audio cassettes and records that had been compiled before.

Many people who have listened to this audio recording for the first time reconsider the list above and prefer to give second place to the blackbird after the nightingale. Perhaps this time the voice of the whitethroat was not recorded successfully, or maybe the reason is that it repeats the voices of other birds while singing and does not *create* a melody itself. Nevertheless, the blackbird that we know, which has its own style, is worthy of second place among songbirds after the nightingale. It is difficult to judge. Some people like the voice of the song thrush more than the voice of the blackbird or whitethroat. As the name says by itself, if you hear the voice of the song thrush at least once, your soul will enjoy this tune throughout the summer, until late autumn. Moreover, it will be 'a moveable feast' for you (Ernest Hemingway).

Wouldn't it be nice if we recorded the voices of Kazakh birds onto audio disc? On many CDs produced in Moscow and St Petersburg, there are bird voices recorded from the Syr Dariâ, Altaj regions and the Ile shores. We don't appreciate, or are not capable of appreciating, nature and its reserves, as other nationalities do and turn these things into a profit. In the same way, the Americans and the British got rich by selling Maṅġystau oil.

Animal voices have been used as a research method in all branches of biology for a long time. Soviet scientists once recorded the voices of birds of prey onto audio cassettes, in order to frighten flocks of starlings that flew into gardens and ate the newly growing buds on the fruit trees.

The biggest collection of 'polyphonic phonetics' in the world is located in the city of Ithaca, USA. Its founders were scientists at the Ornithology Laboratory at Cornell University.

In second place is the laboratory of the Faculty of Biology and Soil Science at Moscow University. The phonetics' collection of St Petersburg and Kiev universities is also rich. Once (in 1972) the full catalogue of recordings published in the Soviet Union was in the library of I.D. Nikolsky, entitled *The Service of the Progress of Bioacoustics*. Today, this is considered a rare book.

The singing frequency of the blackbird is described in many scientific or literary works. As we have said before, there are birds that sing more beautifully (nightingale, whitethroat), and there are birds that have a longer singing duration than the blackbird. For example, pipits reproduce 418–420 melodies in an hour and chiffchaffs sing 470 times in an hour. However, it doesn't mean that they sing better than the blackbird or their song is more pleasant. What is the reason for this? Firstly, our hero sings very melodically. Secondly, its 'unique style' differs from other birds.

So, why do birds sing in spring? Is it proper to even use the phrase 'birds sing'?

Experts who have studied the songbirds divide them into two main groups. The first reason why birds sing is as a 'call' (for example, when a male calls for a female; a female calls its chicks; chicks call their other nestlings (siblings), etc.). The second reason is to warn of a threat, as a form of self-defence, and so on. It turns out that all terms for birdsong such as *sing*, *tweet*, *chirp*, *warble*, *pipe*, *caw*, etc. are bioacoustic phenomena that derive from these two aforementioned reasons.

The time of the blackbird's song is its reunion with its mate. The other cause is when they build their nests. These days –

that is, at the end of May and the beginning of June – they sing from five until nine-thirty in the morning. Therefore, some bird lovers call them the 'forest muezzin'. Indeed, its morning song sounds at the same time as the muezzin's voice that calls for prayers, *azan*. Therefore, it is not difficult to find its nest in nearby forests. It builds its nest on the ground or on the branch of a low tree. The female stops singing during the incubation period. It is interesting when beautiful melodies, which resound in the forest every morning, suddenly stop. In order not to make its absence obvious another bird begins its song – a robin.

Blackbird

Nightingale

*I*t was 22 May. On this evening Muscovites started pouring towards the suburbs, parks, squares and woods. They wanted to listen to the nightingale's song.

Apparently, up to 5,000 nightingales are currently registered in Russia's capital city and its adjacent territories. People call the last days of May 'nightingale evenings'. All the newspapers, magazines, radio and television announce the nightingale's arrival as one of the most important events and invite everyone to listen to its song. Organizations consider this moment a significant cultural event: they allocate special vehicles to transport staff and appoint security guards. It is a good tradition to uphold.

The spring was wet in Almaty. It was cloudy throughout May. They said that in Siberia, the temperature was about 25–30°C, hot. However, in our southern city the temperature did not exceed 15–20°C. As a result, songbirds were returning late. Yes, only because of that. Therefore, the spring looked somewhat sad. If you think how brief the spring is and that it passes very quickly, you feel empty. I looked at some of our winged friends with admiration and at the same time jealousy, as they had the opportunity to move along the spring worldwide. On such sad days you wish to abandon everything and go wherever the road takes you.

At last, even if it was late, nightingales arrived. Actually, nightingales knew that they had priorities in the world; they knew that God had created them better than other birds. That was why they didn't hurry. The nightingale is appreciated more than the starling, the wagtail, the rook, the white-browed tit-warbler, the blackbird or the rock sparrow that arrive in the first deceptively warm days of spring, in March.

In recent years, we've had non-stop cold rain instead of the gentle, warm rain typical of Almaty. Eventually, these cold showers ceased, snowy rains that raged like a lake full of evil spirits from a fairy tale stopped, and everything around turned green and put on colourful overlays. When Almaty basked in the sun, and May brought balmy weather, when trees bloomed and butterflies flitted, like an honoured guest, the nightingale arrived. There is a Kazakh saying: 'There are three indefinite, vague things: a guest is indefinite; abundance is indefinite; and death is indefinite.' Was one of these indefinite things a nightingale – an honoured guest?

As well as on the outskirts of the city, there were many nightingales in Almaty itself in the late 1970s and early 1980s. In particular, nightingales were famous for their night-time

singing near the Alatau cinema, in the park where Lenin's monument was located, in the alleys along Gagarin Avenue, in Central Gorky Park, in the area which was then named 'Kompot', as well as in the Gornyj Gigant and Družba districts. The Botanic Gardens were obviously also on the list. Nightingales were breeding and used to build their nests near the campus of the Al-Farabi Kazakh National University, where Nur-Mùbárak University is now situated. Nowadays, Almaty, which was once famous for its greenness, has become a large bustling metropolis.

In the beginning, nightingales moved to the higher areas and built their nests in the highlands along Dostyk̦ and Navai Avenues. These days, they are rarely found in those areas. This bird is unable to live in the mountains, and dense forest is not its favourite habitat either. Nightingales like to inhabit scrubland or open, wooded areas. The second reason for the decreasing number of nightingales in our mountains is the increasing number of houses and building work everywhere. As Almaty grows rapidly, so the world of trees and the number of animals in and around the city decrease. What will become of them?

Goethe wrote about the Persian poet Ferdowsi: 'After he wrote the history and historical chronicles of Iran, there was nothing left for the next generation, except sharing the stories that have already been told.' It seems that after nightingale's song there will be nothing left for other birds. Nevertheless, nature has its own laws.

Some consider the blackcap the next singing bird after the nightingale. If that is the case, I believe that the blackbird claims third place. Some bird lovers say that the blackbird beats the blackcap at singing. Tastes differ. Yet the first place of the nightingale is hard to argue with. This year its song was heard for the first time last Sunday.

Its arrival is a triumph; the time it chooses to sing is also unique. At sunset, all the birds hide in their nests after singing and having fun all day. Birds rarely fly at night. At some point everything stops. In fact, one of the features that distinguishes birds from people is that they appreciate talent. When the nightingale sings, all the other birds listen silently and don't interrupt, as if by their silence, they praise its great gift. However, the nightingale doesn't immediately come 'on the scene'.

The tree leaves applaud the nightingale continuously as if inviting its lovely song. Imagine a sudden flash of lightning in a dark moonless sky, or suppose, out of nowhere, you stumble upon an old friend who had been missing for many years. You feel the same excitement when hearing the nightingale's song. When you are walking, preoccupied with your everyday problems, you suddenly freeze on hearing a beautiful song among thick branches. The feeling is as if someone had scattered a handful of white coral beads under your feet: it is a pity to step on them, but you have no power to pick them up, as if you were jealous of yourself. Oh, God! This is one of the most precious moments in life …

For Kazakhs, 'It is better to see it once than to hear it a hundred times', as the saying goes. So at least once in our life we would like to see the owner of this magical sound. We would be greatly mistaken if we hoped to realize our goal immediately. This bird is seen very seldom. If you notice its nest by chance, it is better to walk past. As soon as this bird notices someone who has seen its nest, it will transfer the nest to another place, or it leaves the nest forever. The nightingale is not a naive or gluttonous bird that can be lured with food. Discussion about its character is another matter.

Sometimes we call a rose a 'red flower'. It appears that the rose was the most valuable flower of the ancient tribes that inhabited Altaj 4,000 years BC. Most of the silver coins found in ancient tombs were decorated with these flowers. The rose originated in Asia. Herodotus (fifth century BC), in his book *History*, mentioned the roses growing in Midas, the King of Macedonia's, garden. Later, the rose conquered the Roman Empire and then the whole of Europe. Today there are 25,000 varieties of these flowers. This fact might be true. However, the flower found in the Altaj excavations looked more like a flower that Southern Kazakhs, Uzbeks and Uighurs call 'red flower' than the rose as we know it today. (It is told in one of the legends that Turpan, the Province of Kashgar, is the birthplace of the 'red flower'.) There are no thorns on the 'red flower', which grows thick, like lilac. This is not its major characteristic though. Its main feature is unfolded in the legend about the nightingale told in Eastern countries.

Red Flower was the beautiful, moon-faced daughter of an ancient king. She was so guileless that no one ever saw her face; she never cried or was upset. People believed that the old expression, 'At twelve not one of her flowers had opened up', denoting ideal purity, referred to this girl. Days and months passed and the little girl grew into a wonderful lady. At the same time, their rich neighbour had a son named Nightingale. He was very handsome like the Prophet Yusuf himself. He didn't pay attention to any of the girls who were ready to sweep his road with their hair and wash it with their teardrops. The prince wrote poetry. Why did he write lyrical poems about love all the time? One day his teacher said to him: 'My son, don't play with the words. Words are sacred.' The student did not listen to him and continued writing love poetry.

One day after Friday prayer, he noticed Red Flower walking on the corner of the street. She glanced back at him for a split second, and he fell deeply in love with her. The prince was at a loss – he could not eat and sleep eluded him. He kept thinking about red flower and writing poems about her and lost his peace entirely. Seeing his desperate mood, the girl's sisters-in-law said: 'Take pity on poor Nightingale. He is unhappy because of you. Let him see you at least once.' The girl agreed, but did not raise her veil. The prince lost his strength even more.

> Whether it was in Sham, Egypt or Bagdad,
> a man wooed like a nightingale at night.
> He was like a tumbleweed driven by the wind,
> and realized that love was a heavy plight.
>
> Whether he was a madman or a sage,
> a loving soul and longing heart are inconsolable.
> The whole night Nightingale sang,
> Then in the dawn, he wore himself out.
>
> Then in the dawn, he wore himself out and.
> A loving soul and longing heart are inconsolable.
> At that time, his Red Flower showed up
> and kissed the face of the sleeping Nightingale.

According to the legend, what we know as the nightingale's song is the song of this madly-in-love prince and is dedicated to his beloved. Indeed, the 'red flower' (another distinctive feature of other types of roses) opens its petals in the morning, and closes them in the evening. During that time, the nightingale doesn't sing, but goes into a deep sleep. It is difficult to say that it does not sing in the daytime. Sometimes on clear days, you can hear its singing. But when other birds start singing, competing with each other, the nightingale stops singing. Perhaps this noble bird respects its own talent.

According to modern ornithologists, it is the male nightingale that sings, whereas the female lays eggs. When it is time to incubate the eggs, the male nightingale stops singing so as to not to attract the attention of people and animals passing by. In order to preserve its chicks, it is ready to sacrifice its art.

By the way, the tale of Nightingale and Red Flower mentioned above has no happy ending. Its last lines are verses of sorrow of the hopeless Nightingale.

Since ancient times, the nightingale has been considered the best of songbirds. If we apply Darwin's ideas, the nightingale's song and its melodious voice might have made the first human come out of their cave, listen to its beautiful songs and look around with admiration. When we contemplate birds, we claim that birds motivated people to dream of flying and freedom, to strive for the most advanced social formations. Okay! Moreover, if we agree with Dostoevsky's assumption, 'Beauty saves the world', why shouldn't we agree with the speculation that one of the first beautiful things that mankind saw, felt, perceived or understood was the song of the nightingale?

Anyway, seven billion people living on the earth agree that the nightingale is the best singer in the world. In any folk literature there are images of the nightingale, and every nation compares their best singer's voice with that of the nightingale. The famous Kazakh singer Bibigùl Tòlegenova brilliantly performs a popular song 'Bulbul' ('Nightingale'), composed by the Soviet composer Latif Hamidi. The Tatars call this bird *sanduġaš*. It is also a bird that is most celebrated in Tatar folk songs.

Sanduġaš, sanduġaš,
You'll leave, but I will stay.

This sad song brings the listener out in goosebumps. Yes, the nightingale is a seasonal bird. In spite of its small size (almost the same as the starling), the nightingale migrates to southern and eastern Africa and winters in their tropical forests, which is incredible. Think how great the distance is between Africa and Kazakhstan.

In the Kazakh song 'Bu̇lbu̇lym' ('My nightingale') it states:

When you sing, just sing like me, softly,

into the ears of my dear one.

When I sing close to your auyl,

how do you dare to sleep?

My nightingale,

a single day spent around you

is worth a thousand days without you.

The nightingale starts its song softly. It is also true that if the song is good, the impression is as if you hear it in your ears, as denoted in the lines above. The line 'How do you dare to sleep?' hints at the fact that the nightingale usually sings at night. Lukman Hakim compared his good days to the experience of a great year, and so does the song. Beautiful songs prolong a person's life. The lines from the folk song tell us this.

Actually, as any child has a father, so any folk song has its author. In my opinion, the creator of the song might have listened to a nightingale's song too often, or written the lines after he had heard the bird's song. There is a connection between the melody of a song and its lyrics. Moreover, listening to a nightingale is an art. We Kazakhs are brought up to value and respect a person's and a bird's freedom. I haven't heard of a Kazakh man who breeds nightingales. Although it is hard to keep nightingales as pets, in neighbouring countries there are people who do. It is difficult because, firstly, the nightingale feeds mainly on small insects. Where do you find worms and ants in autumn or winter? Secondly, if a nightingale is kept in a cage, it does not sing and may die from depression.

Another Kazakh song describes a singer's voice with the simile, 'he sang like a nightingale … varying his voice in forty pitches'. Where do the 'forty pitches' originate from? Ornithologists who study bioacoustics reveal that nightingales can vary their voice in different tones, and some may accomplish forty different tones, performing a wide repertoire of 250 whistles, trills and buzzes. During the tsarist regime in Russia, people used to pay 2,000 roubles for the most vocally accomplished nightingales. The Russian ornithologist and forester Dmitry Kaigorodov, in his book *Tsarstvo Pernatyh* (*In the Realm of Birds*), described a nightingale that could sing in twelve pitches at the Forestry Institute of Saint Petersburg.

In fact, Turgenev's story 'O Solovyah' ('About Nightingales') is of great significance among the literary works dedicated to nightingales. The story is actually narrated by a bird hunter, Afanasy Alifanov. The narrator varies his story by using the colloquial dialects of the common villagers. I will try to translate a paragraph or two.

Nightingales in Kursk were of high esteem until recently. Nowadays, people love listening to nightingales found near the city of Berdychiv, but 15 *versts* from there is the Treyatsky Grove, and the nightingales there are the best. It is best to catch them at the beginning of May …

Okay, the nightingale sings this way. It begins gently with *twee-weet*, then *took*! The whole song sequence is called a 'riff'; its '*took*' element, 'flapping'. Then it sings again – *twee-weet … took! took*! It *flaps* twice, tweets the third time. When it reaches the third sequence, the miracle begins, so it is difficult to describe such an exultation, as you're swept off your feet.

You might know about Bilal ibn Rabah, the trusted muezzin of the Prophet Muhammad. His voice was reportedly so deep, melodious and resonant that passing caravans stopped to listen to his singing. People thought that the person to whom the Creator could grant such a voice must be handsome. Some people claimed that Bilal was more of an athletic and strong man than a handsome one. People who were arguing this point came to the Prophet and a man with a dark brown complexion and curly, bushy hair greeted them. It was Bilal. In some Eastern folk literature, there is a hidden comparison of the voice of the nightingale with Bilal's voice. The nightingale is not a beautiful bird and does not differ much from a tit, only its tail is a bit longer. In spite of this, it sings brilliantly.

Thus, Ivan Turgenev investigated the nightingale so thoroughly that he was aware of where they existed, which forests they dwelt in and when to tame them. Why shouldn't we admire the knowledge of the writer, the author of *Fathers and Sons, Rudin, Asya* and *Home of the Gentry*, who created such fine works of literature and knew so much about his land, its rivers, even its little birds? Furthermore, in his aforementioned story he describes the ways of catching birds and the differences between nightingales with regard to their age and voice.

I had a friend who loved nightingales. He was short-sighted. Once he heard a nightingale singing and immediately fell in love with the bird and nearly lost consciousness … In the end, when he had almost caught the bird, it accidentally escaped his hands. My friend swore that he felt as if someone had pulled the bird out of his hands when he had been trying to catch it. Well, you can never tell. He tried to catch the bird again, but felt humbled and insecure, and fell silent. Ten days later, he tried to track that bird again. And what do you think? The nightingale didn't make a sound. It disappeared. My friend almost lost his mind. I dragged him home with great difficulty. He threw his hat on the ground and started to beat himself up. Then he stopped and shouted: 'Dig the earth. I want the earth to open up its mouth and die. I'm such an idiot, blind and awkward!' Such was the story of the nightingale and the woe it caused my friend.

According to my observations, the nightingale starts its song slowly. '*Qweet-qweet, ti-yu-tiyu-tiyu*' it sings and attracts your attention. Two sequences are over. Then it sings '*ti-plew, tiplew, tiplew*'. When the melody rises, your heart jumps. Then after it begins its fourth sequence its voice is now free to gallop like an unbroken stallion over the wide steppes, as

The Birds Are Our Friends

if it's hurtling along: '*klug-klug, klug-klug*'. Then it pulls up the reins. '*Trrr, tse-tse-tse*': the bird slows down. Next, the nightingale sings as if in Sùgir's *šertpe kùjs*, '*trey, trey, trey, trey, chu-chu-chu, chuvi-chuves*' and comes to a halt.[116]

It is ridiculous attempting to note the nightingale's song on paper. We just want to share what we know and have heard about this bird. Anyway, there are some things that are out of reach.

---

116 Sùgir Aliuly (1882–1961) was a composer and musician. He is considered one of the most prominent representatives of the *šertpe kùj* tradition: melodic and lyrical tunes, with gentle associations, as opposed to dramatic tunes of *tôkpe kùj* which have aggressive associations.

Common Mynah

S tories about the damage invasive birds cause to the environment and agricultural fields are reprinted periodically in newspapers, and they have an effect on me, just like the onset of stormy cold winds. In particular, if you listen to experts in the field of agriculture, for instance, Chinese farmers who exterminated all sparrows in the second half of the previous century, they would tell you the reasons why they had done so. Another experience of terminating invasive species of birds was heard from some former Soviet countries and their examples of how they had dealt with such birds.

If we begin with ourselves, there was time in Kazakhstan when, if a person killed a hawk, known as 'a winged wolf', and handed it over to the authorities, that person would have received ten roubles as a reward. Many writers, including Maksim Zverev and some ecologists, opposed that bloody war against birds and stopped the campaign. Our attitudes to birds haven't changed since then. If we hear the voice of a little owl, we predict it to foretell something bad. If we notice a black-billed magpie we scare it by throwing a stone at it, and we believe that the common cuckoo is the worst bird in the world who doesn't care for its own chick.

There is a black-headed, dark blue bird that looks like a crow. It is called *rozoviy skvorets* (rosy starling) in Russian, and is also known as *alatorǧaj* (motley starling) in the south of Kazakhstan. This bird is the main predator of locusts. The Russian naturalist and writer Pyotr Manteuffel described the rosy starlings and their vanquishment of the dark cloudy army of locusts as if he were writing a war novel. However, some Mediterranean peoples, including our Turkish brothers, curse these birds as a 'two-faced, sinful' bird. Some Eastern poets also described these birds in negative terms.

A disguised Khannas is next to a man.[117]
It's not on a horse nor on foot.
You looked like an angel on May Day,
But became evil in July, you, scum!

---

117 Khannas is a demon mentioned in the Qur'an, Verses 114: 1–6

The point was probably about crops and the birds' damage to the harvest.

The Uzbekistan Government adopted a plan in 2003 to exterminate 952,000 Indian mynahs, or common, declaring them to be one of the world's most invasive species, with the aim of controlling the number of birds, and they appointed the Uzbekohotrybolovsouz (the Union of Hunters and Fishers of the Uzbek Soviet Socialist Republic) to put that plan into action. To motivate the hunters, they agreed to give a bullet for every two birds killed, and a hunting permit for every 500 birds killed.

The Israeli Government also considered the rising number of these birds in their country as a 'bio-aggression' on the land. Therefore, the mynah was put on the 'black list'. How did this bird appear in the land of the Prophet Moses (peace be upon him), when and why? Israeli scientists claimed:

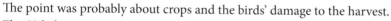

> It all started when Jews moved from South-East Asia and Muslim countries. They brought with them these mynah birds. For some reason, they let these birds out. As a result, Israel became a homeland for the common mynah, which damaged both the economy and ecology of the country.

Until recently, the mynah had not been a common bird in Kazakhstan either. But it's not the only invasive bird in the world that we should be aware of. If an intrusive bird from New Zealand – the kea, also called a 'sheep killer' – crossed our borders, it would be an immediate disaster for the whole country. As keas breed in high mountainous lands, the

Alatau and Altaj, Kôkšetau and Ķaratau Mountains would be convenient habitats for them. According to BBC documentaries about animals, the kea not only harms insects and plants, but is also able to destroy car tyres and any other objects made from rubber, as well as rubbish bins' lids, and linen and blankets hung out to dry. They use their crossed beaks and peck at sheep grazing peacefully in the pastures.

Initially, people did not notice them, as they took them for a type of parrot, but later they killed 29,000 keas. However, the keas did not reduce in number. When they sensed someone coming, they would roll stones down the mountains to defend themselves. Therefore, if we are not careful and alert, our mountains could become a home for keas, rather than 'a homeland for snowcocks', as a Kazakh folk song declares.

Did we ever imagine that these Indian mynahs would drive our local starlings to extinction, who had lived along the steppes and in Kazakh neighbourhoods for many years? Starlings are also like the Kazakhs – naive and humble creatures. If you are humble and naive you will not live in safety.

Eventually, the common mynah was put on the black list, becoming an 'unpleasant' bird in Uzbek and Israeli books. In ornithology it is called a mynah, but in Kazakh it is known as the 'yellow-winged starling', 'Afghan starling' or 'Indian starling'. As it is an invasive species, it does not have an established name in Kazakh. It never lived in Kazakh lands before. First, it arrived on the Uzbek and Turkmen borders from Afghanistan in 1912. People on the borders of Termez tried to scare the bird away, but it didn't go. Instead, over time, it entered the inner parts of the land.

It was seen on the Kazakh borders in the 1960s, on the edges of the Ķazyġürt Mountains. Today, you can encounter the common mynah in every part of Kazakhstan.

In the language of science, the mynah is a synanthropic bird. This means that the bird thrives in urban and suburban environments. You won't find it in the vacant steppes.

It is a funny bird. Its tail is short, but its head is big. Its voice is not pleasant to listen to. Nevertheless, some people appreciate its singing and compare it to the nightingale. For instance, the Ķajnar publishing house printed a book edited by I.A. Yundin in 1973, entitled *Zoopark doma* (*Zoo in the House*), a collection of stories about the animal world, in which one author wrote:

> The mynah's voice is melodious. It is expert at imitating other other birds' voices; it may repeat single words, even say a sentence. Our recently tamed mynah has become a favourite family pet. We have named it Grishka. It has learned about fifteen words. When you ask, 'Who are you?' it answers, 'I am Grishka' in the voice of a man. When asked, 'Grishka, tell me how a dog barks', it answers with a dog's bark.

If mynahs are domesticated, they may live up to 40–50 years. In Isfahan, in Iran, a Persian Kasko (a parrot) learned about 180 words in Persian and Arabic. It even recited Qur'anic *surahs* and names of the Muslim martyrs from memory. Another parrot, Alex, was able to say over 100 English words. It's known that some tame doves can differentiate certain letters. The mynah can do all of this. Therefore, the mynah is a special bird.

Moscow ornithologists are among those who are often delighted by the mynah and its abilities. Newspapers in Moscow print paid advertisements for people who wish to buy mynah birds or exchange them for nightingales, parrots or even song thrushes. Indeed,

The Birds Are Our Friends

Russian bird lovers exhibit rather surprising behaviour. The nineteenth-century Russian poet Fyodr Tyutchev was right when he declared, 'You cannot grasp Russia with your mind.'

There has been a trend since the time of Alexander the Great to keep singing birds in cages. Onesicritus, a Greek writer who accompanied Alexander the Great's army, gifted him parrots brought from India. The king, they say, accepted them, although prior to this, he had denied receiving gifts, and was famous for his righteousness. It is said that bribery originates from that time. As they say, 'Bad habits live long.' Eastern poets wrote the following:

Once upon a time a magpie was a loyal bird,

and once it ate dung, it ate and ate,

until the dung replaced its brain.[118]

As for common mynahs, they live in groups, are well organized and find their food easily. They wake up early and sleep late. They are industrious. Is this a result of their migration overseas? Even the birds that migrate and discover new places and lands are organized and live in groups. As Kazakhs used to say, 'The minority descend from the same forebear.'

Common mynahs are not fussy eaters; they can feed on rubbish. Usually, we divide birds into plant eaters and insect eaters, but the mynah is omnivorous. Their Latin name given by biologists means 'locust eater', although scientists point out that they are also fruit and plant eaters. One mynah bird eats 150,000 locusts in a season. It eats only the head and breast, and cuts the other parts, such as legs and wings, into pieces. Common mynahs also exterminate other harmful insects. There aren't many helpful birds for agriculture like them.

Their beaks are adapted to crunch sunflower seeds, beans and nuts. The mynah's beak is not oval like the hawfinch, but is very strong and tough. A crow puts a walnut into its beak, then rises high into the sky and drops it onto stone. If the walnut does not break, it repeats the action, many times. We have heard stories of crows competing for the broken pieces of walnut on the ground. And many consider crows clever birds.

Oxford University professors tested two crows, Betty and Abel, to check their mental abilities. They placed some food in a bucket, which they then put inside a tube-shaped container, and set it before them. Does this experiment remind us of an ancient Kazakh fairy tale, when a fox was given food in a vase and a crane was given water on a plate? So, what did the crows do? Betty started to bend a piece of metal like a fork, and then began to pull the food from the bottom of the bucket. The second crow did the same.

The common mynah seems even smarter than a crow. This bird doesn't mess around with the walnuts by flying into the sky and throwing to the ground to crack them open. It just rolls them onto the asphalt or throws them under passing cars. It also throws animal bones discovered in rubbish onto the asphalt, and waits until a car runs over them. As you see, they are birds that may go as far as cracking bones to feed themselves. We know if there is a chance, they will eat meat.

Once we noticed a mynah playing with a tin. It was a tin of canned fish. The bird turned it back and forth, but it couldn't find anything in it. Throwing the tin aside, it went away.

---

118 The magpie is considered an insatiable bird by Kazakhs, and people susceptible to bribery are compared to magpies.

After that, another bird flew down and began to turn the tin over again. It was cleverer than the first bird. Moving the tin with its beak, the mynah threw it into a puddle. After a while, pulling the tin out of the puddle, the bird began shaking it. It was clear that it had prepared some 'broth' after softening the hardened meat inside the tin. How did this bird figure that? At this point, the first bird, which had left the tin, flew back. It began fighting with the second bird, because the tin had been its discovery. They started a real fight. Other birds gathered around them, clamouring.

At this moment, another yellow-beaked, yellow-legged bird arrived that must have been the leader of this flock. It drove off the fighting birds. After trying the broth in the tin, this bird gave it to the second 'warrior' in recognition of the latter's work, then it flew away. No one dared to touch this food after that.

In fact, mynahs are terrifying fighters. They are aggressive, but brave as well. If we talk of courage, scientists wrote that in previous years flocks of crows attacked rabbits. Another magazine published how hungry crows attacked a puppy. But when common mynahs fight for food, they even drive off the crows. Even the magpie leaves its carrion and flies away when they see mynahs. Their long legs seem to be designed to fight.

It does not allow any bird from outside to join their flock. It frightens its opponents with its rather unpleasant voice. We often hear that the common mynah is the reason for the starling's disappearance from our lands. Let science figure it out. Although the starling hasn't disappeared altogether from our localities, its numbers have reduced significantly.

Is there a more insatiable bird than the mynah? If you watch it from afar, it seems like this bird doesn't do anything except look for food. It doesn't have a break from this pursuit. Scientists assume that golden eagles can endure starvation for 21 days, owls for 24 days, imperial eagles for 45 days and ostriches for 60 days. Usually, singing birds do not tolerate hunger. Some species may die in two or three hours if not fed. I wonder how much patience these mynahs have. What miraculous energy, what power do they possess?

It easily enters everywhere. Recently, in one of the newspapers it was reported that a mynah flew into a house through an open window and scared all the guests. Usually Kazakhs rejoice when they see a bird that flies through a window into a house, hoping that 'an angel has come'. However, why do people run away from the mynah? Why do they hate this bird? Why is a mynah so unwelcome?

A friend of mine is a person who doesn't want to hear about harming birds. It is difficult to convince him of the mynahs' cunning, treachery and theft. Uzbeks call this bird 'thief bird'. The reason for this is the summer, which is very hot in Uzbekistan, so our brothers do not dine inside their house, but on their veranda. If you leave a table filled with unattended food, then these hungry mynahs will eat all of it in a minute. It seems they are faster than sneaky greyhounds. So, why shouldn't we call this bird a thief after that? My friend believes that people are to blame for such behaviour of this bird. He means that we think only of ourselves. The poor birds only eat leftovers.

We are not surprised by this. Some people love birds, and some people love dogs. My friend doesn't only love, but adores birds. A poet said: 'Love is so tightly blindfolded that you don't hear anything.' After this, how can you not forgive my friend for his love of birds?

If he hadn't witnessed a certain incident, then perhaps he would have continued to think as he used to. He didn't remember the exact time, but it was either when he was going to work or returning from it. As he was going along the alley, he heard the loud tweeting of a great tit. When he looked up, he noticed a mynah throwing small nestlings from a nest at

The Birds Are Our Friends

the top of a branch. Another mynah, probably its chick, began to peck at these nestlings and eat them. The poor tit was flying around and tweeting desperately.

The two mynahs didn't pay attention to it. Seeing such a cruel scene, my friend was shocked and shouted out loudly. The mynahs flew off, but landed not far away. Their yellow beaks were covered in blood. Clearly still hungry, they waited for him to leave. They were like jackals who were not afraid of an unarmed person. Once he heard from someone who had participated in the Afghan War how mynahs pecked the eyes of dead soldiers. At that time, my friend did not want to believe what he had heard, because we usually don't want to hear about bad things. That day he remembered that story. No matter how much he tried, the thoughts of soldiers and the tit's nestlings wouldn't leave him.

In a newspaper article, a famous ecologist named the common mynah as a factor affecting the decrease in Almaty fauna and flora. With regard to fauna, in recent years, crows and rooks have settled in our city. My friend noticed that common mynahs are superior to crows in a fight for food leftovers. They even expel rooks from the battlefield. City dwellers admired the great tit when it pecked at meat that they hung on the balcony. Knowing that the small defenceless bird was hungry, people tried to feed it. Today, if you do not control the food for the tits, then without knowing it, you could be feeding the mynahs.

Last summer, my friend went to his cottage in the countryside to escape from the intensive heat of the city. He hoped to read some books and have a rest for a couple of weeks in the fresh air. His cottage was located in the Medeu mountain gorge. He was pleased that the mynahs had not yet reached these high mountainous places of Almaty. He believed that the city gorge was the only place where the mynahs hadn't settled. However, on the very first night of his arrival at the cottage, he was suddenly woken up by the unpleasant voice of the bird. It was singing '*tryulyu-ryulyu*'. He could not believe his ears. When he looked out from the balcony, there was a mynah in the courtyard on the telephone pole. After some time, a second mynah flew to it with a plant in its beak. Then one of them flew towards the roof. The other one looked around as if it was guarding something. In the evening, the mynahs returned.

My friend was surprised when he saw a nest on the wooden axis of the roof of the house. Look at that! The nest was built in a narrow slot so that a man's hand couldn't reach it. How clever! The next morning, he took a stepladder out of the basement and went onto the roof. He wanted to destroy the nest, until he saw four chicks in the nest. Three of them were sleeping peacefully, the other tried to bite his hand. My friend went away. From that moment, his only problem was those birds. Sometimes, he felt like a poor man who was hiding a criminal in his house. These thoughts made him wake up in the middle of the night. After some time he calmed down and went back to sleep. The chicks grew. The parents brought food to their chicks every day.

The common mynahs were not afraid of anyone or anything. As soon as those birds got used to my friend, they stopped paying the slightest attention to him. Once he needed a stepladder and went onto the roof of the house. Suddenly one of the mynahs attacked him with its sharp claws and he could barely get out of there. After that, he was afraid to go onto the roof of his own house. He seemed to understand the poor starlings, which had gone extinct. His heart ached when he remembered how the mynah had thrown the tit's nestlings from the nest one after the other on to the ground. His blood pressure went up when he imagined the mynah pecking dead soldiers' eyes. However, he didn't dare kill the mynah's chicks or chase them away. The neighbours were surprised by his attitude. He was for them like the holy maiden in a fairy tale that warmed a poisonous snake on her chest.

Common Mynah

Some neighbours used to mock and ask him: 'How are your birds doing?' If adult mynahs used to make noise during the day, their chicks used to tweet at night. So my friend didn't have any rest at all. There was nothing he could do. On one of these restless nights, he woke up in shock. There was a deathly silence. No sound could be heard whatsoever. He didn't sleep a wink until the morning. When he climbed onto the roof, he saw an empty nest. There were no chicks. At last they've flown away, he thought. He was delighted. He carefully destroyed the nest and plastered up the gap in the roof, so that not only mynahs, but other birds could not penetrate it.

It was morning. At the top of the poplar growing in the ravine a robin was singing. It was a wonderful summer day. It seemed the starling would be back soon. Our favourite starling …

Skylark

*I*t has been more than fifty years since Kazakhs became urbanized.[119] It means that two to three generations have replaced one another. A resident of the city never pays attention to the birds that fly over their building, in their yard or at the bus stop. If asked about birds they say they don't know anything about them. Some of them may even be perplexed, surprised that there were birds in the city at all. Out of interest, I tried to ask some city dwellers what types of birds they knew in Almaty, but of those that answered the question the majority did not see or notice birds. However, those who knew about birds replied that they had often seen skylarks. What was the reason for this?

The majority of Kazakhs are aware of the skylark. There is an ancient saying: 'A fisherman rests in a storm, a gardener rests in the rain, a shepherd rests in a tomb.' Here the 'shepherd rests in a tomb' means that a herdsman herds cattle for twelve months, and it is

---

119 This is a reference to the Kazakh saying: 'In fifty years the people will change.' 'Fifty' is not used literally.

especially difficult for them in the early spring, when the grazing land is still poor and the grass is scarce, and the shepherd is exhausted from the heavy winter labour.

It is grey everywhere. The more you look at the miserable fields of early spring, the more deserted you feel. We've grown tired of freezing rain and raging steppe winds a long time ago. Everything you see around is vast and endless greyish steppe; there is nothing to feast your eyes on, or to lighten your mood. You pity the weak wormwood and bleak wheatgrass that hardly rise from the ground and look already exhausted. Suddenly, during these gloomy days, not far from you, near the wormwood growing just under your feet, you hear a very beautiful song. You are surprised, as if you'd stumbled upon an unexpected shiny object hidden under the bushes. It flies off immediately. Your weak bay horse, your dog Bajtôbet with its head down, your feeble flock of sheep that are very thin by this time, all look in the direction of the flying bird. The little bird which has appeared from nowhere soars up into the sky easily and starts its unceasing song.

It sounds as if it is saying to everyone in the grazing field, 'My dears, my brothers, I know you are exhausted from the deep winter, let me sing for you.' Its voice is so caring; a voice that shines through shifting clouds; a very kind voice; a voice that is familiar to you; and a voice that has missed you. In Kazakh, they say 'The person who uncovers *kelin*'s face becomes her favourite in-law', so the voice of the skylark draws close to everyone after such a long winter.[120]

Skylarks arrive as soon as February finishes, although there are occasionally some skylarks that stay for the winter and every one of them hurries to announce the spring. We should be grateful for such a bearer of good news! The skylark is close to Kazakh people and is our most famous, favourite bird. If by chance you live in other parts of the world or move elsewhere, you will remember the skylark's song. Maybe this is the reason why not only I, an outsider to the city, but also any modern Kazakh, a second- or third-generation city dweller, is excited on hearing the name of the skylark.

Obviously, one of the characteristic features of skylark, in addition to the fact that it rushes to our parts with the first signs of spring, is that it doesn't dwell temporarily in the steppes. The skylark doesn't abandon our lands as soon as they become inconvenient, but faces all seasonal changes, such as storm, rain, wind and heat. It is a bird that appreciates its native parts, as we Kazakhs do.

Historically, Kazakhs used to spend their time outdoors; therefore, they'd see skylarks regularly and dedicated different songs and verses to them. In any Kazakh's opinion, the skylark is a songbird. Our people appreciate the skylark's song when it sings in midair. It may sing from dawn to the evening. They say the skylark sings for about eight months of the year. Ornithologists, too, pay much attention to the skylark's singing characteristics. If you wake it accidentally during the night among the bushes, it might start singing immediately while flying away.

The lark is a solitary bird which meets its death singing. Let's talk about this. It nests and finds a mate as soon as March arrives. It is not picky when it chooses places for its nest. Usually, their nests are on the ground, where horses or cows have made prints, or in holes. The lark enlarges the area using some straw, lays some grass in its base, and then lays its eggs. Otherwise, under the wormwood shrub is enough to build a nest.

---

120 *Kelin*, daughter-in-law; according to tradition, when a bride arrives to be introduced to her future in-laws, her face is covered with a scarf. After performing *betašar* – describing every one of her future-in-laws and making her bow to them – the appointed person uncovers her face.

As the poet and military leader Mahambet Ôtemisuly declared:

> A skylark soars on the sky,
> And nests on the marshland.
> When the marshland is in flood
> The skylark faces real troubles.

The poet did not say that in vain. The poor bird is ignorant of spring storms and rain that crashes onto its fragile nest. These are unpredictable natural disasters, but it's a pity when this poor bird falls into the traps of misfortune of its own free will. Female larks incubate their eggs for about a fortnight.

In spring, all the forest animals wake up from their sleep and the steppes start blooming. Insects awake, and snakes too. They are so hungry after the long winter that they begin to lick the earth. Searching for food in vain, snakes often destroy skylark nests. First, they swallow the eggs. If there are chicks in the nest, snakes will also swallow them one by one. Cunning snakes do not eat all the eggs; usually there are 6–7 of them, but may leave one or two eggs and wait until they catch the mother bird, which whirls around the snake to save its nest. The snake lies on the ground heating its body, while the skylark attempts to chase the snake from its nest by chirping desperately. Generally it is only the male skylarks that sing. Nevertheless, that doesn't mean that the female skylark is passive and dumb. The snake does not hurry. It lies on the ground, turning from one side to the other. The bird rises up into the sky and chirps unceasingly. The snake raises its head. The bird thinks that the snake is going to leave the nest, and comes a little closer to the ground. But the snake will not leave. On the contrary, when the skylark is close enough, the snake quickly catches the bird and then finishes the rest in the nest. This must be an example of the snake's magical ability to hex its prey.

We usually think that the skylark is singing when it is chirping and hovering in the air. But it is not singing; it is crying. Whenever you meet a skylark soaring on the air and chirping, look carefully around you for any intruders that might be a danger to a skylark. Rain and storms in the spring may also be a danger and cause a reduction in skylarks. However, skylarks are not easily decreased, they say.

Ornithologists compiled statistics on the number of all the birds in the world at the end of the last century. According to that mathematical survey, the number of skylarks went up to 35 million and their population took third place among the world's birds. In an ancient Kazakh song, there are lines that wish people 'to become as many as skylarks and have many children'. Skylarks can have several broods in a single season. It means Kazakhs knew that skylarks reproduce quickly. In literature, skylarks are famous for their singing in the springtime. In fact, they are not singing, they are calling for a partner to mate with. There is a Kazakh folk song called 'Bulbul torġaj' ('A Nightingale Skylark'). Actually, the difference between a nightingale and skylark is enormous. The refrain of the song: 'Oh singing bird, you soar up in the sky, unable to land …' is a dedication to the behaviour of the skylark. In all Kazakh folk songs, the skylark is described as a treasured and gentle bird that should be cherished. The Kazakh folk composer Žaâu Musa and his famous song about a skylark make anyone pity this defenceless bird. Poet and composer Kenen Aʻzirbajuly also sang about the skylark in a similar manner: 'Skylark, you sing soaring up in the sky, and I'm like you, hungry and bereaved.'

From school textbooks, we are familiar with Sábit Dônenetaev's verses: 'Skylark was enraged by a hawk, and couldn't find peace in the wide world.' The lines indeed describe the pitiful share of the lark. Among contemporary Kazakh poets, Esenbaj Dùjsenbajuly wrote often and masterfully about the skylark. His nickname was also 'Boztorǵaj Balyķšin' ('Skylark Fisherman'). I guess it is not by chance the literary scholar Rymǵali Nurǵaliev and the talented writer Muhtar Maǵauin considered Dùjsenbajuly's collection of poetry, *Bozala Taŋ Boztorǵaj* (*Light Dawn Skylark*), one of the most significant books on poetry.

The skylark does not need much water. During forty or sometimes sixty days of heat in the Myrzašôl region, that Kazakhs describe as 'the heat that will melt the crow's brain', larks may live by drinking warm water from the ditches of cotton fields, and frolic in the burning sand; in the pleasant summers of the Mojynķum area they may live peacefully alongside grazing sheep. During scorching summers in the Maŋġystau and Ùstirt regions, one might see larks drinking drops of rain in potholes around tombs and gravestones. Whenever and wherever I see these humble little birds enduring the inclement conditions of the steppes alongside Kazakhs, I adore their big hearts. If we use the poet Tumanbaj Moldaǵaliev's lines from his verse, 'Only us and wormwood may endure the steppes, my boy.'

Radlov translated the Kyrgyz long poem 'Boztorǵaj' ('Skylark') into German in the 1870s, and published it in Leipzig. In the Introduction to the book he wrote, 'the Kyrgyz, instead of narrating from memory as they usually do, perform this poem looking at papers, and I assume therefore, that it was written by mullahs.'

The text goes as follows: There was a poor fisherman at the time of Hazrat Ali (a son-in-law and successor of the Prophet Muhammad). He could catch only one fish a day. However, he and his wife were satisfied with this endowment. As the saying goes, 'If you are unlucky, even the leaven will go off.' Once, he couldn't find any fish and went to ask for help from an unbeliever who lived next door. The man said to him: 'I will feed you, but every day you will give me a bar of gold for this.' The fisherman didn't know what to do. Then he went to the Prophet Muhammad (peace be upon him) and told him what had happened. After listening to him the Prophet Muhammad (peace be upon him) called for Hazrat Ali and said, 'Help him.'

After a while, so as not to humiliate this poor Muslim before the unbeliever, Hazrat Ali decided to leave his sons Asan and Ùsen (Hasan, Husain) in lieu of the debt and set off. On the way, he saw an old grave. There was a skylark on top of the grave. When he caught the bird to take it for his children, the skylark flew high, taking Hazrat Ali with it. People were surprised by the power of the small bird, and gazed after them until Hazrat Ali disappeared from sight. They flew far beyond the desert and the high mountains.

An old woman they met on their way told them, 'Disbelievers live in these places. Tomorrow all the men will come to the meeting. They will test their knowledge.' After praying to Allah, Hazrat Ali also went to the meeting. The sage of that place told him: 'I see you are a guest who has come from a distant country. This is a very difficult competition. You will be asked ten questions. If God helps, you will answer the questions correctly. And if not, you will be beheaded.'

Indeed, God helped him, Hazrat Ali answered all of the questions, giving the correct answers and defeating the sage. The sage listened to Hazrat Ali's logic and gave in. Soon he realized that Hazrat Ali's insight was based on the divine power of Islam and he and his people joined the ranks of Muslims. They acknowledged that there is no God but Allah; and the Holy Qur'an is a book revealed to the Prophet Muhammad. Hazrat Ali was given a lot of gold for his clear-sightedness. However, he did not spend a penny, but paid that Muslim fisherman's debt and got his sons back. Owing to the skylark, Hazrat Ali achieved his goal.

Here is a short summary of another tale. The cat is the only animal which isn't mentioned in the sacred books, namely, in the Bible. In contrast, one of the most famous birds about which many have spoken is the skylark. Since ancient times, in different countries, plants, animals and birds were used not only as food, but also as medicine. For instance, a person with leukaemia was given a white pigeon's blood; a child with whooping cough was given rock pigeon's blood; those who had a runny nose ate the gallbladder of the coot; and in addition, those who suffered from epilepsy were given snowcock meat.

It is not a sin to kill a bird to use it for medical treatment. However, we cannot touch the skylark and use it for any purpose, because it is a sacred bird. In Belorussia, anyone who sees the skylark first in early spring and speaks about it is given a loaf of bread as a reward. Slavic people also call this bird 'a heaven bell'. Mongols considered this bird a symbol of light and flame. The Ukrainians revered it as a bird through whom people could talk to God, and which spun an inconspicuous silver weft between the sky and the earth. They also predicted that if someone saw a skylark in their dream, they would be very rich. The Germans respected this bird so much that it was a sin to point at this bird with your finger. If you pointed at it accidentally, then a whitlow infection would appear under your fingernail. If someone killed a skylark, then one day that person would be struck by lightning. The British, they say, believed that the soul of the dead turned into a skylark. Probably the spring weather forecast came from the Europeans watching the skylark: if the skylark sang tirelessly during the day, the weather would be fine the next day; if it snowed in spring, but the skylark sang, it would soon get warmer.

As mentioned above, another characteristic of the skylark is that it doesn't take off gradually, but soars straight up to great heights. This feature usually brings trouble. For example, there are people who keep birds at home in the cities. There are bird catchers that work according to the pet shops' orders. As soon as they catch a skylark, they immediately enclose it in a dark cage. In the evening, they cover the cage with a cloth, and in the morning, they remove this cloth. At this time, this bird habitually tries to soar up, but this attempt doesn't work, so it hits its head on the cage, falls down and loses the ability to sing. If the skylark doesn't sing, those who search for it often leave it in the street since such a skylark would be useless for them. The defenceless bird can be eaten by cats or dogs. Many bird lovers from the cities don't like it when the skylark wallows on the ground. You have probably seen skylarks 'bathing' in sand, covering themselves with it during the heat of July. As a result, skylarks look for sand to bury themselves under, and make a mess in cosy city apartments. This is also why poultrymen are not usually fond of them.

According to scientific data, humanity over the past 4,000 years hasn't been able to domesticate any new animals and add them to the list of pets. Therefore, today's pets are those that our ancestors managed to domesticate 4,000 years ago. You and I are only consumers. I believe that the skylark, especially the crested lark, used to be sought after and domesticated by Kazakh children. In one of the versions of the lyric and epical poem 'Ķozy Kôrpeš – Baân Suĺu', written by the Kazakh poet Šože (1808–95), a bird is mentioned that belonged to Baân. This bird was not a swan, a falcon, a nightingale, a parrot or a turtle dove, nor any other songbird. It was a skylark. This version of the poem was published in 2005, in a book called 'Ķozy Kôrpeš – Baân Suĺu' *Žyrynyŋ Nuṡḳalary* (*Versions of the Poem* 'Ķozy Kôrpeš – Baân Suĺu'), edited by the highly regarded folklorist, Professor Suĺtanġali Sadyrbaev. Undoubtedly, this book is of great value for our culture. A reader may be introduced to many versions of the poem that they have never read before. Let's give an example from the work:

One day, Ķozy was grazing livestock in the pasture and Baân was at home. The sky-lark was their messenger. With the help of the skylark, the sweethearts corresponded their cherished feelings. Once Baân sent her bird off with a note and was waiting for a reply from Ķozy. When the skylark nearly reached the borders of the *auyl*, forty-one hawks attacked it on its way.

Having stolen Baân's silk coat, her sister-in-law was milking the cow. The skylark, con-fused and disheveled from the struggle against hawks, mistook her for Baân. The ill-inten-tioned sister-in-law caught the bird with the note once it landed in her hand.

Thus, when the bird did not return, Baân asked her sister-in-law about it. The latter was against Baân's match with Ķozy. She tried to put the girl off the idea of escaping with Ķozy, trying to convince her that kith and kin would blame her. Nevertheless, Baân cared only about Ķozy and nobody else. She didn't listen to her sister-in-law and waited patiently for her skylark to bring good news from her lover. The bird was still missing. Having felt her sister-in-law might have caused trouble, she asked her relentlessly; 'Have you seen my sky-lark?' When Baân's sister-in-law couldn't find out anything from the skylark about Ķozy, she killed it. Baân, who had no idea about this malevolence, begged her sister-in-law, pleading, 'Please give me back my skylark.'

Much attention was focused on Baân's skylark in the poem. Even if the skylark being a messenger wasn't described in detail, it is still clear that the skylark was a pet bird. This bird could recognize Baân by her clothes. Indeed, the skylark is a gregarious bird that is close to people, like the dove which saved the Prophet Noah's Ark from the flood mentioned in the Bible. This description was found in Muķan Mašanov's version of the poem that was includ-ed in the above-mentioned book, as well as in the version published in 1894, in Kazan. The last version ends as the following:

ozy and Baân are buried together,
their tomb is in Aâgôz steppes.
Nobody knows whether to believe the legend or not,
that 'their lark chirps and circles the sky above their tomb'.

Ukrainians call this bird 'neighbour'. The reason is that the skylark easily gets used to people. If a sparrowhawk or a shikra follows it, the bird hides right in a man's body. It also hides under a snowdrift in winter and won't come out when it is afraid of birds of prey. This is its only similarity to the northern partridge, which can also sleep under a snowdrift.

There are many types of skylark. We are talking about the common lark that lives in the Kazakh steppes. They are all similar and look alike. Only the black lark differs from them. Although we call this bird *ķaratorġaj* (starling), it shouldn't be confused with the common starling. This species of the lark mainly inhabits the steppe areas of Kazakhstan. The writer and naturalist Boris Shcherbakov, who lives in Ôskemen, wrote a wonderful article about

The Birds Are Our Friends

this bird. He could easily identify the characteristics of the larks that lived in the town of Zajsan, in eastern Kazakhstan. The article is a good read.

An outstanding ornithologist, L.B. Beme, once came to Kazakhstan and lived in Ķaraġandy in 1938–46. In his memoirs, he wrote:

> It was 2 March, 1945, 8 o'clock in the morning. The temperature was 32 degrees below zero in Arķa! It was snowing and there was a blizzard. Thinking about nothing on a road near Ķaraġandy city, I was surprised to see Kazakh black larks playing with each other, … Sometimes they even sang as if it was spring.

The poet Olžas Sùlejmenov named his poem 'Chernyi Zhavoronok' ('The Black Lark') and dedicated it to Eduard Bagritsky.[121] This black lark is also a steppe bird; to be more precise, a bird that inhabits the sacred Torġaj region. You may understand the poet who says:

The lark in the sky, under a vast cloud
sings its songs about native land in silence.

Other lines from this poem declare:

It was silent, my black lark,
Oh, silence –
This is also a voice.

These lines can be interpreted as revealing the image of larks as native birds of the Kazakh steppes.

Usually, Kazakhs turn their most precious words into poetry. In some of these ancient words, our ancestors were longing for a time of prosperity and peace, 'when the lark will nest on a sheep's back'. When will this time come? People who have a bird such as a skylark cannot be discontented, I say.

Our story about the skylark that shares the grief and joy of the Kazakhs and dwells together with them comes to an end. It is impossible to cover everything about this magnificent bird in a single essay. If something has not been covered, then with God's help, we will talk about it next time.

---

121 Olžas Sùlejmenov (*b.*1936) is a Soviet and Kazakh poet, linguist, politician and Soviet anti-nuclear activist; Eduard Bagritsky (1895–1934) was a Soviet poet of the Constructivist School.

Shelducks

hich bird do we call *itala ķaz* (literally, 'dog-piebald goose'), the 'common shelduck', in the Kazakh language?

If you search for information about this bird in various reference sources, you won't find its name in the list of geese. The reason for this could be that Kazakhs regard this bird as a goose, but modern science mocks this and asserts, 'This is not a goose, but a duck.' We agree with this assertion wholeheartedly. Who knows; the bird that we call a goose, based on its shape, could be indeed a duck. It seems while creating it, the Almighty had second thoughts as to whether to make the bird a goose or a duck.

Indeed, what is the difference between ducks and geese? Usually, the most obvious is that a goose is larger than a duck. But is this the only difference between them?

As we have mentioned before, the names for birds are not only given with respect to their colour and appearance. Names depend on birds' shapes and forms, voice, characteristic features, origins and habitat. If you consult any dictionary, you will see that the name of the common shelduck in Kazakh (dog-piebald goose) is given due to its colour. For instance, some Turkic-speaking countries call it the 'piebald goose'. When we translate its name from other languages, we obtain such names as piebald goose (*ala ķaz*), dark-pied goose (*ķarala ķaz*) or variegated goose (*šubar ala ķaz*).

In recent years, the number of people claiming to have seen the common shelduck in its natural habitat has decreased. In fact, wherever we go, we are used to asking about birds to get more information about them. Unfortunately, we haven't received a complete answer to our questions in this regard for almost a decade. Older people can't add anything, except, 'We used to see them in the meadows when we were children.' As for young people, especially modern youth, nothing is interesting. Why would they think about geese when they are concerned only with how to make ends meet? The third group of people confuses the common shelduck (*itala ķaz*) with the ruddy shelduck (*sarala ķaz*).

What is a ruddy shelduck then? We'll tell you about it later. Since childhood, Kazakhs have heard this folk song; 'A ruddy shelduck flies in the sky. Will a man be happy if he doesn't meet his love?' The name of this bird is not shown in the list of geese. When we talk about geese, first a greylag goose (*ķonyr ķaz*) comes to mind. Anyone who has heard

Ašimtaj's *kùj* 'Konyr kaz' ('A Greylag Goose') at least once, will never forget it.[122] Biržan Sal himself sang 'Biržan sings like a greylag goose'.[123] There is another folk song:

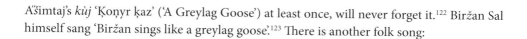

Greylag geese are flying along the lake,
As if creating patterns from melodies,
If you sing, sing like a greylag goose.
Lift your spirits and fly high in the sky ...

And it goes on to say:

---

122 Ašimtaj Karymsakuly (1820–1918) was a Kazakh composer of traditional music and the author of famous *kùjs,* traditional tunes.

123 Biržan Sal Kožaġululy (1837–97) was a famous Kazakh composer, singer and poet.

Greylag geese are singing along the lake,
and the steppe is enjoying their melodious voice.

These greylag geese that share the steppes with us seem to be closer to Kazakhs than other types of birds. The swan is so rare that we hardly see it, there are even fewer eagles, the crane is not so popular and the nightingale is such a short-term guest that we don't even notice when it arrives and when it flies away. As for the greylag, it is always near us, close to us. These birds are like Kazakh people: they move unhurriedly, swim slowly and fly away very late. It is very trusting, as we are. Apart from falling prey to experienced hunters, it even may fall into snares made by children. Are there any lakes between Altaj, which draws the eastern borders of Kazakhstan, and the city of Atyrau, which concludes the western borders of Kazakhstan, to which the greylag goose does not travel?

The ornithologist Anatoly Kovshar wrote that this bird nests in all regions of western, eastern, central, southern and northern parts of Kazakhstan except in the Maṇġystau and **Žezķazġan** regions. However, in the past few years, there are people who have seen the greylag goose in the Tüpķaraġan area of Maṇġystau. Let's look at what other types of geese we know.

The Chinese brown goose is widespread and everyone can recognise it. But how do we distinguish the bar-headed goose? Kyrgyz people call it the 'Kazakh goose'. They probably say this because of its distribution in our mountainous areas. By the way, this species of goose isn't found in Kazakh lands, as apparently it only lives in the southern parts of the Kyrgyzstan Mountains. There are lines from a song performed in a song competition held between two *aķyns* (improvisational poets) of Kazakh folklore, named '*Ķyz ben žigit*' ('An ajtys of a girl and a fellow'): 'There is a tall bird called a *mankus* that drinks water from a pure lake, bending its long neck.'

What kind of bird is this? Modern Kazakhs have forgotten about this species. We as-

sume that *maṇķa ķaz* (bar-headed goose, or literally 'snotty goose') and *mankus* are the same bird. We would be grateful to hear any other opinions on this subject.

Once, the Kazakh poet Maġžan Žumabaev wrote an article to honour Aʼbubákir Divaev, entitled 'Aʼbubákir Aķsaķal'.[124] Aʼbubákir Divaev collected tales about the common shelduck from the regions of Šymkent, Ķazaly and Perovsk, and published them in the *Turkestanskiy Sbornik* (*Turkestani Gazette*). Aʼbubákir *aķsaķal*'s original Russian text states the following:

124 Aʼbubákir Divaev (1856–1932) was a Russian Soviet scientist, ethnographer, linguist, Turkologist and folklorist; *Aķsaķal* is a respectful form of address for an older man.

Kazakhs told marvellous stories about this bird: common shelducks (*itala ḳaz*, that is, literally, *dog-piebald goose*) used to lay their eggs on deserted, elevated hills, in old abandoned graves and in uninhabited holes of different animals. Types of hunting dogs, nicknamed '*ḳumaj*' (greyhounds), used to hatch out of the laid eggs. They were tiny at first. They had black and white chests and were distinguished by their extraordinary speed, courage and dexterity, so none of their victims could outrun them.

Some Kazakhs believed that common shelducks (*itala ḳaz*) menstruated. Therefore, their meat was not used in food. Kazakhs considered that the fate of the greyhound puppy was very sad. As soon as it hatched out of the egg, it was left alone in the nest by the female shelduck. The puppy could die of starvation. That is why there are very few greyhounds (*ḳumaj*). People who adopted these dogs became the happiest people in the whole world. According to Kazakh beliefs, *ḳumaj* (greyhounds) originated from *itala ḳaz* (common shelducks).

Undoubtedly, another question will arise about why the common shelduck is so admired by Kazakh people, as there are so many birds on our steppes. When this legend emerged, it could be supposed that the animal kingdom was richer than today. We believe that these sorts of legends appeared before Kazakhs adopted Islam.

It was not only forbidden to eat common shelduck meat, but was also inexcusable to hurt this bird. If we trace where these attitudes come from, we return to common Kazakh concepts such as kindness, mercy (*šapaġat*), sin (*obal*) and grace (*sauap*). Therefore, the common shelduck is compared to a woman, who is the most respected, honourable and holy of all humankind. Probably, our people had seen in these birds, which dwell near people and go close to them, their own insecure and trusting features. Whereas other birds live near water or at incredible heights, the common shelduck lives near people's dwellings. Have you ever seen a bird that breeds in a hole like an animal, instead of building a nest like a bird? Yes, we mean an ordinary hole. To lay its eggs it uses holes in forsaken places … deserted wintering houses, ravine gaps blurred with water. If it does not find anything appropriate, it may even use an abandoned old foxhole. Before nesting in the hole, the bird first cleans it up inside, enlarges the hole and then spreads hay everywhere.

In his work *Life of Animals*, in the section devoted to birds, Alfred Brehm provided an interesting, funny fact about a common shelduck that lived near a fox: 'They may both live in the same hole in peace. Usually foxes hunt birds, but they won't touch common shelducks. Probably this is owing to the latter's courage.' There is a saying which means there is always someone more powerful than you, and when you meet them, you will yield to them. In this case, the common shelduck differs from other birds. Instead of running away from the fox, the common shelduck is ready to attack it, uttering angry calls and displaying its plumage. And there is a saying, 'Even devout men flee evil', so the fox never comes close to the common shelduck.

Kazakhs who graze cattle see the common shelduck every day. Its head, neck, wings and tail are black and its underparts are white. There is a yellow 'belt' on its chest that resembles a horse's breastplate. It doesn't walk slowly like other geese, but steps quickly and energetically into the thick woods. It moults twice a year. Some of them walk near cattlemen. After some time, they get used to each other and aren't afraid of each other any more.

Perhaps the steppe fox would like to chase the bird that invaded its den, but it's afraid of the herdsmen. Other predatory animals keep away from people, as does the steppe fox. The female shelduck lays 12–15 eggs. In less than two months, its chicks grow up and begin to fly. They multiply very fast. Despite this, their numbers have not increased.

When grazing time arrives, the female shelduck comes out of the hole first. The chicks follow it. Water is far from their nest. Little chicks cannot fly. All predators, including the wolf and the fox, the wild spotted cat and even the smallest bird of prey, the shikra, prey on innocent chicks that follow their mother to the lake. For the common shelduck, the walk between its hole and the lake is simultaneously a very long and a very short walk, just like that between life and death. When they reach the water, the female shelduck begins teaching its chicks to swim. After reaching the water or river, if it notices another common shelduck swimming with its chicks, you will see a real fight. In comparison with other birds, the common shelduck is very jealous. They fight furiously with each other and the defeated one may run away, leaving its chicks behind. In this case, the shelduck that wins the fight just keeps the orphans. Don't be surprised if you see too many chicks on the lake following one female shelduck. Once, Russian newspapers wrote a sensational article when they saw fifty chicks following one female shelduck.

It is inconceivable that greyhounds originated from common shelducks and that female geese menstruate. Science regards such legends as nothing more than nonsense.

In another legend, it was said that the common shelduck didn't only feed on the remains of hay or grain like other birds, but sometimes also fed on the decaying flesh of dead animals, as dogs do. Therefore, it was called *itala ķaz* (dog-piebald goose) in Kazakh. What is this legend based on? As we mentioned before this, the bird grazes with livestock in the countryside. Where there are cattle, there will be losses. Predators gather near the carcass of dead cattle. It seems to me that those who saw the common shelduck next to the carcass misunderstood the scene. It is true that the common shelduck eats grasshoppers and crayfish in the summer time. However, we all know that it is not a scavenger.

One of the birds that has become the hero of as many legends as the common shelduck is the ruddy shelduck. You won't confuse it with other birds. It has chestnut-brown body plumage, a pale head, black crown and blackish legs, beak, tail and edges of its wings. They live in pairs. If one dies, the second grieves deeply. Kazakhs don't kill the ruddy shelduck and don't eat its meat for the same reasons they don't eat the common shelduck.

Kazakh highlanders call it a mountain bird. Almost everyone knows that this bird set-tled among people at the foot of Mount Erenķabyrġa. People who live in the steppe call it a steppe bird. Likewise, people who live around Lake Baikal call it a forest bird. Which of them is correct? We think that all three of these versions are right. A few years ago, pest control experts noticed that, in recent years, the number of ruddy shelducks had decreased. It was later found that poisonous chemicals sprayed to deal with rats might have killed rud-dy shelduck chicks. We know that after their arrival from warm lands in spring, shelducks use the burrows of ground squirrels which are situated in the hills. They live deep in the burrows, expand them and then nest there.

In Kazakhstan the ruddy shelduck inhabits Ile, Žarkent, Šaryn, Balķaš and Lake Sor-bulaķ, which is not far from Almaty. It is also can be found on the waters of the Narynķol district. The ruddy shelduck is one of the favourite birds of Kazakhs who live in China. The well-known Kazakh poet Muķaġali Maķataev, who came from Narynķol district, described

the arrival of spring as follows: 'Ruddy shelduck returned to the meadow; does it mean that the summer is close?'

It might be correct to call this bird 'a goose', like Kazakhs do, but not 'a duck' as science believes. The reason is that this bird flaps its wings and moves slowly before flying, and it doesn't walk quickly like ducks do. Kazakhs are used to exalting and praising their favourite birds, I guess. With regard to the word 'exalt', Kazakhs are not the only ones to sing praises to the ruddy shelduck. Owing to its chestnut colour, our Turkic brothers, Kalmyks and Buryats compare it to Buddha and call it 'The most righteous among birds'. Our Kyrgyz neighbours have the next story about this bird.

One day one of the prophets wanted to marry his only son to a beautiful girl. He wanted his future daughter-in-law to be a righteous, pious woman, able to distinguish between good and evil. According to the saying 'Good things come to those who wait', finally, in a distant kingdom, they found a very clever and beautiful girl. The two young people married. Whether it was happiness or sorrow that occurred to the prophet's family, his daughter-in-law turned out to be very spoiled. Instead of respecting the traditions of her new family, she adhered to her own traditions. She didn't know about the taboos. She did everything she wished. Her sisters-in-law said, 'Dear, young women should make ablutions', to which she replied, 'Why should I? I bathe in the lake every day.' Ignoring the old and the young people, she undressed and bathed in the pure mountain water. She didn't listen to those who asked her, 'What are you doing? The whole village drinks water from this lake.' The prophet uttered angrily: 'May we pray she won't turn into a bird.' The next day, the prophet's daughter-in-law came as usual to the lake, bringing her perfumes and soaps. When she got out of the water, she found herself turning into a ruddy shelduck, and started to cry loudly. As the saying goes, the bird's special sound, '*gag-gag*', resembles a human voice. Before flying away to warm lands, it circles over people's heads as if bidding farewell.

There is another version of this legend. This is a tragic story about a capricious girl who didn't listen to her father, went to bathe in an enchanted lake and turned into a bird. In the same way, the third and fourth versions of the legend are associated with people who 'strayed from the path'.

We may consider all of them just legends. Anyway, it is undeniable that the ruddy shelduck is close to people. In recent years, it began to settle in major cities. Once, we noticed a couple of ruddy shelducks that lived with other species of ducks and geese in the pond next to the Kazakhstan Embassy in Moscow. We watched them and saw how they landed on the roof of the opposite building, and learned that this was not unusual. The Russian newspaper *Moskovskiy Komsomolets* reported, 'Nowadays the ruddy shelduck inhabits Moscow in winter and summer. Furthermore, ruddy shelducks number about 420.'[125]

The third bird in this group is the crested shelduck. Unfortunately, I haven't met anyone who has seen this bird in nature. Ornithologists claim that this species of birds has disappeared, or is close to extinction. I don't want to believe it. When we look at the old Chinese books, we often find birds called a 'brant goose' or 'crested goose'. Similar pictures of these are found in ancient Korean books. How can we say that this bird does not exist at all? Who knows … maybe they exist somewhere, safe and sound.

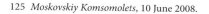

Common Swift

 $\mathcal{T}$ here is a riddle in a series of children's books entitled *Ornithology*. 'It never lands on earth, its life is spent in the sky, it says.' The answer is the common swift (*tùz ḳarlyġašy* in Kazakh; literally, 'steppe swallow'). This may be true or false. The common swift is always seen flying around the sky, with its long wings that resemble a sickle. According to science, it is not a swallow. It belongs to another family – to aerial, acrobatic birds (Apodidae). For instance, the house swallow (*ùj ḳarlyġašy*), which has been known and admired by us since childhood, is a passerine bird of the Hirundinidae family. Therefore, biologists assume that apart from external similarities, both birds are completely unrelated. At first glance, it is difficult to distinguish them; they are both superb fliers. However, there are some quite distinct differences.

Firstly, the common swift doesn't sit on telegraph wires like swallows do. It is constantly in flight. Secondly, if you pay attention to the legs of swallows, you will notice that three toes point forwards, and one toe points backwards, just like other birds. It seems as if God created these swallows specifically so that they could hold their food, or grab onto the branch on which they were sitting. However, *all* the swift's toes are located at, and point only to, the front, and look like a four-toothed rake. What is the reason for this? The reason is that the common swift doesn't build its nest on the lintel of a house, on a wooden axis or in a threshold. It builds its nest on smooth hills and cliffs, or on flat concrete surfaces.

The shape of its claws is similar to climbers' crampons and is very curved. It is amazing to watch this bird cling upright to a concrete wall just like a bat. How does it cling to the wall there and not fall off? It's as if there were glue on its claws. Swallows and other birds are not endowed with such *mountaineering* talents. Obviously, it is impossible to walk on the ground or climb trees with this kind of claw. Probably, the line from the above riddle – 'It never lands on earth' – was used precisely because of this peculiarity. In fact, the reason why it does not land is that it feeds on flying insects. There is no other reason. As the Kazakh pedagogue and poet Ybyraj Altynsarin stated, it 'finds its food with the help of its beak'. If a swift lands, it can immediately take wing like a barn swallow does. You won't manage to blink before you see how it already flies high in the sky. Therefore, all speculation about the common swift – that if it lands, it won't be able to fly again (just like in the fairy tale about the witch Žalmauyz who couldn't sit down if she got up, and couldn't get up if she sat down)

– are totally unfounded. The common swift can fly in and out very quickly, so not everyone notices except for those who study it.

Once, we witnessed an event that many would not see every day. If you go along the Alma-Arasan Gorge, near the *auyl* called Šeberler Auyly (Craftsmen's Village), two roads diverge. If you continue towards the east, you will see a waterfall, and next you see the pure Big Almaty Lake. After having a rest, you can get to Issyk-Kul Lake that is located in Kyrgyzstan. This road will lead you to Kemin (Kyrgyzstan). It is impossible not to admire this virgin beauty, so far from the city. However, it is very difficult to reach the ravine if you don't go on horseback. Because of its dangerous roads perhaps, few people visit this place.

It seems that people have been to all possible lands that could be visited. This is one of the favourite areas for Kazakh ornithologists and their guests to observe birds. Shooting with rifles has been banned there. Everyone can recognize the long-winged common swift at once, and so did we. It didn't fly far. It flew to the opposite cliff and clung to the rock. We looked through binoculars and observed what happened. The surface of the rock was dark black and white. We looked closely and identified common swifts. They did not sit in a row, but were scattered about. They were sitting as if they had decided to take a break after climbing the rocks for a long time. Of course, if they heard a sudden noise they would fly away immediately. The swift that had grabbed our attention earlier looked like an adult bird and then apparently said something to the other birds. After that, those swifts began to fall one by one. We thought that the swifts were sick. It seemed as if they were going to die by hitting themselves on the rock. Indeed, there are birds that kill themselves. Once, the Kazakh poet Ķuandyķ Šaṇġytbaev wrote a ballad that told such a story.

An old eagle hit itself on the rock,
on the rock of Mount Tal ar.
Snow was falling on its head,
on its white bald head ...

The saying 'The eagle finds death on a cliff' is proof of this. This is also one of various mysterious phenomena. We watched those swifts and did not move. Suddenly, a flight of common swifts flew down at high speed until an adult swift began to chirp something. After that, all the swifts took off to the mountainside at the same speed. When they reached the mountainside, they soared into the sky. It was just like the ancient Sufi story, as if the great Sufi mentor, Bahaubaddin, who breathed life into seven corpses, appeared from the unknown and breathed life into these birds too, so that they could fly away again.

That day, the flight of swifts that we met on the mountainside surprised us more than once. After flying for some time, they landed back on the smooth rock. They did not just land there, but clung to the cliffs, and stayed immobile as if sleeping. At that moment, a steppe fox with fluffy fur on its back appeared at the top of the cliff. It noticed the birds and stood still for a while. Then it walked back and forth wondering how to catch the 'naive, dormant' birds below. To carry out its trick, it hid behind a rock. After a while, it appeared again. The birds didn't move and waited for the fox to come closer. Then the steppe fox rolled a stone towards them. The common swifts did not make any sound. *Oh, they are really sleeping deeply*, the fox thought and began to go down in small, vulpine steps.

It tried to approach the birds quietly. It could not attack them at once, as it was very slippery there. When only four or five steps remained, the birds pretended to fall again, and then started soaring into the sky. In this way they repeated their previous trick. The poor steppe fox was frightened by the sudden loud sound of birds' wings and tried to retreat. However, it slipped and fell. The steppe fox is not a cat, is it? When it fell to the ground, it hurt itself badly. It could barely stand and then went in the direction of dense thickets, as if a kite were shouting after it, 'You deserved that.' As witnesses to such an event, we wondered if this was a cunning strategy of common swifts: either swifts were learning to fly, or they just mocked the steppe fox in that way.

The Birds Are Our Friends

Another unusual story happened in Narynķol, in the Almaty region. One day, students of Saryžaz secondary school brought a common swift to the biology classroom. The teacher named Dosan Duanķuľov had been teaching at that school for many years; everybody in that region knew and respected him. He was surprised with the answer to his question about how his students had managed to catch the bird. It turned out that a sudden storm had lifted plastic bags into the air with the rest of the rubbish that had been scattered on the ground. A common swift got caught in a plastic bag that was floating in the air, and fell to the ground. It was just a coincidence, as the children didn't intend to catch the bird.

Another interesting feature of this bird is that it is always hungry. What does it eat? Ornithologists' experiments conducted in specialized laboratories haven't yet yielded results. The composition of its feed is very rich. We are more likely to ask what vitamins are *not* included in their food rather than which components we might find there. Birds are warm-blooded creatures, just like mammals. Usually, a bird's body temperature is high, at about 42°C. Some birds' body temperature is even higher. For example, the blackbird's body temperature is 45.5°C. They have high basal metabolic rates and use huge amounts of energy. In other words, according to scientists, as soon as birds eat, they excrete at once.

If this is the first characteristic feature of birds, then their next feature is their heart rate. For instance, everyone knows the pulse rate of a human being. The usual tit's heart beats 460 times a minute. A small hummingbird's heart rate can easily rise above 1,000 beats per minute during flight. In order to have such a speedy heart rate it is important to eat a lot. We are mentioning hummingbirds that live in distant lands because swifts and hummingbirds belong to the same order of Apodiformes. The hummingbird is the smallest bird in the world. The smallest species that looks like a bee is only 1.6 grams, and its body length is only 5.7 centimetres. Males are a bit bigger than females. This bird is listed in *Guinness World Records* as: 'A bird which flaps its wings very fast. It inhabits the tropical forest of South America. It can flap its wings ninety times a second.' In fact, hummingbirds live only in South America, but swifts inhabit everywhere except Australia. As you see, science is science.

Although South America and the Kazakh steppes are far from each other, science can always grasp the immensity and find links between seemingly unconnected phenomena. This is proved by the fact that hummingbirds and the favourite of our land, swifts, belong to the same family. Kazakhs love swifts. This can be seen from the examples in folk literature. We pay attention to customs and traditions, the interpretation of dreams and the fact that our cherished girls and swift horses are called by this bird's name. Swifts are distinguished by their charm – so much information has been provided previously on this topic.

Perhaps not every Kazakh knows that swifts are divided into different several groups within its species. (There are more than 100 species of swifts, divided into four groups.) However, you are unlikely to find a Kazakh who does not know anything about swifts. The most common species of this bird in Kazakhstan is the common swift. Therefore, our story is mainly about this bird. In recent years, it has even built its nest in our big cities. It has become accustomed to the urban and suburban conditions of Almaty and its surroundings. The common swift is found in the Alma-Arasan Gorge, in the Medeu hollow, in the mounts of Talǧar and Kegen and on the Narynķol cliffs. Like its close relative, the Alpine swift, it loves fresh air and heights. In ancient times a young Kazakh sang to his beloved,

Your eyebrows are similar to swift wings,
oh, my dear girl, if all the girls were like you.

He meant the common swift (*tùz ķarlyǧašy*), not the swallow (*ķarlyǧaš*), since the former has longer, slimmer, scythe-like wings reminiscent of girls' eyebrows (the swallow's wings are thicker and shorter).

At one time, Joanna Burger's encyclopedic guide, *Birds*, caused a sensation in Europe. There was information in this guide that 'The hummingbird feeds on nectar, and the swift feeds on various flying insects. It uses its saliva as a building material to build its nest.' An interesting fact is that the people of South-East Asia turn the white saliva-based swiftlet's nest into a delicacy – edible bird's nest soup. The flight speed of this bird is 160 kilometres per hour (kph).

In some sources, there is a given fact that the swiftest flier in the world is a peregrine falcon, which flies at a speed of 350 kph. In second place is the common swift, which flies at a speed of 180–200 kph. Other sources report that: 'No, the fastest flying bird is not a peregrine falcon, but a common swift. Actually, this is the bird that flies at a speed of 350 kilometres an hour.' In any case, the flight speed of the common swift has caused many disputes. Recently, *Guinness World Records* reported that: 'The common swift might spend two or three years flying without having to land. It sleeps and eats in midair … Moreover, a young swift doesn't land until it has flown 500,000 kilometres.' It is impossible not to believe *Guinness World Records*.

Another interesting feature is that the common swift's body temperature is not stable compared to other birds and mammals. As the saying goes, 'Misfortune doesn't come alone.' If the common swift suddenly gets hungry or the weather changes dramatically and cold weather occurs, then its body temperature can drop to 20°C. Other birds die in such cold weather. For example, in the summer of 1998, namely on 6 June in Almaty, it was -8°C. In the same year, the first snow fell on 26 September. Many birds died, together with their chicks. In such cases, the common swift lay in a half-dead position, as if hibernating.

It is amazing that common swift chicks can endure hunger for a long time. Usually, other birds' chicks tolerate hunger for only one or two days, while the common swift's chicks put up with it for as long as nine or ten days. It should be noted that among the swift genus, only common swifts are able to do this, but not Pacific or Alpine swifts. They say that the common swift leaves its chicks and flies away to warm lands and gathers strength until the cold and snowstorms retreat, then they fly back. According to ornithologists, adult common swifts, in comparison with their chicks, can endure hunger for only four to five days.

They arrive on our steppes when the days get warm and the weather is clement. At the end of April, if you see birds with a white throat and dark wings flying past you and uttering a sound like 'stri-i-i-i' (in Russian this bird is called *strizh*), then you should say: 'Oh, they've arrived again!' It is that favourable time when the weather is balmy and small insects appear. The swift does not arrive every year in April or in a group. This case surprises scientists.

Kazakh ornithologist Anatoly Kovshar mentioned an interesting story in his book *Mir ptits Kazakhstana* (*The World of Birds in Kazakhstan*): 'On 27 March 1960, we discovered a group of common swifts hardly alive, awakening from their winter sleep on the roof of a house in the Šymkent region, in the Aķsu-Žabaģly Reserve. There was no sign of a sunny day, and in that period the snow was still thick on the ground.'

The common swift usually breeds in the Maņģystau and Šymkent regions, but the Alpine swift lives only in Ôskemen, in the Altaj Mountains. Kovshar was the first ornithologist to point out these facts. In terms of weather, common swifts predict changes in the climate quicker than other birds in the region. In a previous chapter, we mentioned how storks sometimes kill their own chicks. It is hard to expect such wickedness from the stork that is celebrated in Kazakh literature as a symbol of fidelity and loyalty. Nevertheless, the story is a true one. Like the stork, common swifts also sometimes throw their own young out of their nest. What does 'sometimes' mean in this context? When does it usually occur? In this case, scientists' opinions differ. A prominent group of scientists suggests that common swifts kill their chicks prior to severe weather changes. The second group holds that the reason for this behaviour as a mystery of the animal world, which we do not understand yet, and which human beings have not investigated in depth. In any case, when the common swift starts throwing its chicks from its nest, storms begin, or long chains of cold days start. It is painful for anyone to see a baby chick dying under its mother's claws. In ancient times, when Kazakhs noticed such a disgraceful act, they would quickly leave the territory where they had been living with the forecast that 'swifts have predicted famine'.

One thing that should be paid close attention to is that the common swift does not usually kill all its young, but spares several, or a couple of chicks. It's as if it's saying, 'I am unable to support all of you. We are going to be hungry. This is the reason for my cruelty, my dear little ones. Forgive your wretched mother!' Then it circles the dead chicks, suddenly soars into the sky and disappears.

Swifts often return to the same nests year after year, rebuilding them when necessary. They build their nests in a hole in a cliff or in caves and nestle in the roofs of deserted outbuildings or barns. Their nest looks like a stretched bed. It will not crash nor break easily. Swifts flock together in a 'flight'.

There is a legend that 'a swift ties a mantis in front of its nest to protect its chicks from snakes'. It is a beautiful idea, but only a legend. It must have been based on the legend when a mantis pecked out a snake's eyes when it was crawling to the nest. 'As a mantis lives near the swift, I want to live next to you.' Probably, the verse above stems from the same legend, and the people's willingness to believe in a creature that can defend poor birds from snakes.

Tales about friendship between the swift and the mantis were also a way for Kazakhs to express their wish to fight against evil. If you really want to believe in a lie, it often happens to be about animals, especially birds. Obviously, when we truly love something, we are not able to convey this feeling. In fact, the swift does not rely on the mantis; it looks after its nest by itself. Usually a swift builds its nest on a cliff, since snakes are unable to climb cliffs. They lay 2–4 eggs, not many.

It is hard to say how many days it incubates its eggs. However, over about 17–19 days both male and female incubate the eggs in turn and feed their young for a month and half. It is reported that the chicks grow rapidly, but in some cases, it takes about 38–39 days, and in unfavourable rainy weather, it can take 56–57 days to bring up the chicks. Unlike other birds, the young swifts fly off the nest swiftly and become independent immediately. This is similar to the hare's behaviour in an old fairy tale. A young hare says farewell to its mother, and as soon as it is forty steps away from its burrow, it says: 'You don't know me, I don't know you.' Scientists haven't yet fully disclosed the inexplicable behaviour and secrets of the common swift.

There are times when parents do not wait until chicks are fully fledged. Science still does not know the reasons why. However, those poor young will survive in the nest, using what they find, exercising by performing 'press-ups' on their wings, then leaving their nest.

Swifts that are unable lay eggs or nest for any reason leave before the other birds. It turns out that they grow old sooner too. As soon as the heat in July cools down a bit, they start migrating (typically in the middle of August). Their voice seems sad, as though saying, 'I have not had any luck in this area. I hope next summer will be different.' The male follows the female in flight. Science claims that common swifts are monogamous and pair for life.

It is a paradox that common swifts are considered resistant to hunger, yet they cannot bear hunger. It was also believed that they did not drink water at all. Scientists, such as Brehm, denied this. It is not possible for a living organism to not drink water. If you claim that swifts rarely drink water, that is more beliveable. This is a story from the East, more precisely from Türkistan.

Once upon a time, Sheikh Kul Kozha Ahmed Yassawi arrived in Syr Dariâ to spread the teachings of Islam, but the locals did not treat him well.

'If you are a sheikh, why are you wandering? If you are poor, then let's find you a herd. If you do not have home, let's build one for you!' they said, as at that time, the concept of 'a dervish' was unfamiliar to locals. Yassawi explained them that he was on the path of Allah.

They asked, 'You come from Arabia and they say that Arabs kill their women if they give birth to girls, and bury their daughters alive in wells when they are seven years old. Is that true, sheikh?'

The sheikh said that this had been true in pre-Islamic times. The Prophet Muhammad (peace upon him) put a stop to these traditions.

People did not trust the sheikh and questioned him further. 'You say your religion pursues close-knit relationships between relatives and family, so how do you explain when siblings and relatives marry each other. Where do you see virtue? … How do brothers and sisters build families if they are co-descendants? … In our culture we never allow such perversions.'

'Turks have good traditions, stick to those!' said Yassawi. His aim was to spread Islam, but for that purpose he had to agree to some of the locals' arguments, and convince them of some of his own.

At that time, there was a *batyr* (hero), who possessed thousands of horses. When told there were enemies on the border of his lands, he used to send eighty men instead of eight, and gave them ninety horses instead of nine. He had a powerful white sword and a spear, and was able to travel in steady storms and wind, through ice and snow, from November frost to January and February cold. His name was Ķožban and he was a leader among his peers. His voice could travel from the mountains to the valleys. When his foes heard his

voice, they lost their nerve and were too afraid to face him. However, he had one weakness – Ķožban ate a lot. That is why he was nicknamed a *voracious batyr*, who could eat non-stop, hence a horse could not carry him. When the horses could not lift him, he travelled by camel, but eventually the camels could not lift him either. Then he travelled by cart and one day, the cart broke. So he came to see the sheikh and asked him for advice. The sheikh told him that he was sick and the name of his malady was gluttony – his addiction to eating. To cure him of that ailment, the sheikh said the *batyr* needed to eat less and fast, and continued to spread the teachings of Islam.

When he returned home, the *batyr* started fasting. On one of the cliffs of the Ķaratau Mountains, there was a high guard post. Every day he had the habit of observing the neighbourhood from that post. One day he saw common swift nests on the rock. It was so clean around it. He thought, *What a tidy bird it is that doesn't leave its droppings in its own environment – presumably it doesn't drink or eat much.* The next day he came again. Hardly breathing, hardly mounting the cliff, he saw the swift fly away from the cliff.

Oh my goodness, usually when birds fly away from their nests they throw away their rubbish, but this bird does not spread its droppings. It seems to be a very ascetic bird. It was sent to me from the heavens, thought the *batyr*. Among the folk there was a phrase: '*Batyrs* are gullible, heroes are clumsy.' According to that rule, Ķožban promised himself, 'That sheikh told me to fast, but I didn't ask him for how many days I need to do this. This bird has been sent to me by the heavens. I will starve for however long this bird starves. I promise!' he told himself.

Then for about ten days he lived without consuming anything except water, and checked the bird – its nest was clean, with no litter or bird droppings. He lived without food for twenty days and the swift was still hungry. After thirty days, he was surprised to find that his chain mail was slipping from his shoulders, his belt stretched out extensively and his fur coat was too large for him. His sad wife Gùlbaršyn was astonished by the changes in her husband's appearance, and became happy again. He was again able to mount his favourite horse, Bajšubar.

'Let me go to my sheikh!' said Ķožban one day, and went to see him. The city of Yasy where Yasawi lived was not far from his dwelling. Ķožban arrived there in a day on horseback. When he entered the city gates, Yasawi was in the centre of the market surrounded by a large crowd. The Sufi was preaching before the gathered men and women. There were more people around him than the last time the *batyr* had seen him. People were nodding their heads. Ķožban listened to his sermon; it was a good one. Even though Ķožban did not understand all of it, he understood the poems.

'These are not bad,' he said to himself. 'Maybe I should announce a competition between my wife and this sheikh.' Then he changed his mind, understanding how inappropriate that would be. *It is better to comprehend, to listen to these verses. These verses have not been created for fun, they are educational. So, let me wait a bit, while the crowd goes,* thought Ķožban. When the crowd left, Ķožban came closer to Yasawi and said, 'My Lord, let me speak!'

Yasawi stopped him and responded: 'Do not say anything, my dear. You have already performed two obligations of Islam, and the other three obligations you will perform without any effort. The first duty is to believe in Allah, to guide you through your life. You have fasted for thirty days. You can see the result for yourself. What would you like to say to me, Ķožban?' Ķožban fell on his knees and asked. 'Lord, bless me!' Therefore, Yasawi uttered,

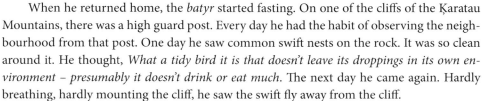

'*La ilaha illa Allah, Muhammad Rasool Allah*!'; that is, 'There is no God but Allah and Muhammad is his messenger.'

Later on, people from all over Kazakh lands went to Yasy and listened to Yasawi's preaching every Friday, saying that if Ķožban *batyr* chose to go to Yasy, then they would also go. Although they accepted the religion, they preserved their culture and their traditions. Since then, Kazakhs have cared for swifts as they care for their sisters. The story I have just mentioned is testament to that, I think.

However, Alfred Brehm wrote that the swift that he kept in a cage died after six weeks without eating any food.

Dove

T he Turkish sultan and caliph Abdulmecid I was anticipating the year 1856. He was the thirty-first sultan of the Ottoman Empire. He felt that the Topkapi Palace, which he had inherited from his ancestors, was not spacious enough for him. He had grown up putting the needs of his people before his own. Therefore, the sultan said, 'Better a thorn sticks in my forehead than be stuck in the Turks' soles'. Thus, the sultan

decided to collect all the innovations of the world in the Dolmabahçe Palace, which was built on his order. The sultan received many gifts at the opening ceremony of Dolmabahçe Palace. Therefore, the sultan's spies and agents had already reported to him about each guest's gifts. For instance, Queen Victoria was going to gift him a Bohemian chandelier that weighed 4.5 tons, the Russian Tsar was going to gift a bear skin, and so on.

According to the grand vizier's calculations, 14 tons of gold and 40 tons of silver were used to decorate Dolmabahçe Palace. When the German ambassador visited the palace, he smiled and asked: 'Is there a place for our gift in this palace, which consists of 285 rooms, and 43 salons?' The next day, Sultan Abdulmecid found out what the German ambassador meant. It seemed that among guests of the event there would be Professor I. Schmidt. He wanted to show the Morse Code Machine to the visitors of the palace. The machine was very useful. It could receive messages from distant countries in an instant. The young sultan wanted to see this device most of all, despite his other royal possessions.

The sultan realized that it was impossible to be victorious in the world with superior armed weapons and force only, as it was a time of intellectual achievements. So, he didn't listen to his wife, who said: 'You shouldn't believe this German. Surely this machine isn't better than our Hatay doves?' Moreover, the sultan, who loved birds, especially doves, from his childhood, called this new device *Gogerchin* (dove), although this name was later forgotten. Unfortunately, this was not the only thing that was forgotten. When other sultans moved from Dolmabahçe to Yildiz Palace, there wasn't even a staff member such as 'dove breeder' in their service book. As a result, the descendants of the Ottomans famous for their love for doves abandoned this hobby. They could only read in history books about this pastime involving dove breeding and watching it fly. The bird that had once provided a tremendous service to the Ottoman Empire in capturing half of the world has become wild today.

Nowadays, you may see doves landing on the mosque's minarets in Bursa or Istanbul, or they build their nests in the ruins of the old Roman city. Only a few people know that today's doves are the same as those that saved the Ottoman Empire from many enemies by carrying good or bad news. For example, on 29 May 1453, doves flew from the high golden dome of the Hagia Sophia mosque, to inform everyone in the Great Empire that Constantinople had been renamed Istanbul, and had become the City of Muslims. In one of the legends, it is told that the sovereign of England snapped a dove's neck and killed it for bringing such bad news. When Fatih Sultan Mehmet heard about this, he sent a second dove. The next dove threw a letter on the roof of the king's palace and flew back. At that moment, the king exclaimed, 'The dove survived. We won't see Constantinople again.' History proved him right. Obviously, we shouldn't think that our Turkish brothers were the first people in the world to use doves as postmen.

Animals have been domesticated from the dawn of humankind. Without dispute, one of the first among these was a dove. Probably you remember the myth of the Great Flood during the Prophet Noah's time. The Flood is mentioned in all of the four holy books that are considered to have been revealed. It is narrated that the Prophet Noah was in the Ark for a long time. Finally, he opened the window of the Ark, sent out a dove – in some sources, it was a raven – and told it: 'See if the waters have subsided.' Before that, many poetic works wrote about this bird; for example, *The Epic of Gilgamesh*, which is believed to have been written near the Euphrates River 5,000 years ago. According to the poem, the dove flew out first from a sunken area:

On the seventh day when it came,

I brought out a dove. I let it loose:

Off went the dove, but then it returned,

There was no place to land, so back it came to me.[126]

Which bird do Kazakhs call a dove (*kôgeršin*) and which bird do they call a pigeon (*kepter*)? What is the difference between them? The difference is that the dove is a tame bird, and the pigeon is a wild one. There is no other difference. We have talked about doves until now. There are many species of them. In fact, doves have been tamed in the East and West since ancient times. Today, if you see birds pecking next to old people, who are sipping tea in the shady corners of Istanbul, Egypt, Sham, Bukhara, Khiva and Kashgar, then don't doubt that they are doves. Don't be surprised if an old dove breeder from the East starts to count dove varieties, such as doves of: Urfa, Marash, Antep, Osmania, Hatay, Kashgar, Khotan, Samarkand, Damascus and Izmir. Each of these was used as a postal messenger.

Imagine you needed to send a message from Samarkand to Bukhara, from Izmir to Istanbul, or from Aleppo to Qarshi. It might have been too late by the time a rider reached the place, especially when the roads were dangerous. In that case, the most suitable postal messenger would have been a dove. It should be noted that every two or three hours a second bird was sent out carrying the same message. Probably it was in order to be sure, in case a bird of prey such as a hawk or sparrowhawk attacked the first dove, or it died at a marksman's hand. So, the second dove could reach the designated place safe and sound.

There are many ways to train doves to be messengers. In the East, only male pigeons were trained in this craft. It turns out that if female pigeons see something interesting, they might delay there or don't reach the designated place.

By researching doves for centuries, the breeders of the East, as well as European scientists, distinguished them according to their colour, shape and voice. They came to the conclusion that there are more than 800 species of pigeon in the world. Prior to this, Brehm proposed that there were 400 species of pigeon. This cannot be considered his error, but rather proof that the science of zoology, like other sciences, is updated every year. A world-renowned ornithologist, Professor S. Petefi, categorized doves (pigeons) into twelve groups:

- Rock dove, rock pigeon or common pigeon;
- Typical pigeon, or true pigeon;
- Giant runt;

126 *The Epic of Gilgamesh*, translated by Andrew George. Available at : https://archive.org/stream/12CPReadingTheEpicOfGilgamesh/12CP%20Reading%20-%20The%20Epic%20of%20Gilgamesh_djvu.txt.

- King pigeon;

- Trumpeter pigeon;

- Curly pigeon;

- Jacobin pigeon;

- Owl pigeon;

- Pouter pigeon;

- Fantail pigeon;

- English carrier pigeon;

- Highflyer pigeon.

Meanwhile, the Czechs, the French and Moscovites also offered other options.

Pigeon breeders are still researching this field. Why do people love pigeons more than other birds? Owing to crossbreeding, pedigree doves appeared in Belgium about 150 years ago. Those doves could fly around 1,000 km a day. According to some sources, millions of doves *took part* in the First World War. Unfortunately, many of them were killed. How could a bird know that a man is able to sacrifice birds to achieve his goals? In 1870–71 when the Parisians were surrounded by the German army, they used to send doves as postal messengers to ask for help. When the Germans discovered these *secret agents*, they sent out hawks and falcons to kill those doves. The French did not worry. As the saying goes: 'A Moses for each Pharaoh', so the French began to tie whistles to the carrier pigeons' tails. The loud sound frightened the falcons, so they didn't even get close to those doves.

Pigeon post was used as a tool not only during war. Smart people used it to make money as well. For instance, the banker Nathan Rothschild used the Pigeon Post effectively to manage financial transactions more quickly and became very rich. Reuters News Agency also used this bird until fairly recently.

Modern science hasn't defined this feature of doves yet. How can it get to a designated place by itself? Where is its compass? Science has no idea. Once, to test the ability of a dove, ornithologists attached a magnet to its wing and blindfolded it. Nevertheless, the result was the same. The dove still found the designated place each time. It is interesting to note that at the beginning of their flight, doves fly aimlessly and without direction. Nevertheless, after some time, they find the right direction.

One day when scientists lit up the nests where the pigeon chicks were, they were scared and began to chirp. When scientists covered the chicks' bodies with black cloths and directed the light towards their eyes, the chicks calmed down. Did this mean that doves could see not only with their eyes, but also with their skin? This is still unclear.

Another strange thing is its milk. A Kazakh proverb says that 'a horse does not have a gallbladder and a bird does not have any milk'. However, some scientists assume that birds have milk. The evidence comes from the fact that a special liquid comes out of the dove's throat when it feeds its young. One group of biologists called this liquid 'vomit-milk'. Another group of scientists called it 'prolactin'. According to researchers, this liquid tastes like butter, and its composition is similar to rabbit meat. A baby dove which drinks this *milk* grows not every day, but every hour. It gains weight at twice the normal rate. Interestingly, there is *milk* not only in females, but in male doves as well. The male dove feeds its chicks until they grow up.

The Birds Are Our Friends

Dove and pigeon pairs are very friendly. They are faithful to their chosen partner and stay with them until the end of their twenty years of life. So how can we distinguish females from males? Experienced pigeon (dove) breeders define them by their beaks. Firstly, if a pigeon breeder pulls on the bird's beak and the bird resists, then it is a male. If not, then it is female. Female doves are quieter. Secondly, when a pigeon breeder pats the bird's chest, it pulls its legs up if it is a male. Females do not do this. These are all the results taken from bird breeders' practice and experience. Nevertheless, it does not mean that these are the only ways to determine the bird's gender.

Basically, the dove is considered a symbol of peace and many associate it with Picasso's famous painting *Dove*. A well-known Kazakh composer, Ahmet Žubanov, called his beautiful song '*Aķ kôgeršin*' ('White Dove'). The Kazakh poet N. Bajmuhamedov wrote the lyrics of the song.

> *A white dove, a helper of men,*
> *Soar high and see the lands*
> *For the sake of your people.*
> *I'll send you to the world,*
> *As a symbol of justice.*
> *I'll wish you to bring good news,*
> *And will observe your flight.*

The white dove is described as a symbol of peace and a happiness in this song. History claims that the dove is the first domesticated bird. Unfortunately, the most murdered birds at human hands are doves too. One species of dove even disappeared from the earth. It happened as follows. On 1 September 1914 at the Cincinnati Zoo, the bird-keeper came to work early in the morning, and saw a dead pigeon named Martha in one of the cages. He hurried to the phone to report what had happened. After some time, the mass media reported that the 'passenger pigeon' bird breed no longer existed. Martha was the last known example of that breed.

American ornithologists offered to pay US$1,500 to anyone who found a passenger pigeon, its nestling or its egg. Alas, until now, no one has seen or heard about that bird. Thus, another breed of pigeon is now extinct. According to some superstitious ornithologists, every year at the beginning of September pigeons do not fly for the whole day. They either walk on the ground, or sit in the branches of trees. There are those who believe that doves mourn their lost brothers. Who knows … maybe this is true.

What did the passenger pigeon look like? There was a pigeon endemic to North America and Canada which retained this name in science. Today it sounds like a fairy tale. One of main peculiarities of this breed was that it multiplied rapidly. In present times, we talk a lot about locusts and their attacks on fields and gardens. At one time newspapers stated that locusts were not as terrible as passenger pigeons. For example, when a flock of these birds flew high, they said the flock stretched up to 360 kilometres. Mathematicians calculated that there were 2,230,272,000 pigeons. John James Audubon, an American ornithologist, claimed that the total number of passenger pigeons was 1,115,136,000. 'It wasn't hard to kill so many birds,' wrote the Soviet author Igor Akimushkin. American soldiers chased those pigeons with the help of dogs and birds of prey. They also threw stones at them, beat them with sticks, poisoned them and tried to catch them with different traps. To exterminate them in the end soldiers even shot them using cannon.

Moreover, anyone that killed a dove was given an incentive of US$10. Have you heard the story of Americans who used different strategies to prevent a thick flock of pigeons from obscuring the face of the sun, and flying straight to the agricultural fields to attack the plants? At that time, Americans walking in the evenings watched how military men fired at an army of harmful pigeons with cannons and after that, the ground would become dark with dead pigeons. Farmers were certainly happy at having got rid of pigeon disasters, whereas the Government was pleased to receive more taxes from the farmers' profits. At that time, Americans heard about and used the method of the Spanish and the English, who had driven a harmful bird called the dodo to extinction. The dodo inhabited the island of Mauritius in the Indian Ocean. It is a pity that the announcement of the last dodo's death in 1638, in London Zoo, did not stop people's cruelty towards birds. At the present time, we only have the dodo's picture.

Finally, what made an end of passenger pigeons? Did the end come to them because they were harmful? No. Passenger pigeons became extinct because of their tasty meat and abundance. For instance, chicken meat consists of 71 per cent water, but pigeon meat is only 49 per cent water. Pigeon meat is six times richer in protein than chicken. However, one thing should be clarified: people who love and domesticate pigeons do not keep them for their meat. Why do you think is this?

It is difficult to find an answer to the question. There are racing pigeons, along with decorative ones. Racing pigeons are able to do various exercises: they ascend high and descend, demonstrating different *dances* in the air. And there are pigeons that are completely useless as messengers: when the wind changes direction, these pigeons stray from their path. Therefore, not every pigeon is designed to serve as a postal messenger.

There are many pigeon clubs in Almaty. They used to gather at weekends in Tastak market, Malaâ station, before the Èkran bus stop and at Vernyj market. You would hardly see Kazakhs among them. The most valuable prized bird species among the club members were the peacock pigeon, the pectoral sandpiper and the peacock. These birds were able to ascend so high and then did somersaults like real acrobats. To watch that scene was incredible. A pigeon which can do many somersaults is a valuable bird. There are Kazakh folk songs about pigeons, and such verses can also be found in folk poetry, in the works of *žyraus* such as Aķtamberdi.[127] Those verses prove that steppe Kazakhs have been familiar with pigeons from olden times. However, Kazakhs were not interested in domesticating them. The reason is that we do not have a culture of hobbies or interests like this. There might be some exceptions, of course. For example, I heard of some men in the region of Šymkent who tame these birds. Another reason for the disinterest in dove breeding is that our ancestors did not lead a settled way of life. They considered domesticating quails and pigeons, or fighting dogs and cockerels as something only people with no worthwhile occupation

127 Aķtamberdi Saryuly (1675–1768) was an influential Kazakh *žyrau* (poet), performing his topical verses to music, but also an epic storyteller, military commander and counsellor to the rulers.

would be interested in. Nomadic Kazakhs would think that going to market every week to fly pigeons was silly. Even today, it is not common for Kazakhs to domesticate quails, or use their animals for dog and ram fighting and so on.

Other types of dove, such as the turtle dove and the common wood pigeon, are common on our steppes. A pigeon that has a stripe around its neck is an 'Egyptian pigeon'. Another nickname is the 'laughing pigeon'. This is because its song resembles a laugh. It is a very beautiful bird. The difference between a laughing pigeon and other pigeons is that it never flies high. It eats food on the ground. It is neither arrogant nor showy. It is a very modest bird. Some arrogant doves look at it as if blaming it, and saying: 'Why do you need those wings then, if you don't fly?' In the 1930s, this bird inhabited the Middle East and the southern regions. Ten years later, it had spread to the whole of Europe. In the twentieth century this topic was discussed widely at scientific conferences, as it was considered an invasive bird.

The common wood pigeon weighs up to 600 grams. It is larger than other types of dove and widespread. Their body feathers are darkest on the upper side, where they are coloured in dull tones of grey and brown, with shades of lavender on the nape. It is paler on the lower part of its breast, where a tint of pinkish lavender is usually present. Its legs are red and its beak is brownish. They have white fringes and conspicuous white tips on their otherwise slate-grey tail feathers. They usually call '*ghooo*' and breed 2–3 times a year. The common wood pigeon sleeps at the top of trees at night. Unlike other types of dove, it does not only feed on fruit, berries and seeds on the ground, but also plucks them from the trees. Often it has a little branch in its beak. Maybe that's why when people paint the bird of peace, it is a common wood pigeon with a branch in its beak. When fighting, male ring doves can be aggressive, showing real male strength. If the males fail in battle, they accept their loss. Two pigeons can flap their wings and jump at each other. when sitting on a branch, and he who falls first is the loser. Females choose and surrender to the winning male.

We can see turtle doves every day. Their voice is exceptional and heard from afar as '*turr- turr*'. Their Latin name is also the same as its name, derived from '*turtur*'. Initially, it was called a *turtur*, but then this changed. If you were travelling in the steppes of semi-arid Torǧaj and Mojynķu̇m and accidentally saw among the bushes and old graves a couple of turtle doves flying away, you would be surprised when thinking where you saw them. Do not be surprised, as you have seen them in the cities. It is a very sensitive and careful bird. Its speed exceeds 185 kilometres an hour. It feeds mainly on fruit seeds and drinks water twice a day. It breeds very quickly. Turtle doves may cause problems with their droppings and waste in large cities and parks, where city councils argue about how to clean up after them in the squares. What is good is that we are still not in danger of destroying the turtle doves as the Americans did. Many Eastern healers used dove's droppings to cure illnesses. Uyghur folk medicine still utilizes dove droppings to treat a person's back and urinary tract.

There are several folk legends about turtle doves. The first is about their relationships. It is true that these doves live in pairs and appear to be loyal. They feed together, and help each other when nesting. It has become a custom for newly married couples to fly doves at their wedding, to symbolize love and peace. However, when they fight, they are unstoppable. People who have observed turtle dove fights reject the idea that these birds are an appropriate symbol of peace and accord, and have written many opposing articles. Nevertheless, I personally consider turtle doves to be very convivial birds. I think we can excuse animals for fighting, while so-called intelligent human beings cannot stop fighting with each other.

The second story is about how doves kiss. The famous Kazakh poet Muḳaġali Maḳataev declared in one of his verses:

I'm afraid I hardly have any friends,
Does it mean that my life is wasted?
I came to this conclusion though,
Watching two cordial doves kissing.

As Dostoevsky mentioned, if you see two doves kissing each other during mild spring evenings, you will not believe that there is boredom and sadness in this world; then the world will seem to sing. In reality, doves do not kiss each other; they feed one another.

In the Kazakh steppes and in Almaty, the rock pigeon is quite common. Rock pigeons inhabit not only our cities but also all parts of the world. Rock pigeons are recognizable at once. Wild rock doves are pale grey with two black bars on each wing, whereas domestic pigeons vary in colour and pattern. We see few differences between males and females. They breed four times a year and usually have two chicks. Both parents care for the young. These doves are not afraid of people. The type of dove described at the beginning of the chapter, and which survived in the Prophet Noah's Ark, was a rock dove. Rock doves feed on plant seeds. Another of its characteristic features is that it can find its nest from 5,000 kilometres away. The references about these birds report that rock doves were domesticated 5,000 years ago. Egyptians regarded these birds as sacred, and they were the first, along with Indians, to tame the rock doves. The Ancient Romans also regarded these birds as holy. Later, they became wild and in around the eleventh century, disappeared completely from the list of domesticated birds. There are not many animals or birds that became wild after they had been tamed.

I wonder if doves are fond of people these days because they were domesticated in the past. Sometimes, they suffer from this tendency to come too close to people: cars run them over, and they are caught when trying to eat from human hands. Biologists consider these doves susceptible to disease. About 35 per cent of them may die before they fly from the nest. That is why we should be careful when feeding them in the street.

Similar to the rock dove is the blue-headed wood dove. It has black patches on its wings, and a reddish breast. It used to inhabit the Alatau Mountains, but lately, it has also been seen in the city. It is very fearful. It sips water like a horse, syphoning the water up, and it is amusing to watch it.

The most beautiful dove is the crowned pigeon. We do not have them in the Kazakh steppes. There are no diamond doves in our parts, as they inhabit Australia. One other species, the Socorro dove, inhabits the islands of the Pacific and Indian Oceans. Lately, they have been reported to behave like nocturnal birds. It is not interesting to talk about birds that you have not seen, and it's not too bad if you learn just enough about the birds that inhabit your own country. Therefore, we finish our story. May our friends, the birds, be safe!

Peregrine

The largest bird: ostrich, weighs up to 156 kilograms.

The smallest bird: bee hummingbird, weighs only 1.6 grams.

The highest-flying birds: crane and swan.

The most beautiful bird: peacock.

The best singer: nightingale.

The best runner: once again, the ostrich, which runs up to 72 km/h,

The fastest bird: peregrine.

As scientists have proved, the peregrine can fly at 320–370 kilometres an hour. Obviously, it doesn't mean that as soon as the peregrine spreads its wings it will zoom at this speed, only when peregrine is focused on its prey will it fly like lightning.

The peregrine is called 'terror of the birds', as well as 'travelling falcon'. Both are acceptable.

Usually, people are amazed by the chestnut tree, which changes its colour three times a year. So does the peregrine. I suppose the chestnut tree and the peregrine are somehow related in the linguistics of both Slavic and Turkic languages. Russians call the chestnut tree *kashtan*, and the peregrine *sapsan*. Our Bashkir brothers also call it *sapsan*. The root of this word, I suppose, is *šapšaṇ* in Kazakh, which is usually connected to Turkic words meaning 'fast', 'agile' and 'fierce'. There are a lot of Turkic words in the Russian language, so it is for linguists to judge.

The peregrine comes out of an egg as a white baby chick, later turning a brownish yellow, and looks around restlessly. Its breast line is straight, its legs yellow, its eyes as sharp as a knife. The similarity of its screech to that of an eagle is so evident that pigeons, blue tits, ducks and geese fly away whenever they hear it. After some time, its back darkens, the vertical lines in its breast become horizontal. Its chest builds up, its eye socket turns black, its moustache stripes grow, its beak becomes iron-hard, and it grows into a real falcon. And that is the black peregrine which is often mentioned in Kazakh poems: 'My black peregrine, the girl didn't fall for me, so let her be.'

The first person to name it *Falco peregrinus* was the English ornithologist Marmaduke Tunstall, who published *British Ornithology* in 1771. Since then, this Latin name has circulated in scientific papers. In Kazakh, the peregrine's name means 'sickle-winged'. Languages other than English – German, French, Italian, Romansh – also imply that the bird has sickle-like wings.

Its other name is 'wandering falcon'. As its name suggests, before returning from warm countries with other migratory birds, the peregrine visits northern parts of Europe, Asia, America, as well as southern Europe and Africa. Brehm wrote that it nests on rocks, high trees, sometimes even in the towers of the gothic-style churches that are often found in Europe. However, the present situation doesn't concur with Brehm's information. According to recent facts, the peregrine is extinct in Germany, Poland, Denmark and Scandinavia, as well as the eastern states of the USA. It is rare in Baltic countries, as well as Belorussia and Ukraine. The sole reason for this is the excessive use of poisonous chemicals as pesticides for agriculture.

Nonetheless, its keenness to travel is not a feature that distinguishes the peregrine from other birds. Scientists focus mostly on its cruelty; specifically its fierceness, when it strangles a bird it catches and starts feeding on it immediately in midair. Once a group of hunters saw a peregrine clasping a white goose far bigger and heavier than the peregrine itself. When they saw it land, they fired a gun and the predator instantly dropped its prey and flew off.

However, it circled around as if observing the people's reaction. It had been only five or six minutes since it had grasped its prey when it managed to break the neck of and smother a large 3–5-kilogram goose. Moreover, a 20-kilogram swan is no difficulty for it. And the peregrine itself weighs merely 1 kilogram.

Falconers of the past knowingly gave peregrine names like 'the Executioner', 'Bloodthirsty' or 'Black Sword'. People even saw a peregrine attack a hawk to protect its nest. It doesn't seem to be afraid of anything. It hatches once a year and eats for about 300 birds during the nesting season. The peregrine breaks its prey's breastbone and feeds only on soft meat.

Once we witnessed it clasping a duck in the middle of a crowded duck pond. This time it didn't kick its prey when coming down through the sky, but seized a flying duck, grabbing it in midair. A horseman, who was watering horses on the shore, rushed with his ķuiryķ, but the peregrine took no notice.[128] Instead, it sat on the nearby tree for a while, then later landed clutching its prey and proceeded to try to feed it. Occasionally it gave out a screech. The horseman charged once again, his eyes fixed on a twisted fat duck in the predator's claws – he wanted to snatch it. The peregrine wasn't afraid, but slowly withdrew to the top of the tree. At that moment, you would understand the saying about one's eyes 'blazing fire': a look that does not yield and does not fear; a look that is ready for anything. Among all four-legged creatures, only the wolf possesses such vigour.

Supposedly, all types of falcons are brave. They swing easily into a flock of flying ducks and drop them one by one. Even a small sparrowhawk, or its fist-sized 'little brother', the shikra, are considered the scourge of all pigeons. Pigeons and blue tits alike are so terrified that when a sparrowhawk or a shikra cuts through the air, they fly onto an open balcony in fear of their lives.

However, none of them is like the peregrine. The saker falcon may have bloody eyes, but it hesitates when it encounters a stronger bird. However murderous a hawk might be, it doesn't strike against a golden eagle. On the other hand, a peregrine, especially when provoked to defend its nest or chicks, can easily attack vultures and eastern imperial eagles. If the old Kazakh poem 'Charge your enemy boldly, you won't die till your time comes' is about birds, could it be about the peregrine? No one has heard of a peregrine being attacked by another bird.

A hobby is also considered a swift bird. It's true. It's so fast that one doesn't notice it seizing a swallow in the blink of an eye. One fact that makes this such a mean act is that the swallow is a nice, innocent bird. The hobby's bravery is a consequence of exaggeration, it seems. God knows what the origin of the Kazakh phrase 'tussled like a hobby' is. It's evident that few people regard the hobby as bold. Few Kazakh falconers have ever hunted with a hobby; the Russians hardly ever. Some years ago, there was a falconer outside Almaty who was the only person who had a hobby. When asked why, he said, 'In summer, birds of prey get hungry. They are fed up with the same meat bought from the bazaar, or the house rabbit and corsac fox. They might starve by eating nothing. If I give it a taste of pigeon or duck, the hobby is a best choice to hunt for such small birds.' It turns out eagles are similar to horses in having dietary preferences.

Just as 'the fox's beautiful fur is its misfortune', the peregrine's predatory talents might bring it bad luck. Alfred Brehm discusses peregrines in the 'Birds' section of his *Life of Animals*. He writes:

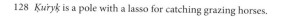

---

128 Ķuiryķ is a pole with a lasso for catching grazing horses.

One can't treat the peregrine's predatory nature lightly because of the innumerable damage it causes. The peregrine isn't satisfied with only killing birds for its sustenance. It chaotically thrusts itself left and right, and slaughters everything in its way. It kills so many birds at once, as if a whole flock of other raptors might have done this. Its own 'brothers' from the falcon family drop their prey the moment they spot a peregrine. It goes without saying that it does more harm than good. Consequently, they all should be eliminated.

If Brehm, who is acclaimed for his love of animals, states his opinion so furiously about peregrines, does it mean that Kazakh people, who concluded that the 'peregrine is like the wolf of birds', felt animosity rather than sympathy (as we used to believe) towards it? On every occasion people observed its predatory characteristics.

A famous Soviet zoologist from Tashkent, Roman Maklenburtsev, suggested culling buzzards annually. Ornithologists from the Soviet Union, who were alarmed that the birds were becoming extinct, were shocked by this statement. The scientist didn't give in:

Didn't we plan to raise muskrat in a region near A'mu Dariâ? We did. However, why is it not happening? The number of buzzards, which feed on muskrat, is growing, that is why. The agricultural plan will not advance until we get rid of them, or the Central Committee of the Communist Party will have to look for other solutions. Hence, the extermination of buzzards should be our main prerogative.

No sooner said than done. Shortly, hunters with guns on their shoulders were hidden in the reeds of A'mu Dariâ. Afterwards, buzzards died like flies. Was it only buzzards? Not all the hunters were professionals; among them were a lot of men looking for fun, holding guns, free bullets from the Government, authorization in their pockets, and no control whatsoever. As well as buzzards, 20,000 hawks died in that period. More than half were peregrines. What can you say about that? Those rascals didn't distinguish the buzzard from the red-footed falcon, the saker falcon from the peregrine, or the hawk from the sparrowhawk. However, the number of muskrats never did increase. People should not interfere with the providence of Allah. The devil always follows wherever man goes. Ornithologists who fear the buzzard's vivacity ought not to read Brehm's book. God knows, they'll start more bloodshed.

When peregrines are being discussed, buzzards, hobbies or the red-footed falcon should not be mentioned at all. The peregrine is a peregrine. A talented poet, a reputable master, who knows his worth in Kazakh poetry, might have complained about our audiences, who didn't distinguish the good poetry from the poor:

I am a stallion that trots, even when saddled a thousand times,

that strokes and aims afar,

I am a peregrine flying high,

that a kestrel doesn't dare approach.

Some people say that peregrines do not land on dead people. They are compared with the gyrfalcon, saying that they are as pure-bred as them. We do not know. There is no need to argue. The fact that it feeds on pigeons, ducks, geese, lapwings, larks and gulls is without question. Does it eat mice or gophers? Quite possibly. The zoologist Ralph Pfeffer, who was born in Kazakhstan and later moved to Germany, wrote about peregrines in his book *Ptitsa na Ruke* (*Bird in the Hand*), in which he kept mentioning Alik, who is the Kazakh falconer Aʹbilhaḳ Tùrlybaev. Previously, we mentioned Aʹbilhaḳ in the chapter 'Gyrfalcon'. As Ileke, Iliâs Žansùgirov, remarked about Molyḳbaj the *kùjši*, 'The only *ḳobyz* player left is him', the most knowledgeable falconer in Kazakhstan nowadays is Aʹbilhaḳ.[129] In his book, Pfeffer mentions Aʹbilhaḳ, attributing the following words to him: 'A peregrine is the best to put forward to a hare. The hare's brain would be scattered around once the peregrine kicks him.' The experienced falconer, the most respected Aʹbeke, wouldn't have said this unknowingly.[130] However, the peregrine is famous for being able to attack a flying target rather than something that is on the ground.

Speaking of attack, in Mahambet's poem 'Ḳyzġyšḳuš' ('The Lapwing'), he wrote:

> Oh lapwing, lapwing,
> Your wings are firm, your neck is soft,
> Having lost Isataj,
> I befriended solitude.
> The peregrine's powerful kick
> Made you lose your lake.
> Žangir Khan's powerful pressure
> Made me lose my native land.[131]

Consequently, people have long known the peregrine's tenacity, specifically, its unique tactic for catching birds. Speaking of the old days, plenty of legends and stories suggest that the people of the Middle East and Asia Minor have known how to raise peregrines since ancient times. In one of those legends, when one of the gossips led to dispute, a peregrine was the reason for both sides coming to a mutual agreement. 'If he wants to be friends, let him give his peregrine' was a condition to which the village leader had resigned himself half-heartedly. This is a legend. In truth, from ancient times people used peregrines less than saker falcons, the eagle or even less than the gyrfalcon, though it has always been respected. For example, in Egyptian mythology the God of the Sky, Horus, is drawn with a hawk's head. In 1405, the King of England, Henry IV, bestowed the Isle of Man on John

---

129 The citation is from Iliâs Žansùgirov's poem 'Kuishi', and describes 'the last *ḳobyz* player', Molyḳbaj.

130 Abeke, shortened respectful version of Aʹbilhaḳ.

131 Mahambet Ôtemisuly (1803–46) was a poet and leader of rebellions against Russian colonialism. He and his friend Isataj Tajmanuly (1791–1838) organized initial rebellions against Žángir Khan (1801–45) of the Bôkey Horde (1801–72).

Stanley. In exchange, the Stanley family was obliged to bring two peregrines to the future coronations of Henry's descendants. This tradition continued until 1821.

The Holy Roman Emperor Carl V sold the Maltese islands. What was the price, you ask? Not money, but one peregrine. Later, the American writer Dashiell Hammett wrote a novel called *The Maltese Falcon*. In 1941 a film adaptation was made with the same title.

When we talk about the peregrine, we recall an old saying: 'When two wealthy people become in-laws, they present pure-bred horses to each other.' The peregrine has also been a bird of the privileged. According to another poem:

You are a peregrine among birds,
A jewel a commoner can't aspire to.[132]

Yes, only the rich, who had everything in abundance, could afford peregrines. Firstly, they are not easily acquired. Raising them is highly problematic, like snatching prey out of the lion's mouth. As a species they are few, stubborn and not easily tamed. Secondly, even if it is caught, it won't yield straight away. In falconers' terms hawks usually start eating from the gauntlet after 1–2 weeks. The writer Táken Álimķuĺov has a story 'Sur Ķaršyġa' ('Grey goshawk'), based on the life of Aķan Seri.[133] In this story, when Aķan caught a young goshawk, he was asked when it would be ready for hunting, and he said, 'It seems that the breed is spiteful, so he will probably mellow in half a month.' The peregrine is not a goshawk; it takes a lot longer to tame. Thirdly, grooming a peregrine is very difficult. That's why most peregrine-catchers gave them to wealthy people as a gift. Gentlemen appreciated hunters' work, and gave whatever they were asked. We would like to tell the story of a man who took the risk of following this tradition. This is the story.

Seser lived in Ulaanbaatar, the capital of Mongolia. He had graduated from the Moscow Agricultural Institute and started work as an economist in an iron-ore refinery. Our hospitable Mongol brothers did not alienate a Kazakh son. Instead, they respected him as 'wheat amongst the barley'; that is, they treated better than they would treat each other. He wasn't deprived of authority, fame or promotion. Having the power and position that he did, did he think that in one night he would be coming back to Kazakhstan, crying for his homeland like the antelope which has left the black forest behind?

This song was committed to his memory:

Is it the Kobda we see from afar?
Why hasn't the Kobda become my home?[134]

---

132 The citation is from the 'Ajtys of Kùderi and Ulbike'. *Ajtys is* a poetry improvization contest accompanied by *dombyra* (traditional Kazakh instrument) music. The given *ajtys* is a well-known example of the genre, and was a contest between Kùderiķoža Kôŝekuĺy (1820–58) and Uĺbike Žankeldiķyzy (1825–49).

133 Táken Álimķuĺov (1918–87) was a Kazakh writer and literary critic. Aķan Seri Ķoramsauĺy (1843–1913) was a Kazakh poet, singer and composer.

134 The River Ķodba.

Whatever people say, he was happy when he moved back. His daughters and sons were accepted into Kazakh school immediately. They studied Kazakh. He didn't tell anyone that the reason he had returned from Mongolia was his children's education. When the Mongol people gained independence from the USSR in the 1990s, they advocated abandoning the Cyrillic alphabet and adopting their previous writing style. One day when he had returned from work, he had seen his young daughter scribbling something. He didn't ask what it was. He recognized that ancient Mongol script. His heart ached at the thought that in the next five or six years, his descendants and siblings would be deprived of their ancestral culture. The proverb 'Head home while you have your senses' might have referred to this situation.

Shortly after, he quit his job and returned to his homeland of Bayan Olgii.[135] There people were also much disturbed. It had been half a year since most had migrated to Kazakhstan. He followed the crowd and came to Almaty. The city that Seser and his relatives had dreamed of didn't give him a warm welcome. Although his children attended a Kazakh school, they couldn't find a common language with the local Kazakh children, who spoke Russian. What to do? These two lines come to mind.

> Is it the Ķobda we see from afar?
> Why didn't the Ķobda become my home?

They decided, 'No, that city is not for us,' and moved to the countryside. There was no work there either. Both he and the local administration were exasperated by him asking for a job and them declining. The mayor and other authority figures grew annoyed and said, 'We are not the ones who invited you back from Mongolia. You are welcome to go back where you came from.' The Mongols were kind, and also had discipline and manners. But here, people in offices were impatient and could blurt out everything in a mix of Kazakh and Russian. Even women swore in Russian. He had studied in Moscow, so was also acquainted with the swear words, but he couldn't keep up with the locals.

His neighbour Mizamhan, who had migrated from China, became wealthy rapidly because of trading goods from Ghulja and Urumqi in China. Only he and the elderly Tağajmurat from Uzbekistan were left out. Tağajmurat *aķsaķal* resembled the Kazakh people of the past – wise and deliberate.[136] He was poor. The poor are usually generous. Sometimes he was dismayed at himself when they talked in private, saying, 'How did I not learn how to trade after being raised among Uzbeks?' He had neither trading skills nor Urumqi, no Ghulja connections to rely on. Quite the contrary; when he visited relatives in Uzbekistan, they expected him to treat them with presents.

Once the weather became colder, Seser stopped paying visits to the administration. A pox- and wrinkle-faced mayor, a squat man, who fashioned his hair like a young hedgehog, didn't seem like a bad person; he didn't mumble a greeting like the others. On the other hand, he first said, 'Yes, boy', then pausing for a while, turned his whole body and said, '*Uagalei-kumus-sale-em*.'[137] But warm greetings were far from the promise; Seser accomplished nothing. He was put off, worn out by hearing, 'Come tomorrow, or the day after tomorrow.' One day he met the mayor near the shop and turned to greet him. After greeting him back,

135 Bayan Olgii – a province in Mongolia with a Muslim and Kazakh majority.
136 *Aķsaķal* is a respectful address for an elderly man.
137 *Uagalei-kumus-sale-em*, a greeting in Arabic that means 'Peace be upon you too'.

the mayor asked out of nowhere, 'Ei, Gengis Khan? Why were you named Seser?' He added, 'Seser sounds like *eser*.'[138]

Seser grinned, 'The right version is Ôser, *aga*.[139] The Mongols made a mistake when they wrote it down.' He lied. Previously, when Mongolia was allied with the USSR, they had been in the habit of giving their newborns Russian names. Also, the superstitious Kazakhs used to say, 'If you name your child with a kaffir name, he won't be jinxed; if you give the name of a swindler, he will live long.' There are no secrets about the name Seser. Nowadays no one would believe that it's actually from the word 'USSR' (or 'SSSR' in Russian). It was a time when the Kazakhs of Kazakhstan also named their kids Iliych, Michael, Ivan, Nicolai, Mels, Kim, even Kaganovich. The Kazakhs of Bayan Olgii weren't going to give in to the others, so they named him 'SSSR'.[140] In Mongol phonetics it is read and written as 'SeSeSeR'. Later the syllable 'se' was omitted, and he became Seser.

'Okay, Ôser *batyr*, tell me this.[141] Are there any Kazakhs who hunt with an eagle in Mongolia?'

Seser wanted to boast 'You should learn hunting from us', but refrained, saying only, 'There are.'

The mayor asked, 'So, do your Mongols hunt with the peregrine?' He didn't wait for Seser to answer, just looked at the sky saying, 'If only I had a peregrine.' Seser also looked at the sky. It was crystal clear. Just like the sky in Bayan Olgii.

'Why hasn't the Ķobda become my home?' he mumbled.

'What are you talking about? What's the Ķobda?' asked the mayor.

'Nothing,' he replied.

A bird was flying high in the sky. Not a peregrine, probably a black kite. Peregrines didn't fly that way. 'Do you hunt with birds?' he asked, wanting to change the subject.

The mayor knitted his brows. 'I did that in the past. Now everything is fucking different.'

Seser asked himself, 'Why did he swear in Kazakh, not Russian?' The mayor turned and went on his way.

As the Kazakhs say, 'Oh, it turns out it's just a frog.' Seser understood his *aga*'s affection for the peregrine. His hint was clear, although he didn't say it directly: 'Catch one for me'. He assumed it to be right, since he didn't have any cattle or money to put in the mayor's pocket to win his sympathy. Probably the mayor assumed if anyone would be able to get hold of a peregrine, that would be this poor lad. For crying out loud, wasn't Seser the one referred to as the 'Wild Mongol'?

The next morning, he got up with the sun's first rays and headed towards the woods. A little earlier that year, he had been stuck for 1–2 hours on the road with thick woods along both sides. He had been coming from Almaty, and the bus had broken down. That day he had heard peregrines screeching in the woods, and thought, 'So, there are peregrines here in Kazakhstan as well.' Today he seemed to hear them once again.

One of the four pigeons he had caught the night before in the old club's roof had died. He judged it a good omen, since 'the owner contributes to his own loss'. He tied the legs of the three remaining pigeons. Pressing them beneath his arms he recalled a song that started

---

138 *Eser* – a fool, reckless.

139 *Ôser* means 'will prosper'.

140 SSSR, Russian for USSR.

141 *Batyr* – originally a term for 'hero' or 'valiant warrior', roughly equivalent to the European 'knight'. Nowadays the term signifies military or masculine prowess.

The Birds Are Our Friends

with the line 'Tie a horse in the Kalmyk way', and chuckled. He did not even have a stick, let alone a rifle, only a small yellow-necked hoe. With a net tied around his waist, casual clothes and trotting calmly, he looked like a man taking a walk. He was humming. 'Why hasn't Ķobda become my home?'

It was the middle of the fourth month – 'cuckoo month', as Kazakhs call it. Why cuckoo? Cuckoos do not arrive that month. They only arrive when the sun is hot, and summer has reached its peak. According to Kazakhs living in China, the second month is already Nauryz (March), so farmers start preparing their ploughs and other tools.[142] In central, northern and western Kazakhstan, they say 'February will challenge us for forty days', and face this month with fear. Winters are long in Mongolia too.

The lark was tweeting, and not too far away, the magpie was cawing. Hence, spring was close. The peregrine would nest at that time, and after 28–29 days its chicks would fledge. Although Seser considered himself an urban Kazakh, he had spent his childhood in the countryside, near livestock. Memories of childhood cannot be erased from one's memory. He was startled how local Kazakhs had distanced themselves from nature. They didn't know simple things. In youngsters' case this was understandable, but silver-haired elderly people couldn't differentiate a yearling from a weanling. Hardly anyone could identify birds either. For them, every sparrow was a blue tit. Every tree was a willow. If you asked them for the reason, they'd give the excuse, 'Eh, ķaraģym, we left native parts a long time ago.'[143] Shouldn't they rather speak the truth: 'I was easy-going, careless, indifferent from the beginning, and later, because of Russian vodka, I didn't pay attention to anything else.'

The song kept coming back to him: 'Why hasn't the Ķobda become my home?'

The sun was blazing hot by then. As Seser wondered if he could distinguish the saker falcon's egg from the peregrine's, a pied raven swooped from the black woods. There was definitely a bird of prey there somewhere. The peregrine does not build its nest itself. It seizes a raven's or magpie's nest. In that instant a white-grey bird bolted, fluttering its wings from the nest on an elm tree at the edge of the slope. When Seser observed carefully, stretching his neck, he saw that the nest was a raven's. A magpie's nest is domed; you can see that it leaves a hole in one side, so that only it can enter. There is usually one more 'door', however, it's hard to find. It is shut all around. The raven's nest is spread more widely; individual twigs stick out from the sides. You might have seen that, in the East, people mix straw with sand and form bricks to construct a house. It looks as if a raven uses the same technique, and plasters its nest's foundations with clay. Anyone who sees its nest might wonder, *What a great work of a master*. In this case the *master* is the raven.

Seser halted, misty-eyed, disappointed that he hadn't noticed what kind of bird had just flown away. Never mind, he thought, and began climbing the tree. The white-grey bird flew round the nest once more. He recognized it. A saker falcon. The raven lays eggs in winter. They lead their chicks before the harsh winter ends. Thus, firstly, that saker falcon was looking for a nest. Secondly, it meant that there was no peregrine close by. Other hawks do not nest near the peregrine. It was the opposite of 'The pious run from evil'.

Speaking of neighbours, however vicious they might be, surprisingly, peregrines never trouble small birds nesting in nearby rocks. If its nest is on one tree, sparrows and blue tits

---

142 *Nauryz* – Kazakh annual holiday. In Kazakhstan, spring arrives fully on 21 March, the day when Nauryz is celebrated, signifying not only the Spring Equinox, but also the renewal of nature; Nauryz is also the word for the month of 'March' in Kazakh.

143 *Ķaraģym* – diminutive form of address for a younger person.

can nest freely on the next one. In other words, it has its own *auyl*. It does not bother its *auyl*, and does not let others do so. It hunts far from the *auyl*, without disturbing small birds in adjoining areas. It does not attack them. In this way peregrine resembles the wolf which is a highly social animal that lives in packs and does not interbreed with its close relatives.

Seser went back. Birds generally search for food before dawn or at night. He wanted to examine the brown mountains along the big road, especially under that black ledge. If only he had come at dusk, he would have known where each bird was flying. He had no horse to saddle. What had he to do? Who should he ask? Who was going to give him a horse if he asked? Had he been in Mongolia, he wouldn't have worried: Kazakhs and Mongols, even the most indigent ones, would at least have lent him an anthrax-laden horse. Relatives always had one if you did not. He who comes not boasting but asking is considered the same as God.

'Why hasn't the Ķobda become my home?'

Hoping for the best he progressed towards the mountains. After a short distance, the long narrow asphalt road became full of potholes. Later with all the stones around, the road had fallen apart, but seemed as if it had often been patched up, and gradually led to a big road once again. He went off-road, following the mountain spur far away, where he could only see the shadows. When he was circling the ledge, he saw a flock of ducks heading towards the city of Ķapšaġaj. But there was no peregrine chasing them. He went further, where an old Uyghur man on a donkey was herding sheep.

Seser lay down his net. He tied the two pigeons he had been clenching under his armpit to either side of the net, as the saying goes, with 'long harness, wide straps', and tied their knuckles to a stake with a 5–6 ķùlaš long rope,[144] with a loop at the end, like a ķazyķbau.[145] Then he hid under a silverberry. The second end of the rope was at the bottom of the net. A pigeon that is on a 'long harness' can fly up to a man's height, but then it feels as if 'dragged down by its hem' by a thin rope, and it lands. Whenever the pigeon flew up, other pigeons became restless. After midday, the pigeons settled down. Even if they didn't, a predator attacking them was unlikely to show up. However, Seser tried to poke them with a stick, as if saying, 'Why are you so quiet? Move. Call for a peregrine.' They didn't budge. *Had they been in their nests, they wouldn't have been so calm*, he thought. They were still, as if they were afraid or worried about something.

'Why hasn't the Ķobda become my home?'

By then he was exhausted as well. He stood up, tired of lying down all day long. Suddenly, the pigeons started fussing. The old man's sheepdog from before came running, so he warded it off with bricks. Silence once again. Wings rustled; one or two pigeons flew by. They didn't even glance at their kin, who were prisoners on earth. He packed up his net and went home. He reached the main road and hitch-hiked. All of a sudden, the pigeons under his armpit started twitching and jerking. Apparently, they were being suffocated. So, he loosened his hold, but instead of coming out, they hid further in his arms. While he was wondering, *What has happened to them?*, a car heading from the city swooped and stopped right in front of him. The driver was from the *auyl*. Seser knew his father. He was a teacher from China, but now he herded sheep for another farmer. They were outsiders, like Seser. As the saying goes, 'People who have less are each other's kin', so they found a common tongue quickly enough. The lad was very talkative and polite, enquiring about an

144 Ķùlaš is an age-old Kazakh measurement of length, equivalent to an arm span.

145 Ķazyķbau is a way to tie a rope to a stake.

older companion's health and well-being, as befitted a Kazakh. He dropped Seser next to his house.

Next day Seser woke very early and returned to the same ledge. As he was crossing the road, the pigeons started shuffling again. The instant he opened the chest-side button of his *bešpet*, all three birds burrowed further into his chest.[146] The wind seemed to swish at his head. He looked at the restless birds in his arms and thought, *Can you not fight one another when it's already cramped*? They seemed to calm down. After a while they became agitated again, then calmed down once more. He passed the place from the day before, and lay down his net next to a thick caragana bush. The wind seemed to blow again round his head. The pigeons cowered in a corner. He saw a peregrine nearby, flying swiftly upwards. As 'a duck taken aback swims backwards', rather than wishing an unexpected peregrine to fall for the trap, he started shooing it away with stones. As he was wiping the sweat from his forehead, he thought, *Oh my, has this peregrine been following me since yesterday? I wondered why the pigeons were so restless. Poor little things. They sensed the peregrine's presence, unlike me.*

The predator didn't show up again. It was midday, noon, afternoon, way past noon, dusk, and there was no sign of the peregrine. He walked home. He pitied himself. He freed the pigeons and recalled the song once more. 'Why hasn't the Ķobda become my home?'

Time passed. It was already May. He tried to avoid the mayor. He felt like a person who couldn't fulfil his promise. Later, the man from China who was herding the farmer's sheep became unwell so he was asked to fill in for him for one or two days. He agreed readily. *It's better than quarrelling with my wife, sitting at home and doing nothing*, he thought.

In the spring sheep didn't tend to stay in one place, rather they roamed from one hill to the other in search of grass. Ashamed to ride the herdsman's donkey, he went on foot. The donkey grazing with the sheep didn't raise its head. Teal feathers were scattered under a silverberry tree. Poor bird seemed to have become prey to a red or corsac fox. He halted when he approached what was left of the teal. No, neither a red nor a corsac fox had done this. It had become a meal for a peregrine. How did he know that? One distinguishing fact about peregrines is that they leave their prey's wings, head and legs uneaten. They eat only pure meat.

As had happened a while ago (when he'd tried to catch a peregrine using the pigeons), a swishing wind went by above his head. What if the peregrine had a nest nearby? He started studying his surroundings carefully. On a lone rocky cliff, there was no place for a bird's nest nor a hillock on which to clasp their feet. Just as he was thinking that by this time peregrine would have shown itself if it had a nest, the swishing wind returned. It turned out to be a peregrine. In the blink of an eye it was already up in the sky. Even further. He sat still, wondering about its next move. The peregrine hovered overhead and darted down. Like a rock from a slingshot it came, its wings grazing the tops of bushy trees, then it rose swiftly. He ran after it. He saw a large nest lying on the thick branch of a big tree. He took off his boots and started climbing it. The peregrine definitely had an egg or chick, or else it wouldn't be diving so hard. By diving in this location, the bird was declaring, 'Stay out! This is my place.'

Now Seser had reached the nest, but when he saw it, he nearly fell backwards. His excited heart calmed down. It was not the absence of chicks that shocked him, nor the presence of four or five eggs instead of chicks – it was the squishy softness of the eggs, like rubber. They flexed when he squeezed them, like something wobbly. He had cold sweat on

Peregrine

---

146 *Bešpet* is a light, embroidered, knee-length outer garment worn over a dress or a t-shirt.

his forehead. Was it a devil or a jinn?[147] 'God help me', he muttered. No other word came to mind. Wasn't an egg supposed to be hard? What was this? He recovered himself and looked sideways. One or two eggs were squished, like soft *ķùrt* left to dry on a shelf.[148] It couldn't even be called squashy, or else it would have been scattered all over the nest. That nest had some disease; a disgusting smell overpowered him.

Why was he hesitating? Was he imagining malformed babies born at the Semej test site?[149] Had the illness spread to them as well? While he was pondering, something caught his attention. Long talons sliced at his face. He swayed and held on to the brunch. The thick tree broke with a thud. The first thing he saw was the black peregrine falling, taking the branch with it. Even as it fell, the peregrine kept threatening him and screeching. The peregrine, who was protective of its chick and who was risking its life to save even dead eggs, was rather pitiful. Seser jumped down, wiping the blood from his face. Generally, the peregrine strikes with its back claws. God had protected him. If it had reached its target, it would have torn out his eye. Not too far away the donkey was trailing. The injured peregrine couldn't fly away, and was falling and rising. It was heading clumsily towards the ravine. Seser caught up.

The peregrine slashed at him with its claws, not wanting to let him any closer. He took off his *bešpet* and threw it at the bird's head. Amid the mayhem he managed to catch the bird. The poor bird was breathing hard. It seemed its wing was broken. Its one leg was dangling. Seser had tears in his eyes. 'God has doubled his misery.' The peregrine did not understand his pity, and was struggling to break free. 'I will set you free. Heal first. In this state you could be anyone's prey,' he said.

At dusk, a large man was seen riding a donkey, following the sheep, a wounded peregrine laid on the front of his saddle. At that specific moment, he hated everything: those successive mountains, blood-red clouds, skipping spring waters, the mayor in the *auyl*, the innumerable sheep, the donkey that didn't obey however hard he tried, and Kazakhstan.

In his ear, he heard a familiar song: 'Why hasn't the Ķobda become my home?'

---

147 *Jinn*, an intelligent spirit created from fire (as opposed to angels created from light and humans created from earth), invisible to humans. Jinns can be male or female, Muslim and non-Muslim; they can be born, marry and die. They appear in different forms and move at great speeds. It is believed that non-Muslim jinns can possess human beings and do harm, whereas Muslim jinns heal people and fight evil jinns.

148 *Ķùrt*, hard, salty dairy product made from a drained yoghurt-like beverage, *ķatyķ*; *ķùrt* comes in different shapes.

149 Semej (now in the East Kazakhstan region) was the primary testing site for the Soviet Union's nuclear weapons from 1949 to 1989. Over 200,000 villagers in the region were thus exposed to radiation, often deliberately, so Soviet scientists could determine its effects, and over half that number continue to be affected. Soil, water and air remain highly contaminated, and serious physical deformities in children were and are a common occurrence.

Peacock

*I*t has been said and written many times that the peacock is the most beautiful bird in the world. Why is it so beautiful? The answer to this question is certainly 'because God created it like this'. Scientists at Fudan University, China, have tried for many years to reveal the secrets of this conundrum. Recently, they announced, 'We have uncovered the mystery of the peacock's beauty.' The reason is its pigmentation and colour structure. A substance in the body of a peacock emits colouring peculiar only to these birds. Therefore, each of its feathers shimmers with blue, gold, brown and light blue. The scientists revealed that each of its feathers consists of two-layer crystal structures, made up of melanin and keratin proteins. Usually, ordinary people are not interested in these details. They are only interesting to experts.

Let's suppose that we could explain the colour of the peacock feathers, how then do we understand the behaviour of the peacock in the evening? The peacock that grazes quietly together with the hens during the day becomes anxious, then flies and lands on the top of the tallest tree at twilight. After that, it stares at the sunset. Even if the sunset has ended, the peacock continues to sit there. It doesn't move from its place, as if it won't be able to see the sunrise again. Even when the Pleiades appear in the sky, it doesn't stop looking to the west. I wonder how its neck doesn't get tired. Only with the onset of sunrise does the peacock turn its neck to the dawn. This means that the ancient Eastern riddle is true:

The peacock is a bird of God,
it is not an ordinary one,
it is a sunflower among them.

Indeed, this bird is compared to a sunflower among the birds. If there are two birds that love the sun, one of them is the peacock. Perhaps this bird loves the sun's rays so much because it naturally inhabits hot countries and originates from India, Sri Lanka and the island of Sumatra. Among the first European visitors who encountered this gorgeous bird in these lavish lands, there were those who thought peacocks couldn't fly. They were wrong, obviously. Probably, one who saw the long tail feathers of the peacock would have said that 'it cannot fly, because it can't lift its heavy body'.

Moreover, in the aforementioned countries, no one scares this bird or throws a stone at it. In 1963, India declared the peacock to be the country's national bird. This doesn't mean that the peacock has become an honourable bird only since that time. According to ornithologists, the peacock was domesticated about 3,000 years ago. In Sri Lanka, you may also see these birds grazing on the street. Since they walk in the street or in gardens freely and loosely, those who see these birds grazing blithely think that peacocks cannot or are not supposed to fly.

In fact, peacocks can fly. They are as large as 2.5 metres in length and have significant weight. However, they can take off easily and fly swiftly. In 2004, in the Russian newspapers *Izvestia* and *Komsomolskaya Pravda*, it was reported that one of the peacocks had escaped

from its enclosure in Moscow Zoo during the evening. They asked people to contact the zoo administration or the newspapers' editorial offices if anyone saw it. Soon the peacock was found. The zoo authorities were pleased that 'the peacock wasn't caught and eaten by drunkards who roam the streets'. In another article, it was reported by the same editors that some unemployed people had caught a Japanese crane and had eaten it as a snack accompanied by some vodka.

It is said that the peacock was first brought to Europe by Alexander the Great. Of course, this didn't mean that the bird was brought in the king's personal carriage. Probably, it merely means that peacocks moved to this region in those times. In one of the sources it was stated that, in eleventh-century Rome, there were more people who kept peacocks at home than those who kept quails. The Romans honoured this bird; they used to eat its meat, and gave each other its feathers as a gift.

An ancient Eastern couplet reads like this:

The peacock's tail adorns its beauty
It must be Great Almighty's will.

Indeed, as we said before, the peacock's beauty comes from its long tail feathers. Only peacocks have these tail feathers. Peahens, like female pheasants, are smaller in size, and drabber.

When the peacock opens its colourful tail feathers into a fan, it doesn't mean to display its beauty as everyone supposes. It wants to attract the peahens' attention. By doing so, peacocks invite the females to nest. A Turkish theologian, Harun Yahya, wrote: 'The peacock itself cannot see its beautiful tail feather, which fascinates everyone.' Indeed, there is a deep philosophical meaning here. In ancient Eastern literature, the peacock was always regarded as a subject for philosophical writings.

Modern ornithology states that there are white peacocks as well. In 2002, an interesting article was published about the abduction of an albino peacock from a British zoo. It is interesting to note that no one had paid any attention to the thief, who had hidden a white bird similar to a goose in his shirt and left the zoo. It is still unknown whether this bird was ever found or not. More likely not. The reason is that peacock meat is highly prized in some foreign restaurants as a delicacy.

Peacocks don't differ much from other species of *Phasianidae*. When peacocks are two years old, the females begin to lay eggs. In two months, they hatch chicks. Sometimes, for some reason, the female is unable to lay eggs. When the peahen is sick, dies or weakens because of climate changes then a turkey can hatch its chicks instead. There is much in common between these birds.

Since the 1990s, modern Kazakhs have started to domesticate peacock chicks in Almaty and keep them at home. The first experiments were unsuccessful and led to the birds' deaths. There were two reasons. Firstly, since these birds are accustomed to a warmer climate, they couldn't adapt to the changeable weather of Almaty. Secondly, the people, who didn't know about the special care needed for these birds, were to blame. Instead of raising peacocks that were already acclimatized to Kazakhstan, ambitious and competitive people ordered peacocks from distant foreign countries. The bird is as pure as an angel. It dies or flies away from those who have bad intentions.

In the Ancient East, ambassadors that visited a king's palace when visiting another country didn't pay attention to gold, silver or wealth, but to pets. A king that met an ambassador with birds of prey was regarded as a cruel and bloodthirsty leader. A king that had many songbirds was regarded as a good-natured and wise ruler. And the owners of the palace that had weak or sick birds were regarded as unstable, unprincipled, unhappy rulers that didn't have willpower. A king with a leopard was supposed to be courageous; a king that kept deer loved beauty; and a king with many colourful things was considered a womanizer. Whether these assumptions were true or not, as a Kazakhs saying goes 'When people say something, there is always a reason.' When kings sent each other gifts like peacocks, parrots, nightingales or falcons, there were definitely hidden messages in them.

There are some superstitions about peacocks. If someone keeps them at home, a misfortune can happen to that person. Another one is if someone is poor and can barely feed himself, but keeps a peacock at home, it won't bring any luck for that home. I guess both of these are false. In this case, I remember a Kazakh proverb: 'Kazakhs believe in omens; but their omens don't come true.' The peacock cannot cause misfortune. Happiness and unhappiness are sent by the Creator, or caused by a person's own actions, not by a bird.

It is true, however, that you can hear the peacocks' mournful voice in the courtyard of those who keep this bird as a decoration and to show off to others. Again, what else do you expect to hear if they are not cared for or are deprived of freedom? In addition, this bird is not a songbird. As has been said before, the Almighty doesn't gift everybody with everything at once. It would be great if such a beautiful bird had a beautiful voice. (There is a saying in the East: 'The peacock is proud of its appearance, but is shy of its legs.')

People who heard the bird's plaintive voice thought it was a bad omen, just like a dog's howl. What other reason could there be? People presumably considered it a bad omen when a destitute person kept a peacock at home, because they were concerned about the poor. How could a man who barely feeds himself take proper care of the bird? It is not so easy to look after such a large bird, after all.

Some tourists were surprised to see wild peacocks in the American states of California and Florida, as well as in New Zealand. Don't be surprised by this. In the beginning, many rich people in these places wanted to keep this unusual bird for decoration. These people could not be bothered to look after them, and instead, they set them free. Perhaps there were other reasons: maybe the peacock's unpleasant voice early in the morning used to wake a sleeping child. Anyway, those peacocks were difficult to tame and were set free.

Farid-ud-Din Attar's famous work *The Conference of the Birds* and Alisher Navai's *The Language of the Birds* both attach great importance to the peacock. Jalal-ad-Din Rumi, in his poem 'Masnavi', narrated a story: 'One day a jackal was escaping and it fell down into a bowl of paint. It became so colourful with the paint that having forgotten it was a jackal, it announced that it was a peacock.' There are many other examples in Eastern literature about peacocks.

Turkish folklore scholar Nezihe Araz connects the legend 'A Peahen Woman from Turkistan' with Rumi's work. When we hear the word 'Turkistan', it is clear the talk will be about our land. Therefore:

> Once upon a time, a woman arrived in Konya city and set her tent in the distant countryside of Konya, in Gulditobe. Nobody could see the peahen woman. People were interested to see the person who indulged in playing the *rubab* every day and they wanted to see her.[150] Among the people who were intrigued by her mysterious, beautiful music was Rumi. One day they did not hear the sound of the *rubab*. Therefore, Rumi ordered several strong guards from his palace to find out what had happened to the woman. When the messengers came to her place, they couldn't find the woman. Instead they saw some feathers lying on the ground.[151]

It is clear that the legend belongs to Sufi literature. However, the next story does not belong solely to the East; the whole world knows it.

Shah Jahan (1592–1666), although he raided India, is considered by some to be one of the most revered rulers of the past, but is a contradictory personality. We say *contradictory personality* for the reason that he came to the throne by murdering his siblings and all other rivals for the throne. Having been a cruel emperor he built the Taj Mahal, a mausoleum in Agra, dedicated to his wife, Mumtaz Mahal. His Pearl Mosque (Moti Masjid) is also an example of wonders of the world. According to researchers, Shah Jahan moved his capital city from Agra to Delhi in 1648 and lived among the Indian people. Turkic (Mughal) culture thrived alongside Indian culture.

Between these cultural connections a respect and love for the peacock appeared. The emperor was surprised by the Indians' care and attention to this bird. Maybe because a peacock was regarded as 'the guard of the heaven' in Islam, and he wanted Indian people to adopt Islam and feel connected to it through such details, he decided to call his throne the 'Peacock Throne'. Or it might have been caused by his love of beauty. Anyway, he commissioned a new throne to fit the name. According to that order, the main body of the throne was to be built from the mango tree and covered in precious stones, and its shape was to be that of a peacock. The throne had twelve pillars. In Indian architecture, sculpture, jewellery, art and literature, even in music, folklore, design and dance the peacock plays a significant role. The British valued that throne at about £61.2 million at that time.

A Kazakh proverb says: 'There are three non-virtuous things: the throne, a horse and luck.' Perhaps this was said when one was upset about life. The Peacock Throne was also not virtuous. The Persian Nadir Shah invaded the Mughal Empire in 1739, and seized it. The

---

150 *Rubab* – a lute-like musical instrument originating from central Afghanistan and popular in west Asia.
151 Araz N., *Turk folklorunda kuşlar*, Ankara: Ersa vatbaası, 1993.

destruction of the Khanate built and founded by Babur greatly affected the future of both Turan (Central Asia) and Iran.[152] There are some lines which describe that historical event:

> A precious jewelled wonder was demolished.
> What can you say,
> this mortal world will come to an end one day.
> Shah Nadir took the Peacock Throne
> and the Mughals were out of luck.

> Persians got the Peacock Throne.
> Since then the foes of the Mughals have ruled.
> If you lose your luck you lose it all,
> Pity! The Mughals never had the throne back.

Meanwhile, after Nadir Shah's victory, the Mughals lost the precious throne and never recovered. The believers in legend thought this defeat was connected with the loss of the Peacock Throne. Who knows …

Not long after, Shah Nadir was defeated by the Kurds and his wealth was plundered. Kurdish nomads broke the Peacock Throne, taking the precious stones and throwing away the wooden frame. After they became stronger, the Persians captured the Kurds, took the throne back and reconstructed it. The Mughal throne went to the Persians again and it served them for many years. It stood in Tehran for about 200 years. Shahs changed. Each shah prayed blessings to Shah Nadir. They were grateful for the event that 'transferred luck from Turks to Persians'.

History knows other emperors who renewed and restored royal possessions passed from generation to generation. For instance, the Emperor Fatikh Ali (1797–1834), reconstructed the Peacock Throne and bought about 26,733 precious stones weighing 230 kg. It is valued today at US$804 million.

Ancient chronicles provide interesting facts. During Shah Nadir's reign, many parts of the Caucasus, the central and eastern parts of Georgia, were part of Iran, so the Persian kings used to invite the elite of the lands to their feasts. When Persian leaders were sitting at the top tables, Georgian dukes used to make their toasts, taking the feathers of the peacock into their hands. The feathers indicated that people were foreigners who the Persians dominated.

In 1926, the Emperor Pahlavi, and in 1941, his heir the next Pahlavi, sat on this jewelled throne. The Peacock Throne did not bring happiness or luck to Iran either; it brought famine. The last heir of the Pahlavi dynasty, Mohammad Reza, was forced to abandon both his throne and homeland when Ayatollah Khomeini overthrew him and came to power in the country.

When I visited Iran recently, I witnessed the importance of the peacock for this country. I took some pictures of them in the capital city, Tehran. In the city you often encounter tall sculptures of peacocks. The sculptures are embedded with colourful lights and are usually kept clean. Tehran is famous for its dance and art. They connect the origins of the 'Peacock Dance' with the history of the throne. The Peacock Dance is widespread and popular throughout Asia and mirrors the beauty and grace of the peacock.

152 Zahir ud-Din Muhammad Babur (1483–1530), founder and first Emperor of South Asia. Great-great-grandfather of Shah Jahan.

Our world is full of controversies. If you hear the legend of the Peacock Throne from the Kurds and ask them how they destroyed it, they would state that it was a made-up story to blacken their nation, and that the Kurds would never do that. Probably, they might not have done it, because there are many pitiful and grievous events in the history of this nation.

One of these stories is again related to the peacock. A particular section of the Kurdish people are Yazidis. We may reflect on this religion for a long time. Yazidis pray to and believe in Melek Taus; that is, the 'Peacock Angel'. As we know, the peacock is sacred, a divine bird for Kurds. That is presumably why they deny the charges of Iranian historians regarding the Peacock Throne. Actually, no one should harm birds. The saying 'A bird and an angel are twins' is not used for no reason.

Birds of Turkey

*I*t is impossible to not to be surprised by Ancient Ottoman buildings that have survived from olden times. One month would not be enough to see the beauty of magnificent mosques, palaces and caravanserai, of covered markets and domed mausoleums, of fountains, parks and gardens designed by the chief Ottoman architect, Sinan Mimar (1490–1588) and his students (*mimar* means 'architect' in Turkish). The Europe-centric perspective of a lot of people changes when they see Islamic design, in particular Turkish art. One wishes that Istanbul had existed as one of the best examples of building construction for thousands of years. There are some buildings to which most visitors and even city dwellers whose ancestors were born and raised in Istanbul (it became an Islamic city in 1453) do not pay enough attention. Yes, buildings!

Perhaps, those objects should not be fully classified as buildings. The Eyub Sultan Mausoleum, Sultan Ahmed, Sultan Mehmed Fatih, Nure Osmaniye, Suleymaniye, Selim, Beyazit, Sehzade, the Aya Sofya, Irina Church, Small Ayasofya, Egyptian Market, Kapalis Square, Dolmabahçe, Böselsbay and the Yildiz Palace are all buildings. For example, the Topkapi Palace alone occupies 700,000 square metres. However, the largest *building* I'm going to describe is no larger than 0.7 square metres. No, it doesn't look like a dwarf's house. You decide for yourself if it can be called a building or not. However, the Turks called these constructions *kuş köşkü* – a 'bird villa' (palace, house, settlement, place, etc.)

The Topkapi Palace, which was the palace and home of the Turkish sultans for three centuries, consisted of three parts: the harem, the *birun* and the *enderun*. The harem was not designed in the way that outsiders described it; that is, as 'the sultan's place of entertainment and dwelling of his numerous wives'. In fact, the harem was the most secluded part of the palace, where the sultan's mother, wives, sisters, daughters and their guests resided. Women needed privacy according to Turkish etiquette. The *birun* was an external courtyard. The *enderun* was an interior courtyard, designed especially for people close to the sultan. One of the most prestigious locations in the interior courtyard was known as the House of Falconers. Falconers took part in important ceremonies.

Before the construction of any grand building in the city, architects had to preview and discuss the plans with the sultan and the grand vizier. The sultan used to ask the architects, 'My *mimar* [architect], are there any places for my dear friends and visitors?' Who were these visitors and friends? They were birds. Truly, birds are our friends, aren't they?

Architects who had unwittingly forgotten to include birdhouses in the design, or didn't find them necessary, might have left the palace in shame. They would probably never serve the sultan again.

The bird villas of Turkey are different from the bird boxes common elsewhere, made of wood and attached to buildings, trees or posts. On Turkish buildings, just below the frame of the roof, there are elaborate, ornate birds' nests, which are not attached later, but are built in from the start. They balance the buildings beautifully and look like an integral part of the external design, adding a touch of sophistication to the walls. It is known that in Europe, putting up bird boxes became more common in the nineteenth century, but in Turkey, from the thirteenth century onwards, bird houses were placed on all sorts of structures: palaces, mosques, bridges, schools, houses, tombs, and so on. When Europeans discuss Anatolian architecture, they talk mainly about Ancient Roman and Greek temples. However, the bird-house tradition deserves attention as well, as it has a long history and demonstrates the Ottomans' love and compassion for birds.

Turkish people have numerous songs about birds, and there isn't probably any nation that has not dreamed about flying like birds. There was a person named Hezarfen Ahmed in the fifteenth century who admired birds. He designed wings, flew from the top of the Galata Tower and landed safely on Ushkudar. People who watched and saw that event certainly dreamed of flying; some of them took the risk of repeating Hezarfen Ahmed's exersice and the majority of them failed, or ended up dead. Murad Khan (1612–40) ruled the Ottoman Empire at that time. The khan granted Hezarfen Ahmed a sack of golden coins and exiled him to Algeria. Probably the ruler was thinking of his people's safety. So Hezarfen Ahmed died in the foreign country.

It is unlikely that a visitor travelling to Istanbul would miss Sultan Ahmet Square, which stretches along to the Blue Mosque in the city centre and is one of the most beauti-

Birds of Turkey

221

ful landmarks of the city. At the time of the Byzantine Empire it was a hippodrome: a site for horse-racing and chariot-racing. During Ottoman rule, there was a bird market in this square. The sultan used to visit it, not just for fun, nor purely to listen to the nightingales, blackbirds or other songbirds. Why do you think he visited the market? To buy caged birds and set them free. It might have been a wonderful activity for those noble men to observe and watch the released birds flying free through the Istanbul sky.

However, we can't possibly consider this area as a land of peace and quiet, because in 532, the Roman Emperor Justinian murdered about 30,000 people during the Nika Revolt, and later, another relentless ruler, Sultan Mahmud II, beheaded thousands of Janissaries who rebelled against the disbandment of the Janissary Corps in 1826. Today, sultans are no more, and the tomb of the last sultan, Mehmed IV Vahideddin, is in the city of Sham (Damascus). He was unable to die in his own country where his magnificent ancestors Osman and Orhan had ruled. The difference between rulers and poets and prophets was that their lives usually had a sad ending. As Kazakhs used to say, this fleeting life is 'treachearous and false'. The Hippodrome of Constantinople (Istanbul), or the horse-racing track, was closed long ago, and the site of former bloodshed is now covered with flowers and fountains. The single mark left of those periods is the gulls that soar high above the top of the Blue Mosque. I imagine they might be the souls of the dead.

Anyone who visits museums in Istanbul learns that birds are sacred to the Turks. In Ottoman palaces, like in all Eastern palaces there were professional staff to look after birds. There is evidence that kings ordered the most talented artists to paint birds. One of those painters was the Russian painter Ivan Aivazovsky (born into an Armenian family), who lived in the sultan's palace for many years and painted there. Many of his artworks can be found in Turkish museums. However, Russian historians tend to omit this fact from Aivazovsky's biography.

The Turks used to name their beloved sons and daughters, as well as their favourite places, by the name of birds. That is why there are names such as: Akdoğan (the White Falcon), Akkus (the White Bird), Kumru (Dove), Doğanalyp (the Mighty Falcon), Suna (Duck), Çalıkuşu (Kinglet), Turna (Crane), Bulbul (Nightingale), Başdoğan (the Leader of Hawks), Keklik (Quail), Karabatak (Coromorant) and Kuşhan (the Khan of the Birds). Don't be surprised if you also encounter geographical names such as: Akbaba (Vulture), Atmaşa (Accipiter), Balaban (Bıttern), Kartal (Eagle) and Bulbul (Nightingale).

Africa is home to 2,341 bird species of which 1,500 are endemic to the continent. Turkey cannot be compared to Africa in terms of the number of birds that live there; nevertheless, it has many birds that are native to the country's climatic zone. Since olden times, many sea and water birds that inhabit Kazakhstan and Siberia migrate to Turkey. An old Kazakh proverb says, 'There's no place girls and birds can't reach', meaning you may meet girls getting married and settling in distant places, as well as discover birds in any part of the world. If you see gadwalls soaring over the Mediterranean in February you will be moved. Why? Obviously, these birds have migrated from our home – Kelintôbe, Šalķar, Narynķol, the Aral Sea, Lake Zajsan …

Although there are frosty winds and cold snowstorms in February in our parts, the shores of the Mediterranean are tranquil, with ripe bananas, oranges and tangerines in the

The Birds Are Our Friends

market. Our plants may be buried under thick layers of snow during this season. In the Mediterranean, however, plants thrive and blossom, colourful butterflies fly around them and attract attention. Speaking of butterflies, there are some that migrate as soon as the autumn cold arrives, as many birds do. They escape cold weather in warmer countries, including Turkey. Can you imagine that these tiny creatures, the painted lady (*Vanessa cardui*), flew over the mountain flowers of Almaty and Alma-Arasan last summer and are now in Turkey, almost 3,500 kilometres away? Isn't it fascinating?

Akdeniz![153] Asia, Africa and Europe surround it and it stretches over a total area of 2.5 million square kilometres. The Mediterranean Sea is connected to the Atlantic Ocean to the west, and in the east, to the Sea of Marmara and the Black Sea by the Dardanelles Strait and the Bosporus, respectively. To the north, it borders Southern Europe and Anatolia. In the south-east, it is connected to the Red Sea by the Suez Canal. Its year-round warm waters and wetlands are the breeding grounds for birds that love warm water and good conditions, especially over the winter. There are some 417 species of birds found here and 17 of them are listed as endangered. This area is an age-old habitat for seagulls, ibis, pelicans, flamingos, ducks and other water birds. It is an overwintering site for the greylag goose, the greater white-fronted goose, the lesser white-fronted goose and the bean goose that Kazakhs love and write songs and *kújs* about.

Let's say you are walking in this abundant land, where the soil is fertile, the trees are green all year round and the water never gets cold, or as Ancient Kazakhs would put it, 'the numerous fish frolicking like a herd of yearlings, the frogs making constant noise like a flock of sheep'.[154] Everything in this land seems familiar, yet a little alien at the same time. It seems everything is mixed up in nature. Suddenly, you hear the familiar voice of a bird. No, it's not the whoop of the graceful swans gliding on the tides. Nor it is the honk of the geese. It can't be a songbird either. What bird is it? You hear it and listen again. Eh, it's our own rook! You are surprised to learn that they also winter in these parts. They make so much noise, as if following a tractor pulling a chisel plough somewhere in the Aķmola or Ķostanaj regions. Yes, they will return to Kazakhstan soon. They'll be one of the first to arrive there.

The thrush, the European robin, the common whitethroat, the tree sparrow, the Eurasian skylark and the crested lark all return to Kazakh lands as soon as spring arrives. Of course they do. It is fascinating: these lands are much warmer than Kazakhstan and have a milder climate. Apart from the warm rain, or occasional strong winds, there is no sign of winter here. That is why you can meet Russian tourists swimming in January or February. In the meantime, the Kazakh steppes are wrapped in snow, and it would be unlikely to be warm enough to do this until May. In addition, considering the distance, it seems like there is nothing in Kazakh lands for birds to strive for. But despite this, birds will hurry to reach their native parts, leaving the bird-friendly and flowering Turkish lands for the rigid steppes of Kazakhstan. They will fly both day and night, and hurry, as if it is a matter of urgency to get there. Unfortunately, not all of them will make it home.

They say that the French, who settled in one corner of the Mediterranean, kill about 30–40 million songbirds each year and send the meat as a delicacy to restaurants. Spain shoots about 3.5 million and Malta consumes about 300,000 blackbirds annually. Italians catch about 40 million birds each year, and nearly 30 million of these are snared by glue

---

153 *Akdeniz* (Turkish), literally the White Sea, the Mediterranean Sea.

154 The citation is from the *tolgau* (an age-old genre of Kazakh poetry) 'Ķajran da meniṇ Edilim' by Ķaztuǵan Sùjinišuly, a seventeenth-century *žyrau* (poet, composer, warrior and councillor to the khans).

traps. Birds stuck in glue traps often suffer injuries to their delicate wings, skin, feathers, body and legs, and even in the unlikely event that they free themselves, they do not recover. It is hard to understand people. Europeans were the first to introduce Laws of Nature Conservation, but some of them don't obey this law. There are frequent reports of hunters that cruelly shot, glued, trapped or poisoned songbirds across Europe, not to mention the illegal killing of the ortolan bunting, which is cooked and served whole in French cuisine.

When, a decade ago, there was an outbreak of bird flu in Turkey, some print media recommended that Europeans should avoid visiting the country. This seemed unreasonable. The Mediterranean Sea borders a number of countries, so does the Black Sea. One cannot keep birds locked in the territory of a particular country. They may fly from Turkey and land in Greece or Italy in 2–3 hours; the birds of the Black Sea can be in Russia in a blink of an eye. That is because birds have wings. But many countries considered bird flu exclusively 'Turkey's problem'. It was not the only time when Turkey faced a misunderstanding regarding birds.

There is another bird in Turkey – the stork. It is a beloved bird of not only Turkic people, but other nations around the world too. Kazakhs usually greet it with a song: 'The stork has arrived, the summer also!' During the Ottoman Empire, storks used to build their nests not only on the roofs of the houses or on the tops of trees, but also on the tops of mosques and tombs, even on the roof of the sultan's palace. If you ever go to Istanbul, then you should visit the Eyüp Sultan Mosque. Although it is not Mecca, for Muslims, especially for Turkic people, it is considered almost as holy as Mecca. Eyüp was a holy man who carried the flag of the Prophet Muhammad (peace be upon him). His tomb is enclosed by a white shiny silver net. When I saw a stork's nest on the roof of this mosque, I recalled a sad story. Do you know that storks, which are so dear to us, were destroyed ruthlessly by the Greeks?

Once I visited Athens. I couldn't see a single stork there. This was surprising considering the geographical features of Greece. On that journey I managed to visit several places in Ancient Hellas (Greece). There weren't any storks or even their nests. Later, I learned that from ancient times, the Greeks killed storks wherever they saw them. First of all, there was an age-old belief that storks stole newborn babies. I learned that some Greeks would also say, 'This is a favourite bird of the Turks, who deprived us of our homeland.' They would drag stork nests from rooftops to the ground and burn them. After 1830, storks became extinct in the areas where Greeks lived. In 1839, the English archaeologist and explorer Charles Fellows, who visited Asia Minor, wrote the following about the city of Miletus: 'It is obvious what part of the region belongs to the Turks and what part to the Greeks. If there are no pigs, then this area must belong to the Turks. If there are no storks, it's the domain of the Greeks.'

Izmir is one of the most beautiful cities in Turkey. This historical place is familiar to us from school textbooks, and is where different peoples enabled the development of various cultures. This city is located on the Aegean coast where Alexander the Great and Marcus Aurelius left their traces. There is the famous 'Kuşadası' island (or 'Bird Island') next to this city, but that is another story. This island is blessed by Allah as there are different types of birds. One traveller wrote in 1857 that it would be possible to recognize the areas where Greeks lived in Izmir not by their churches, but by the destroyed stork nests.

The waves are gentle and mild in the Aegean Sea, as if the waves are happy to discover that innocent storks will not be killed any more. If silent old churches, where these peaceful birds nested, could talk, then perhaps they would say, 'You fought with Turks and lost the

The Birds Are Our Friends

war to Turks. Why did you hurt those innocent birds?' Most water birds that fly and play over the warm waves are birds that live in our lands as well. Here, we remember the Kazakh poet Tôlegen Ajbergenov's verse:

Even when you see a quiet sea,
It will make your heart tremble.[155]

There are some other birds that have suffered because of the Turks' tenderness towards them. Let me tell you another story. In Turkey there is a dove called a ringed turtle dove. There are many of them in our lands too. Another name for this bird is the Egyptian turtle dove. You can recognize it by the black 'ring' on its neck. It is a mistake to call this bird a native Turkish bird. Nevertheless, in German, Spanish, French, Finnish and Slovenian its name remains the 'Turkish turtle dove'. Probably it was interesting for Europeans who visited the Ottoman Empire to find this bird there in abundance. However, this bird inhabited this territory well before the founder of the Ottoman Empire, Osman I, or his father, Ertugrul, were born. Why is it called the Turkish turtle dove then? What happens if we divide 100 billion birds across the globe, by saying, 'This is your bird, and this is mine'? Unfortunately, so many bad things happened to this poor turtle dove.

Over the centuries, these innocent birds were exterminated, as well as the storks. During the reign of the Ottoman sultans in Europe, Christians used to kill turtle doves. They explained this behaviour: 'Thus we are demonstrating our resistance to Islam.' Is it a reasonable explanation though? When the Ottoman Empire collapsed, among the localities of the Balkan Peninsula, such as Bosnia, Herzegovina, Montenegro and Albania, these birds only inhabited the villages where the Turks lived. In fact, neither the stork nor the turtle dove were Turkish birds. It is wrong to consider birds our property. However, there are birds native to Turkey. Let us write a few words about them.

When Urfa, a Turkish city with a 9,000-year history, is mentioned, the Prophet Ibrahim (Abraham) comes first to all Muslim minds. It is said that this renowned messenger of God in Islam, to whom a sheep was sent from heaven, was born in this city. The legend echoed in the Holy Qur'an, that the Prophet was thrown into a fire but the flames turned into water and burning logs turned into fish, was also set in this city. Balıklı göl (Lake with fish) is considered holy by locals, and fishing there is prohibited. There is a record that Jesus Christ once visited this city. Tarsus, in which the Prophet Daniyar (Daniel) was buried, is not far from this place. Urfa is a sacred place. The locals, descendants of the great steppe nomads, still prefer the mountains over the sea. They also prefer meat to fish. They have begun to adopt maritime transport only recently.

The second thing Urfa is famous for is the *kelaynak* bird (northern bald ibis). Turkish people believe that the northern bald ibis only inhabits Turkey, namely, Urfa. In fact, in the seventeenth century, this bird could be found not only in Asia Minor (Anatolia), but also in the Alps, in modern Switzerland and in Italy. In the beginning, Europeans neglected this bird, calling it the 'forest raven'. Over the years, they started catching this bird because of its delicious meat. As a result, Europe bid farewell to this bird forever.

155 The citation is from Tôlegen Ajbergenov's poem 'Žurekke ajtylǧan ôleŋder' ('Poems written to the heart').

225

According to some ornithologists, there were times when this bird nearly disappeared from the planet. Only thanks to the villagers of Urfa did it continue to survive. It was a sin for Turks to kill a bird.

Recently, archaeologists excavating the Egyptian pyramids found mummies of the northern bald ibis. Their discoveries concluded this bird was sacred for the Ancient Egyptians. In contrast, for Europeans, this bird was associated with tasty soup and meat.

In neighbouring Morocco, there are farms where northern bald ibis are bred. In any case, this bird is included on the international Red List. Of course, we cannot state that there are no indigenous birds in Turkey. For instance, local ornithologists believe that the black francolin, the white-throated kingfisher, the paddy field warbler, the bluethroat and the lammergeier are all indigenous. Birds such as the ortolan bunting, Cretzschmar's bunting and the Dead Sea sparrow do not inhabit our lands, nor neighbouring Russia and Central Asian countries. This shouldn't be a surprise. Each climatic zone has its own bird species. For example, in modern ornithology it is said that the Eurasian oystercatcher, the ibisbill, the red-throated loon, the Calandra lark, the white-winged snow finch and the coal tit are native to the Kazakh steppes. Indeed, thanks to research, in recent years, these birds have been found in the deserts of America. This story may be similar to that of the Alakôl gulls told by the Kazakh ornithologist Ernar A'uezov (see page 99).

In English, the word 'turkey' (a Turkish hen) is used for a bird which the Turks have never considered native to their land. Recently, Armenian ornithologists reported that a new species of crane had been discovered on the Turkish border. This crane, of course, lives in Turkey as well. Nevertheless, the Armenians prefer to consider this bird exclusive to their own country.

Approximately 456 bird species inhabit Turkey – in comparison, according to the latest data, there are more than 512 bird species in Kazakhstan – 304 of which are native and 152 visiting birds. The largest number of any one species consist of sparrows, at more than 15 million. Small birds are welcomed everywhere. There is a songbird, the goldcrest, that is smaller than the sparrow. Anatolians love this bird, which is considered to be the smallest bird in Turkey. It weighs approximately 3.8–4.5 grams, is 90 mm in length and its egg weighs 0.7 grams. We suppose that Kazakh viewers still remember the popular Turkish TV series *Çalıkuşu* (also broadcast in Kazakhstan), which was named after this bird. The goldcrest nests near Almaty every year.

Why do people like small birds? Probably the reason is that God created people to take care of their smaller brothers.

Birds are a frequent topic in Turkish folk literature. In general, Turkish literature is similar to Kazakh literature, yet at the same time, very different. We will talk about this another time. Europeans always write with surprise about the Turkish love of birds. As Edmund de Amigos used to say:

> For Turks all birds are sacred. For instance, ringed turtle doves protect peach trees in the garden. Swallows forewarn the house about fire. Storks are sacred as they winter in Mecca. It is also believed that the common tern delivers Muslims' souls to paradise.

Here we have translated some of their myths. It would be great if there were scholars who would explore Turkish mythology and present it to Kazakh readers.

Once there was a married couple. For some reason they lost each other and spent their days mourning and dreaming of reunion. They were far from each other and could not hear each other. God had mercy on them and transformed them into the scops owl. Therefore, this bird's voice is bitter, sad and unpleasant.

Another legend about the Eurasian scops owl is associated with the subplot of the story of Tahir and Zuhra. This subplot is often mentioned in Eastern epics, such as the Kazakh text 'Ķozy Kôrpeš and Baân Sulu'. Just like the two separated lovers, Ķozy and Baân from the Kazakh epic poem, Tahir and Zuhra were also unable to live a happy life, but they were buried together. There is a tall poplar tree that grows next to their tomb. Every year a red flower blooms near the poplar tree, but a thorny plant grows between them each year and separates the poplar tree from the flower. In another version of the legend, the poplar tree is associated with the male scops owl, the red flower with the female scops owl and the black thorns with an imperial eagle. This legend mentions the bitter voices of the two separated lovers. These two lovers only meet once a year. They miss each other so much that when they meet, they even drop the food that they bring to each other. Therefore, they wait for the next year. There are many other beautiful legends in Turkish literature about the fate of pining lovers.

The legend about the black francolin, which is told by Turkish Cypriots, is also interesting. Before turning into a bird, it was a very beautiful, moon-faced girl. She didn't pay attention to any of her admirers until she met her true love and married him. Young men consumed with jealousy began to gossip about the young bride. The two lovers ignored them. After that the jealous ones decided to turn her mother-in-law against the newlywed bride. The woman believed their slander and started to test her daughter-in-law. One day the woman asked her daughter-in-law to bake twenty-four loaves of bread and a pie. Then she mixed up the pie dough with the bread dough when her daughter-in-law was not looking. When the bread had been baked, there was no pie among them. The woman began to accuse her daughter-in-law of eating the pie up. The bride was very ashamed in front of her beloved husband. Therefore, she prayed, 'My Lord, it would be better if I turned into a bird than to endure these torments.' Her prayers were heard and she turned into a bird. Since then, when people hear the tragic voice of a bird sounding from a dense forest on moonless nights, they curse gossipers and liars.

The partridge is called *keklik* in Turkish, just like in Kazakh. Kazakh people believe that it calls its own name. Why does this bird do that? In ancient times, a prophet hid in the mountains to escape from his enemies. At the same time a partridge was sitting on the top of the poplar. Then it started to invoke its name and betrayed the prophet to his enemies. The enemy killed him at once and the prophet's blood spattered the partridge's wings. Before dying, the prophet cursed the bird, saying, 'Let the one who looks for you, find you easily.' Perhaps that is why the partridge falls easily into the hunter's hands.

By the way, Turks compare the human soul to a bird. Yunus Emre, in his famous poem, said:

To this true word God will attest:
The Spirit is the body's guest,

Birds of Turkey

Some day it will vacate the breast
As birds, freed from their cages, fly.[156]

The poet Baki said, in his turn:

The bird, his soul, hath, human-like aloft flown to the skies;
And naught remained but some bones here on the earth below.[157]

Here, the words of the Kazakh poet Kempirbaj also come to mind: 'A gadwall flew from my chest bidding farewell.'[158]

Let us say a few words about the names of birds. A well-known scientist, Ilhami Kiziroglu, who wrote a monograph entitled *Birds of Turkey*, translated the word 'ornithology' into Turkish as 'the science of birds' (*kuşbilim*). The science of birds is well developed in Turkey. It would be interesting to compare bird names in Kazakh and Turkic languages; Turkish in particular. All this information is the topic of another discussion. Until next time then.

156 From '*Geldi geçti ömrüm benim*', available at: http://www.turkishculture.org/philosophers/yunus-emre/se-lected-poems-ii-431.htm

157 From 'Elegy on Sultan Suleyman', available at: http://devdergisi.com/Makalel-er/322022088_20170912180520.pdf

158 From '*Kempirbajdyŋ Ašetpen ķoštasuy*' ('The Farewell of Kempirbaj and A'set'), a poem by Kazakh poet Kempirbaj Bôgenbajuly (1834–95).

The Birds Are Our Friends

A Purposeful Life

Fly thou to the untroubled East ...

Goethe, 'Moganni Nameh'[159]

All good people write poems in their childhood. Later, poetry probably leaves us. Sadly, poetry is like a bird that might fly away.

Nowadays, about 230 large and small countries unite more than 2,000 nationalities. However, it is not easy to earn the respect and love of everyone, even for individuals who are internationally famous. However, there was a person, one of the greatest sons of humanity who was worthy of deep admiration. Alfred Brehm. How do we know that Alfred Brehm acquired such fame? I believe, if it hadn't been for poetry, Brehm wouldn't have achieved any of his accomplishments. It seems poetry appeared before God created the Prophet Adam. In the ancient Islamic book *Noor Namah* (*The Book of Light*), it was revealed that Allah first created Light. When you read about the lives of such people as Brehm, you wonder whether poetry is that Light.

Alfred Brehm was born on 2 February 1829 in the village of Unterrenthendorf (now called Renthendorf), in the small duchy of Saxe-Weimar, Germany. He was born into a family where everyone adored poetry including his father, Christian Ludwig. He was a pastor in a small church in that village, but he was never without a book of poetry in his hands. He used to read aloud passages from the Bible, and was particularly fond of the phrase 'In the beginning was the Word'. The pastor also loved birds.

The whole countryside named him *Der Vogelpastor* (the bird pastor). This nickname hadn't been given to anyone else in the history of Christianity. The number of stuffed birds that the pastor collected was about 9,000, of which 700 were birds of prey. Everything about all types of birds could be found in old Brehm's home. The pastor loved children very much as well and especially had great hopes for little Alfred, one of his two sons by his second wife. Indeed, Alfred followed in his father's footsteps. He used to walk with his father through the

---

159 From 'West-Eastern Divan', available at: https://archive.org/stream/westeasterndivan00goetuoft/westeast-erndivan00goetuoft_djvu.txt

woods when he was a child. He could imitate the sounds of bird voices. He could recognize and distinguish any kind of bird at first sight. When he was eight years old, his father bought him a hunting rifle.

Alfred's mother, Bertha Reitz, was a woman with a poetic soul. She didn't only write poetry, but also promoted German classics throughout her life. Later, the Eastern editions wrote about her, that she was *Atin Bibi* – 'a woman scientist'. Since the Prophet Muhammad's time (peace be upon him), this title has been conferred to literate and educated women.

The mid-nineteenth century was a time when there was a special respect for art among German intellectuals. It was the time when readers didn't visit Schiller's grave without taking a bunch of flowers, and Goethe was not long dead (1832). Goethe's book, *The West-Eastern Divan* – which included 'Moganni Nameh' ('Book of the Singer'), 'Hafis-Nameh' ('Book of Hafiz'), 'Uschk Nameh' ('Book of Love'), 'Tefkir Nameh' ('Book of Reflection'), 'Rendsch Nameh' ('Book of Humour'), 'Hikmet Nameh' ('Book of Maxims'), 'Timur Nameh' ('Book of Timur'), 'Suleika Nameh' ('Book of Zuleika'), 'Saki Nameh' ('Book of the Cupbearer'), 'Mathal Nameh' ('Book of Parables'), 'Parsi Nameh' ('Book of Parsees'), and 'Chuld Nameh' ('Book of Paradise') – became very popular.

It was a wonderful period for the East. Europe began to take an interest in Arabic literature and culture. People were more focused on Voltaire's work *Muhammad* rather than on articles written by Goethe about Napoleon's reception and the brief aphorisms said by the Great Emperor. The East! Eastern poetry! The might of the Holy Qur'an! Napoleon was surprised by all this beauty. If Persia and Arabia were proving yet again that they were the golden cradle of not only the exotic, but also of aesthetics, science, and artistic and ethical studies, then it should have been clear that Europe realized where true civilization was.

There is a Kazakh saying: 'Only a goldsmith knows the price of jewellery.' The Turkic Sultan of the Ottoman Empire, whose ancestors had migrated from the Kazakh steppes, held half of the world in his hands at the same time. Constantinople was renamed Istanbul (in other sources 'Islambol' – 'be Islam'). A green flag with a crescent on it replaced the cross on the top of the Hagia Sophia's dome. An Eastern proverb remains from that time and states: 'Persian is a soft language [i.e. the language of poetry], and Turkish is a hard [iron] language [i.e. the language of warriors]'.

Little Alfred seemed to be a born dreamer. In particular, he dreamed of visiting the East at least once in his life. By the age of thirteen or fourteen, he had already read books published in German and French about animals that inhabited the Middle East, Ancient Egypt, the city of Baghdad, the gardens of Iran and the banks of the River Nile.

His mother loved reading the German romantic poets of that time such as Joseph Eichendorff and Ferdinand Freiligrath. It is interesting to note that the poet Freiligrath, who wrote about various kinds of birds that inhabited and flew over the blue waters of the Nile, and about different species of animals that inhabited the African savannah, never travelled out of Europe. Anyway, he became an example of imitation and Brehm's teacher after Goethe, who educated him to worship nature and aroused his interest in literature. People thought that Alfred would become either a poet or an ornithologist. As usual, talented people's lives consist of unexpected events. In 1844, after graduating from primary school, instead of going to the *Gymnasium*, Alfred entered the technical school.

Probably he did so because of his interest in Eastern architecture. While studying at a special school in Altenburg from 1844 to 1847, to become a bricklayer, unexpectedly he was acquainted with the wealthy Baron Johann Wilhelm von Muller. People always look with suspicion and gossip on people who suddenly become rich. There were also many rumours about Muller, who considered himself a 'nobleman by birth'. Some people gossiped about his humble origins; others laughed at his illiteracy. People discussed the stupidity of his wife and the brainlessness of his daughter. Whatever people said about him, Muller had some influence at that time.

In reality, he wasn't as stupid as people thought. He knew that wealth was not an eternal thing and that he would only be remembered if he did good deeds. He wanted to become famous by exploring the wildlife of the East. Nevertheless, wherever he went, people who knew of his origins and state avoided him. Then, by chance, he met Alfred, who was getting bored at technical school. Alfred was young, talented, literate and a dreamer, loved travelling and at the same time knew a lot about Eastern and Western culture. Muller recognized that potential immediately, and the two men quickly reached an understanding. Travelling to the Middle East! Researching different types of birds and animals living in Egypt, Asia Minor and Greece and introducing them to Europe!

Alfred's dream would soon be realized. He immediately signed the contract proposed by the Baron. On the morning of 31 May 1847, he said goodbye to his family and embarked on a long journey, accompanying Muller as his secretary. They went to Leipzig first, then to Vienna, from Vienna to Trieste, and then to Athens. After that, he arrived at the port of Alexandria by ship. When he arrived in Cairo, he and the Baron both got sunstroke, as they had never experienced such heat. The Lord was merciful to them and after their recovery, Muller planned to leave Egypt for Sudan. They sailed along the River Nile and then spent the rest of their journey travelling on camelback.

Alfred finally understood the Arabic folk poetry he had read in his childhood. He saw the birds he had read about in Bedouin folklore for the first time. On one side, everything around was far from his understanding, and on the other, all of it was known to him. The lion, the ostrich, the camel with its calf, the Arabian horse, the bare steppes, a single well, gritty sand … all of these were familiar yet unfamiliar to him. He saw a lark singing above his head. Later in his travel narratives, he wrote that:

> Wild birds of North Africa sometimes flew far to the edge of the desert. The African fish eagle that inhabits the Nile Gorge also flies away to the boundless steppe after eating its fill. In north-east Africa, there are four types of sand grouse. There are several species of birds such as black grouse, black-bellied sand grouse and the common rock sparrow, which are not, however, endemic desert birds. The native bird of that area is the lark.

Today, looking at these texts, it seems as if his adventures were written about the Kazakh steppes. He wrote:

> If you see a much-praised Arabic horse in the city, you will be surprised. It looks like a cart-horse: meek-eyed and floppy-eared, slow and timid. Moreover, his master looks like a wretched man. What bandit looks as sluggish and weak as this man? Only his piercing gaze through his thick eyebrows betrays his true nature. As soon as that fellow mounts his horse, he becomes unrecognizable. In such cases, the lines from Ferdinand Freiligrath's poem comes to mind:

O, Bedouin, when you get on your horse,
You become unrecognizable in an instant.

These lines also seem to be about steppe Kazakhs visiting the city.

Although Muller spent his time expressing negative emotions about the country and its inhabitants, Brehm moved away from the noise to where he could devote his time to exploring and investigating new species of animals. If you have ever watered a dry indoor flower, then you will know how that flower will bloom again. Brehm, who had dreamed of visiting the East since his childhood, had exactly the same state of mind. He was fascinated to learn and discover new things. Perhaps such moments should be called happy moments of life.

The capital city of Sudan was Khartoum. In January 1848, upon arrival in that city, they contracted malaria. Despite his illness, Brehm prepared 130 stuffed birds in one month,

The Birds Are Our Friends

and yet Muller was displeased with him. Instead of finding rare animals, preparing them to be stuffed and sending them to Europe as fast as they could, and earning a large amount of money, the pastor's son had made friends with some Africans and spent his time chatting with them. Because of this, they argued with each other several times. As the saying was, 'The borzoi will take its anger out on the crane.' When Baron became angry with Brehm, he argued with the Arab guides. Sometimes he fought with them, but ended up hurting himself.

Egypt and Sudan were ruled by the Ottoman Empire at that time. Brehm suggested the Baron should wear Turkish clothes to be closer to the local people. At first the Baron was against it, but when he thought about the benefit, he agreed. Brehm didn't stop there, but began to learn Arabic and Turkish languages. Thus, winter passed and summer came. When Muller realized that this business wouldn't bring an immediate income, he left Brehm alone in Alexandria and returned to Europe the following year.

'Wait for me here!' he said. 'I will come back in a couple of months.' However, he didn't come, either in a couple of months or a year. At that time, Brehm, who was alone in Cairo, became interested in Islam. He shook the *ishan* [an Islamic spiritual mentor] Musallam's hands and began to live as a Muslim. His Arabic and Turkish became fluent. He learned the Holy Qur'an so well that he became an expert reader. He even translated the Holy Qur'an into German with the help of the *ishan* Musallam. Therefore, rumours reached Europe that 'the pastor's son, Brehm, had adopted Islam and become an imam in Cairo'.

We don't know for sure whether he actually converted to Islam or if it was just Muller's gossip to keep the young man in fear for his job. Nevertheless, it is true that he renamed himself Ibrahim, shaved his head, dressed in Turkish clothes, prayed five times a day, read the *surahs* (chapters) and *ayahs* (verses) of the Holy Qur'an in Arabic, read Hadiths (a collection of traditions containing sayings of the Prophet Muhammad, peace be upon him) and went to the mosque. These were Brehm's own words.

The members of Baron Muller's original expedition had weapons and were accomplished marksmen. Sometimes they forgot that they were on a scientific expedition and engaged in bloodshed. Brehm, unlike them, was tender with animals: he ran after reptiles when they escaped and rejoiced with mammals when they were happy. He didn't destroy birds' nests.

Some newspapers later reported that 'he became blind before his death'. But his friends attested, 'No, this was false. Brehm could not become blind, because he was a real man who received gratitude not only from people, but also from animals.'

On the way back home after Muller had filled a ship with animals, birds could be heard chirping in the port, lions, wild bulls and camels roared and sheep bleated. Then a Turkish translator from the Sudanese province, named Ali Ara, said: 'Ibrahim Bey, they aren't only mourning for us, but also for you.'

It was true. Brehm's relationship with Muller began to deteriorate slowly. The Baron, who had been less considerate about animals from the beginning, didn't think of anything except money and power. He began to make unrealistic claims such as how he was going to go to Suakin (Sawakin) through the Red Sea, then get to Sudan and Khartoum with the help of a caravan, in a short time and on a small budget. After that, he wanted to sail along the River Nile where no one else had ever gone, and find a 'tribe of wild people'.

Muller announced that he would introduce these wild people to European culture, and then travel to the west across the Atlantic Ocean and reach the Gulf of Guinea by ship. There were no comments on the boaster's empty words. Needless to say, he wasn't as good as his word. Even experienced travellers such as Samuel Baker and Stanley were barely able to accomplish these travel goals much later.

Oscar Brehm, Alfred's brother, joined him on this expedition. The two brothers sailed along the River Nile in 1850, but Oscar became ill with malaria. After some time they continued their journey and one day when Oscar was swimming in the Nile in early May, the waves suddenly intensified and Oscar began to sink. Sadly, no one could save him. Alfred had suddenly lost his brother and was unable to do anything for a long time. Then he decided to travel to Khartoum. Baron Muller, instead of expressing condolences, sent Alfred a telegram in which he said: 'I don't have money, so don't rely on me any more and do whatever you want.'

Alfred could not trust the Europeans any more. He went to Latif Pasha, his old acquaintance, the new Governor of Sudan. Latif Pasha was Turkish and a generous Muslim. Thus, Alfred continued his expedition with support from him. Consequently, he wrote his internationally popular book, consisting of six volumes, named *Life of Animals*. His book became a best-seller and was translated into many languages. Unfortunately, the book hasn't been translated into Kazakh yet.

The Kazakh steppes also play an important role in the creation of this renowned book. Some volumes of the book might even have been written in our land. This topic needs special research. If we divide the book into volumes: the first volume is devoted to mammals, the second to birds, the third to amphibians, then reptiles, invertebrates and fish. Each animal in the book is illustrated in detail.

Undoubtedly, there are different views about Brehm's *Life of Animals*. Some people said that this was a poetic work written by an amateur naturalist, whereas others assumed that it was a work about nature, written from a poetic state of mind. However, neither before Brehm nor after him had there been such a wonderful work about animals. It was written: 'Naturalists and ornithologists considered that he was either a writer or a poet, while writers believed that Brehm was a naturalist and an ornithologist.'

Indeed, when reading each volume of this book it is like reading an exciting epic. So, it can be regarded as a poetic work to a certain extent. The love of poetry given to Brehm by his parents inspired him throughout his life. Owing to his love for poetry and birds he was saved from all the troubles and hardships that occurred in his life. Probably this was the reason why he became one of the greatest people in the history of humankind.

There were many interesting adventures that occurred in Brehm's subsequent life. When

Muller found out about Brehm's fame, he wanted to become friends with him again and offered him a lot of money. Alfred, who was a principled man, didn't trust him any more. His principles guided him when he quit from the University of Leipzig, the Zoological Garden of Hamburg, then the Berlin Aquarium.

In 1852 when Brehm returned safe and sound back to his hometown of Renthendorf, he realized that he wasn't satisfied with the expedition in which he had taken part. He decided to write travelogues rather than scientific works. Therefore, in 1855, he wrote a book entitled *Travel Sketches from North-Eastern Africa.*

We see a great literary talent in Chokan Valikhanov's works like *About Our Trip to Kashgar and back to Alatau District* or *Description of Kashgar or Altyshaar.*[160] When someone reads Brehm's mentioned works, they will appreciate his great gift of writing as well. However, neither Chokan nor Brehm wrote works of fiction. Maybe they were right not to do so. How wonderful when each person knows his own business! Both of them were educated and intelligent people. Today, you can meet people who write stories or an account of their trips from their *auyl* to Almaty, or travelogues from Almaty to Istanbul. When Brehm received a fee for his book, he went to Spain with one of his brothers. He was worn out after his Spanish journeys. Although he brought back many stuffed birds with him, he was not willing to write about his travels to Spain.

Our Tajik, Uzbek, Iranian and Arab brothers, as well as Europeans, have traditions of marrying their relatives. Brehm married his cousin Mathilde Reiz, with whom he had five children. In Kazakh culture we never marry our relatives. From a genetical standpoint, it is more beneficial for the children resulting from the marriage. Brehm might have preferred this cultural tradition if the science had been more advanced in his times.

In 1861, Ernest II, the Duke of Saxe-Koburg and Gotha, wanted to hunt in Abyssinia (Ethiopia) and invited Brehm and his new bride to travel with him. Unfortunately, after a few days of hunting Alfred Brehm became ill and returned to Germany. On his return he wrote two books, *Ergebnisse einer Reise nach Habesch* (*Results of a Journey to Habesch*) and *Tiere des Waldes* (*Forest Animals*). These books gave him new ideas.

We realize that Brehm was excited by the idea of writing a book about the animal world for the public. By that time, Comte De Buffon's *Histoire Naturelle* (*Natural History*), published in the eighteenth century, was an obsolete source on which to rely. Therefore, Brehm accepted the offer to become Director of the Zoological Garden in Hamburg. Together with the professional zoologists Ernst Ludwig Taschenberg and Eduard Oscar Schmidt, he started to investigate insects, frogs and invertebrates. I can't help wondering where he drew the energy from. He acquired respect and fame quite young, but he always strived ahead and invested his money in his favourite subject. Birds and Brehm were inseparable friends. He was a sincere admirer of nature; he wasn't after fame or fortune. That is probably why his works were also successful with readers. How happy is the writer who can explain himself to his audience! Unfortunately, most writers are not recognized until it's too late.

Nobody recognized Brehm as a patron of science and nature, but he always reasoned and acted as a man with abundant spiritual and financial resources. We Kazakhs seem to be lucky in comparison to many other nations, as many of us are provided for. But there are not many wealthy Kazakhs who have donated large sums to global charities. Those that promote knowledge are also rare. Who among Kazakhstan's wealthy has attempted to translate

160 Chokan Valikhanov (1835–65), a Kazakh scholar, historian and folklorist.

The Encyclopedia Britannica or Confucius' works into our native language? We haven't even compiled and published the 'Red List' of endangered animals of Kazakhstan yet.

Usually, we do not care about the animal world. Any bird is just a sparrow to us and the greenery around us is just a tree. However, the fauna and flora of the Žetisu and Altaj regions in particular are fascinating, but our writers are not interested in exploring and explaining them. Even worse, there hasn't been a single naturalist among Kazakh writers.

If we return to our story about Brehm, he did have one adventure after another. He experienced many hardships in his life. His father and then his mother died, his children died one after another and then his wife died in childbirth. In spite of these hardships, he carried out his favourite work. Brehm travelled to European countries and to America (1883), and became an honourable member of scientific academies in many countries. In 1874, he visited Saint Petersburg to take part in the Western Siberia expedition. From there he went to Kazan in Russia, Tyumen and Omsk, sailed on the River Ertis and stopped at Semej. The Governor General Poltaratskyi supported him in his journey, so he travelled to Alakôl, Maķanšy, from there to Alatau, the Tarbaġataj Mountains and then to China. There, in Tacheng (Šáuešek), he conversed with Kazakhs and on his way back he travelled

through the Altaj Mountains, and made friends with people from Buḵtyrma. He wrote several articles as a result of this expedition, such as: 'A Trip to Siberia', 'The Asian Steppe and Its People', 'The Kazakh Community and Its Family Relations', 'Siberian Timberland, Animals and Hunting Craft', and 'Nomads' Cattle'. However, none of these has been translated into Kazakh.

It is interesting that Brehm, being a German, had various disputable opinions about other European nations. For example, he said of the Italians, 'Every German despises Italians'; about Greeks he said 'They are cowards and mean'. I consider his opinions to be a result of being a friend of other racist people such as Muller. However, Alfred Brehm underlined Kazakhs' hospitality, innocence, bravery and proficiency, and wrote about the animals and birds of our country. For instance, about the argali he wrote: 'In Central Asia and Northern America there are the largest wild sheep, known as "arḵar" in Kazakh and "argali" in Mongolian. They inhabit the regions of Aḵmola to Altaj, in the Alatau Mountains'.[161]

In his volume about animals, he stopped near some *kulans*, wild donkeys, in the steppes of Türkistan. 'The kulan is really a steppe animal, but also lives along the shores of rivers and in the hills.' Of course, he couldn't give a complete account of all the Kazakh animals during such a short trip, and some of his facts are inaccurate.

Once, in Semej, Brehm went hunting with local officials and shot an argali. He presented his trophy to the Governor General's wife as a gift. A Kazakh immediately created a poem about the visitor's marksmanship. Brehm jotted down a translated version of the poem in his notes.

He travelled several times after his Kazakh steppe journey. During one of those journeys, the great traveller caught a cold, and died on 11 October 1884 at his home.

So, what is happiness? Brehm didn't answer this question. He led a secluded life, far from journalists, the noisy bourgeoisie and even from his relatives. He didn't attend parties, or if he did, he left those gatherings early. In contrast, if his environment were favourable to him, he could be cheerful and talkative, joking and chatting. When he entered his aviary, his winged friends sat on his head, shoulders, knees, back, everywhere on his body. At those moments Brehm would cry, said his biographers.

But did he know that he was the one who led a truly happy, purposeful life?

A Purposeful Life

---

161 Brehm A., *Life of Animals*, Terra, 1992, Volume 1, p. 430.

Why Did Levitan Not Paint the Birds?

*T*here is a saying in the East: 'There are thousands of people in the market. However, everyone greets whom he prefers to.' Among the masters of art, especially among landscape painters, my personal favourite is Isaac Levitan.[162] Instead of a wonderful summer, or bright, sunny, cheerful spring days, he concentrated mostly on the dark brown, cold and dull colours of autumn. Observing this sad painter's works, a poem translated by Abaj comes to my mind involuntarily:

The drizzly autumn mist sprinkles moisture,

And makes the velvet bespet wet.

Bitter tears a fellow sheds

And wipes his face.[163]

There is a feeling of nostalgia in many of the artist's paintings such as, *Autumn Day, Sokolniki* (1879), *Oak* (1880), *By the Whirlpool* (1892), *The Vladimirka Road* (1892), *Autumn, The Manor* (1894), *Over Eternal Peace* (1894), *Golden Autumn* (1895) and *Fortress, Finland* (1896). This feeling of wistfulness that makes the heart ache is familiar to each of us. But instead of sharing these emotions with someone, sometimes we don't even acknowledge them and hide them from ourselves. Does Levitan's greatness lie in the fact that he manages to connect us with the known and unknown worlds living in most people's souls? Maybe for this reason his gentle sadness and hope are as close to us 'as the inner lining of a warm coat', as they say.

Nevertheless, each time when faced with the magnificent heritage left by the great artist, and I feel, as the Ancient Greeks used to say, as if I were among the gods; something

---

162 Isaac Levitan (1860–1900), a famous Russian impressionist painter, a master of landscape and founder of the 'mood landscape' genre.

163 From the poem '*Surğylt tuman dym bùrkip*' by Abaj Kùnanbajuly, translated from the Russian poem '*Neosenni melkii dozhdichek*' by A. Delvig.

bothers my soul greatly. There is a sense that something is missing. I feel that if only I had waited a bit longer a missing traveller would have arrived to fill the emptiness in my heart. However, what was missing? Indeed, autumn is the season of expectation. Perhaps it isn't about the painting at all, but about the magical autumn melody, which renews old pain. No, it was not that.

Autumn is a hectic time of sadness, when your heart aches, recollecting misery. What about the sunny summer? Mainly, Levitan's paintings about spring express a melancholic state, the sadness of a lonely soul devoid of human presence. Let us have a look at his famous landscapes such as *Spring, High Water* (1897), *Sunny Day, Spring* (1876) and *March* (1895). Each of those paintings contains all the colours that characterize spring. Moreover, the fragrance of various flowers can be smelled from the pictures. The pleasant song of a breeze and the rustling sound of water can be heard. Nevertheless, something is still missing.

As the Kazakh poet Tôlegen Ajbergenov described in his poems about Maṇġystau, which were dedicated to the Kazakh composer Šặmši Ḳaldaâḳov: 'Alas, in these lands, a source of inspiration is missing, like yourself.' In Levitan's paintings, birds are missing.

The flutter of birds' wings, their inspired dawn chorus, their radiant presence as they land and fly are omitted. Look at the painting *By the Whirlpool*. Even if there are no geese or ducks, I think there must be coots on that pure water. But they are absent. There are also no birds in the painting *Sunny Day, Spring*. Is it possible to live without birds, to meet spring without birds? Oh, it would be so nice if there were birds in every painting about autumn and spring.

By the way, in the painting called *March*, the snow is just beginning to melt. You feel the presence of spring in the pictures. In a few weeks, there would be the scent of the thick pine trees, those naked tall birch trees would turn green and flourish. Even the chestnut horse harnessed to a sleigh, after getting rid of its shaft, would be fat and playful again. Everything is awakened. It is like waking up after a deep sleep, then having a sweet dream at dawn! It is as if the artist once said: 'Indeed, why do I offend the birds?' Perhaps one of his critics said that spring and birds shouldn't be separated. Anyway, he painted a starling nest at the very top of a birch tree.

To be honest, it is not very well balanced with other parts of the painting. Probably he added the nest after completing the work, but anyway it doesn't combine with the general view. It looks artificial. On the one hand, weak and tender branches would break if carrying such a nest; on the other, the nest of a starling shouldn't be white. Unexpected colours scare birds.

In the painting *Over Eternal Peace* it looks as if the painter himself turned into a bird. From above you can see a small lonely church on the shore of the eternal water, ancient graves with curved falling trees, an island isolated from the world and heavy moving grey-white clouds on the horizon. Standing in front of this famous painting, whose artist lived several hundred years ago, you wouldn't stand motionless when you saw the ancient world. On the contrary, you would fly away like a winged bird along the edges of the eternal river. Below, you could see the ancient cemeteries and the roof of a lonely church surrounded by newly blossoming green trees.

The Birds Are Our Friends

Finally, we think and look for the images of birds in the paintings. Why? Why didn't Levitan paint birds? Was it possible that he couldn't paint them? Maybe he didn't like them? It is unbelievable. Can we take it as fact that Levitan liked birds when we see two or three hens in the painting *Sunny Day, Spring*, or find images of three or four seagulls in the painting *Fresh Wind, Volga* (1895)?

It is true that landscape and animal painters are similar in their work, but in reality, they are not connected or compatible with each other. It is not about that, I think. It is about the inner world of the artist, his worldview. Let us take as an example the famous painting *Golden Autumn* to convey our thoughts. In a meadow that has not been mown, in a pristine grove, among white birch trees, you can see the autumn sun and its rays. The owner of this grove wants to expel the black shadows that have entered that secluded forest without permission. But the black shadows do not want to leave, implying that they are the owners of that grove. Conflicts are everywhere. Obviously, if you added birds to this beauty, you would not turn your attention to the conflict of the sunbeams and the shadows; you wouldn't consider the state of the artist's soul; you wouldn't see anything but those winged angels.

Birds are the closest beings to humankind. They attract attention among the living and non-living creatures that Almighty God created. They are close to us, as they also love freedom, will and movement, just like people.

Thus, the great artist made the right decision to not include birds in his works. Otherwise, in the exclusive and original world of art, his masterpieces would lose their place forever.

Like all great things, birds also do not like half-finished things as well as a lack of attention. If we paint the birds, they should at the forefront. Otherwise, it is better to leave them out. The Kazakh poet Muḵaġali Maḵataev said:

People, who have never written poems, are still alive.
I may live just like them, if I do not write.

Birds can live without us painting them; they can live without people. Can we live without birds?

Autumn Idyll

*I*t was the same quiet autumn.

It was the time when birds were migrating to warm lands again.

'If you are lucky enough to have lived in Paris as a young man, then wherever you go for the rest of your life it stays with you, for Paris is a moveable feast.'[164] If someone, whether young or old, man or woman, visits Paris for the first time, that person will remember Ernest Hemingway's words as a prayer.

Nevertheless, I remembered an event that had happened before Ernest Hemingway. I remembered those Kazakhs involved in the Napoleonic War, in early 1812, who had watered their horses in the River Seine. I read the *ayahs* (Qur'anic verses) and I prayed to the Almighty for the repose of A'men Bajbatyruly and Narynbaj Žanžigituly's souls. (It was said that a third Kazakh adopted Christianity and was given the Russian name Yakov Belyakov.)

I wonder how the Champs Élysées, Notre-Dame, the Louvre, the Pantheon, the Palace of Fontainebleau where Napoleon once lived, and Montmartre impressed the steppe Kazakhs. Or Place de la Bastille, and the beautiful squares and flower gardens of Paris. I am sure that they did not dare destroy or burn elegant houses in Paris, the city of dreams and the pearl of world civilization.

Earlier, people could distinguish between good and evil, and were aware of such concepts as *obal* (doing something bad is a sin and one has to have compassion for others to restrain oneself from such deeds) and *sauap* (good begets good, and kindness is a mark of humanity). Unfortunately, nowadays people are forgetting such concepts. Long live the memory of our great ancestors, who never forgot their Lord and didn't abandon their humanity wherever they went, and whatever hardship they had to endure.

Oh, our ancestors … Perhaps, while watering their horses in the River Seine they sent their greetings to their homeland via the birds flying high over the horizon. Only a verse makes someone forget their greetings about yearning. Only a verse can draw the feeling of longing for a homeland. Here is one of these verses:

---

164 From 'A Moveable Feast' by Ernest Hemingway, available at: https://archive.org/stream/in.ernet.dli.2015.208 021/2015.208021.A-Moveable_djvu.txt

Our people arrive early and leave late,
And the birds are always beside them, it is their fate.
There is grief in the leaving birds' voice,
It moves your soul and makes you howl in pain.

Birds fly away to warm lands. Where they fly to and how? Let us discuss it today. As for the above verse, we don't know its author. Probably that poet was one of those people who were forced to abandon and then missed their homeland. Indeed, if there are two things that Kazakhs don't part with, one of these would be poetry.

Today, Paris is flourishing again, after the ruthless Russian cannons that once thundered. Indeed, it is a very beautiful city. There are flower gardens, as well as ponds at every step. Birds swim in those ponds. They are not afraid of anyone or anything. There are birds familiar and unfamiliar to us among them. There are church roofs and the bell towers of Paris: not every one of them is Notre-Dame, but each of them is quite grand. Against the houses of God, birds flying in the Paris sky look like angels.

Cathedrals and birds …

Beyond doubt, while they were in France, Germany and Poland, A'men and Narynbaj saw many of those cathedrals before returning to their homeland. Did they know about the endless debates between birds and those European cathedrals?

As well as the various speculations of the Middle Ages, the whole of Europe, especially the Christian world, held many beliefs about the migration of birds. Some hypotheses leave much to be desired. Once, a scientist who was well known throughout Europe, named Carl Linnaeus, explained that when it became cold, swallows and tits hibernated under the mud of a pond. Some scientists responded, 'No, birds hide under tree leaves in the autumn and stay there half-dead until the summer comes.' Another group of scientists were surprised at their own *discoveries* and said, 'No, rooks turn into ravens, and cuckoos into peregrine falcons, as they look alike. When spring comes, the peregrine falcon turns into the cuckoo again. This is the omnipotence of God.'

The Dutch considered that black geese didn't come out of eggs like other birds, but from the seashells scattered on the seashore. As soon as they had wings, they turned into birds. The reason for this was that no one saw black geese eggs anywhere in the Netherlands. On the other hand, the North Sea shores, as well as small and large rivers and lakes, are full of shells. How could the Dutch, who had mastered the technology of making guns and ship-building best of all, not realize that black geese laid their eggs in other countries and only arrived in Holland to spend the winter?

I suppose devout Christians are still ashamed of the Bishop of Hereford's claim to the entire world community from the tribune of the Church:

> Ladies and Gentlemen, the time has come to put an end to all disputes about birds. It is nonsense that birds turn into insects with the onset of cold weather, as well as the fact that they hibernate under the mud of ponds. It seems God honoured us to tell you the truth. In fact, birds migrate to the moon for the winter … The Lord has given wings to birds. And those that have wings can fly. This conversation is over. Stop arguing with each other and wait the birds' arrival from the moon in the spring.

Frederick II Hohenstaufen, the Holy Roman Emperor (1194–1250), went on a Crusade to the Mediterranean. When he saw birds flying over the sea, he thought: I guess our bishop's hypothesis is wrong. It seems these birds are flying to the east. After that, he appointed someone to investigate everything about birds. As a result, he made the following assumption: 'Perhaps birds don't hibernate in the mud of the ponds and migrate to the moon, but winter in other lands.' When Pope Gregory IX heard about this, he said: 'Oh, this sinful world. Maybe one day people will doubt that the Jesus Christ our Saviour is the son of the Holy Virgin Mary.' Thus, he cursed the emperor as an apostate.

In May 1822, (eight years after our heroes, Narynbaj and A'men, returned to their homeland in 1814) in Mecklenburg city, Germany, children that were grazing pigs caught a stork and brought it to a clergyman. The stork was wounded. It seemed that it had been shot from a bow at close range. An iron-tipped arrow was stuck in the stork's neck. Progressive scientists said to the clergyman: 'So much for the evidence. Today, such an arrow is used only by wild African tribes. In other countries you cannot find an arrow like this. It means the stork came from Africa. But you say that they come from the moon.' Christian clergymen, who adhered strictly to the rules of religion, cursed the disobedient *apostates* and the rotten stork that the devil had brought, and killed the bird. I wonder why the truth has always had a thorny path.

Without any dispute, there were always honest and intelligent people who recognized the truth. There weren't only a few people, but entire nations. What did Kazakhs think about the arrival and migration of birds, when Europe was misunderstanding this topic? Let's give an example from folklore once again.

The reeds of the lake are tall and thick,
the winds blow, waving from the lake.
Our sisters who had left for Misr,
came back, making noise all around.

Anyone who knows the structure of the Kazakh language, or world folklore in general, will understand that these lines weren't *composed* recently. As we see from the old riddle, even the most ignorant of the Kazakhs knew that birds migrate to warm lands in autumn. This is revealed by the line, 'Our sisters who had left for Misr'. And the line, 'came back, making noise all around', refers to their arrival in spring from warm lands. There is another riddle:

A caravan heads to the city Šam (Damask),
to a distant place, where the khan lives.
They bid farewell to freshwater lakes,
and sing their bitter song at dawn.

The answer to the riddle is the migration of birds in autumn.

The next riddle that the poet Amanhan A'lim heard from the old men of the Ķožatoğaj *auyl*, in the Ķyzylķum district of South Kazakhstan (now Tùrkistan), and wrote down, reads like this:

Our winter palace is on the River Nile,
We alight along its shores.

We make up a caravan of thousands in spring,
and take off from Baghdad, Šam, and Misr.

The line, 'Our winter palace is on the river Nile', means that birds spend their winters in Africa and return to their homeland in spring. No Kazakh ever said that birds migrate to the moon in winter or hibernate under the mud of ponds. No one would have believed in such nonsense.

Now, let us see if the folk verses above have any scientific basis or not. Modern ornithologists prove that many ducks, when leaving our land, fly over the Mediterranean Sea and then land in Egypt, Algiers and Tunisia. The crane, bald coot, curlews, pied avocet, common whitethroat and lapwing indeed winter on the shores of the Nile; storks and swallows fly to West Africa. How was an *uneducated Kazakh* aware of this fact?

Meanwhile, we should not think that birds usually overwinter only in Africa. Some finch species spend the winter in England and Germany, and some duck species stay in Iran, whereas others such as the dusky moorhen overwinter in Italy and France. We call the hazy band of light seen in the night sky *Ķùs žoly* (the Birds' Way). Slavs call it the 'Milky Way', perhaps because the galaxy looks as if milk has been spilt on the sky. Kazakh legends say that this is what birds use to navigate when they travel back and forth when migrating from one land to the other.

The coot, cuckoo, woodcock, wryneck, starling, quail, robin and other small birds fly at night, whereas large birds that hunt their prey in midair travel during the day. These may include such birds as the stork, crane, bittern, bearded vulture, Himalayan vulture, black kite and other birds of prey.

You might know about *The Epic of Gilgamesh*, or the myth of Noah. In both stories the dove that is sent returns to the Ark. Therefore, about 5,000 years ago, people knew that birds migrated back and forth without getting lost. In scientific terms, they knew about birds' navigational talent.

On an Ancient Egyptian papyrus there are lines that say that every crane, when leaving for warm places, carries a spotted crake on its back. Some scientists took this legend for granted and concluded that the birds that never lost their way were the large birds, and the small ones just travelled on their backs. For example, they speculated that when a crane migrates it carries a spotted crake, whereas storks carry little robins under their wings.

The English naturalist Frank Lane and the ornithologist Ernst Mayr said that they had seen twice 'a robin flying on the back of a bustard' in Africa. Also, the English explorer Samuel Baker stated that he had seen tiny sparrows 'riding' storks. They explain this behaviour by the feeding habits of the smaller birds.

To the question 'Why do cranes fly low and make a trumpeting sound in autumn?' Native Americans, experts of nature, had a single answer: 'They announce their departure and call for birds that are flying to Africa, to give a ride to smaller birds. If one shot a crane or a goose in autumn, one would see sparrows fly out from under its wings.'

As a rule, you will not find such *scientific* evidence in ancient Kazakh sources, perhaps because our ancestors were against utopian dreams. I do not feel any shame about my ancestors, but for those of us who are living in the time of money and trade, what will the next generation say about us? 'Though I stand on my heels I'm unable to see my future'.[165]

Birds fly both by day and night. Why don't they lose their way? The answer is that the sun is their guide. A number of experiments were conducted, aimed at finding a scientific basis for this hypothesis. In the end it was concluded that, in the course of the birds' journey, they navigate relying not on the earth's magnetic field, nor the gravitational force, nor the wind, water, air or mountains; they use the sun to navigate, as human beings do.

There is a phrase that ridicules scattered philosophers of Ancient Rome: 'First, I'll get my stomach full, my friend, and then we will discuss the philosophical subject of why, how and when a human being should eat, and who with.' As has been said before, people used the navigational talent of birds long ago, before the scientific discussions on how they navigate appeared.

The Birds Are Our Friends

165 From '*Žigit bolyp, bel buyp, bekemsinseŋ*', by Kazakh poet Žúmeken Názimedenov (1935–83).

The historical records from Ancient Egypt, Ancient Greece and Ancient Rome mention messenger pigeons that carried messages. In modern times, the French and the British were the first to learn and study Pliny's manuscripts on how to teach birds to carry post. During the war, they were the ones to send secret messages via pigeons and this proved to be a secure form of communication.

Thank God. Europe has shown itself as a model of bird care and protection. In every city there are gardens and parks full of birds. They are not frightened of people. In Rotterdam (Netherlands), pheasants sit on traffic lights and common geese eat from people's hands. Common geese used to inhabit our Caspian shores about forty or fifty years ago, and the Maṅġyšlaḳ Peninsula. Obviously, they left these lands where people now extract oil day and night. Nowadays, they inhabit Bulgarian and Romanian lands. It is clear that migrant birds do not observe international borders. They are opposed to the idea of separating or discriminating countries, religions, races or nationalities.

The USA and Canada made an agreement to protect migrating birds in 1916. Their communities used to mock them, saying that 'it looks like our Governments have settled everything important for their people, so they are now taking care of the birds'. Not long after, Mexico signed the same contract. The Japanese Government suggested signing such an agreement with the Soviet Union, and the USA and Australia did so in 1972–73.

Because of similar agreements, these winged angels live freely and reside in every European city. No one poisons, shoots, kills or frightens them. This is certainly a crucial achievement of humanity. To summarize: 'In the end mankind lost the game!' How does this phrase sound? It does not sound good. Better to say, 'In the end, mankind got over itself!' When we get over ourselves, we succeed. Maybe this is called 'civilization'. Nevertheless, if we think of Kazakhstan and its state, it is a pity to lag behind civilization in this sense.

The autumn has come again.

Birds are departing. It is the saddest season, a season of yearning. The song born of dream, 'If only I had a pair of wings the birds had', might describe this period. Never-ending dreams. Never-ending melancholy. Stories about birds will never end.

Modern science claims that it has already investigated and studied about 8,500 birds (some references show 10,000). I do not believe this. If we knew everything or had discovered everything, what else would be awaiting us?

As far as I am concerned, it is better when birds are an undecipherable mystery to us, always soaring high in the skies. What do you think?